An Introduction to Islamic Law

The study of Islamic law can be a forbidding prospect for those entering the field for the first time. Wael Hallaq, a leading scholar and practitioner of Islamic law, guides students through the intricacies of the subject in this absorbing introduction. The first half of the book is devoted to a discussion of Islamic law in its pre-modern natural habitat. The author expounds on the roles of jurists, who reasoned about the law, and of judges and others who administered justice; on how different legal schools came to be established, and on how a moral law functioned in early Muslim society generally. The second part explains how the law was transformed and ultimately dismantled during the colonial period. As the author demonstrates, this rupture necessitated its reinvention in the twentieth-century world of nation-states. In the final chapters, the author charts recent developments and the struggles of the Islamists to negotiate changes which have seen the law emerge as a primarily textual entity focused on fixed punishments and ritual requirements. The book, which includes a chronology, a glossary of key terms and lists for further reading, will be the first stop for those who wish to understand the fundamentals of Islamic law, its practices and its history.

WAEL B. HALLAQ is James McGill Professor in Islamic Law in the Institute of Islamic Studies at McGill University. He is a world-renowned scholar whose publications include *The Origins and Evolution of Islamic Law* (Cambridge, 2004), *Authority, Continuity and Change in Islamic Law* (Cambridge, 2001) and *A History of Islamic Legal Theories* (Cambridge, 1997).

An Introduction to Islamic Law

Wael B. Hallaq

CAMBRIDGE
UNIVERSITY PRESS

CAMBRIDGE
UNIVERSITY PRESS

University Printing House, Cambridge CB2 8BS, United Kingdom

One Liberty Plaza, 20th Floor, New York, NY 10006, USA

477 Williamstown Road, Port Melbourne, VIC 3207, Australia

314-321, 3rd Floor, Plot 3, Splendor Forum, Jasola District Centre, New Delhi – 110025, India

103 Penang Road, #05–06/07, Visioncrest Commercial, Singapore 238467

Cambridge University Press is part of the University of Cambridge.

It furthers the University s mission by disseminating knowledge in the pursuit of education, learning and research at the highest international levels of excellence.

www.cambridge.org
Information on this title: www.cambridge.org/9780521678735

© Cambridge University Press 2009

First published 2009
13th printing 2021

Printed in the United Kingdom by TJ Books Limited, Padstow Cornwall

A catalogue record for this publication is available from the British Library

ISBN 978-0-521-86146-5 hardback
ISBN 978-0-521-67873-5 paperback

Dedicated to my students

Contents

Introduction

One out of five people in our world today belongs to the Islamic faith. Yet we know very little about Muslims, about their culture, their religion, their history. Our bookstores are crowded with titles about Islam, mostly negative and nearly always concerned with "Islamic violence." Islamic law, or Shariʿa, has in particular become an ugly term, as often associated with politics as with the chopping off of hands and the stoning of women. An endless array of popular books have distorted Shariʿa beyond recognition, confusing its principles and practices in the past with its modern, highly politicized, reincarnations. Considering Shariʿa's historical role as the lifeblood of Islam, we have little hope indeed – given these distortions – of understanding the history and psychology of as much as one-fifth of the population of the world in which we live.

This book attempts to correct misconceptions about Islamic law, first by giving a brief account of its long history and then by showing that what happened to it during the last two centuries made it what it has become. While, historically, it did its best to distance itself from politics and to remain an example of the rule of law, it has now ironically become a fertile political arena, and little else in terms of law. The book therefore attempts to provide the knowledge needed to explain why any mention of the Shariʿa provokes distaste and even fear on our part. What brought this about? Was the Shariʿa as harsh and oppressive as it is now depicted in the media? What were its doctrines and practices in history? How did it function within society and the moral community? Under what conditions did it coexist with the body-politic? How was it colonized and largely dismantled? And, finally, how were its remnants transformed into an oppressive regime, wielded above all by the relatively new nation-state (perhaps the most important factor in Shariʿa's modern transformation)?

In order to explain how Islamic law worked, I begin, in chapter 1, with some introductory remarks about the people who made Islamic law what it was and about what they did as jurists and judges. In chapter 2, I discuss the ways and methods through which these jurists arrived at the law, showing the importance of interpretation in approaching the Quran and other sacred texts. In chapter 3, I explain how these jurists came to belong to different schools, but more importantly what these schools meant in terms of giving authority to the law (an authority that the modern state was to replace). In chapter 4, I turn to legal education, the means by which the juristic class reproduced itself over the centuries. This chapter offers a brief account of the workings of the "study circle" as well as of the law college, which has now become the infamous *madrasa*. The college, we will see, provided not only a point of contact between law and politics, but also an effective venue through which the ruling class attempted to create and sustain political and religious legitimacy. Topics covered in this chapter are no doubt important in themselves, but they are also fundamental for understanding nineteenth- and twentieth-century developments where the appropriation of the Shari'a by the modern state was made possible through dynastic control of traditional legal education.

Chapter 5 takes into account the interaction between law and society, especially how the moral community constituted the framework within which the law court operated. Customary practices of mediation are shown to intersect with judicial practice and to complement it as well. Finally, this chapter provides a look at the place of women in the traditional legal system, a theme relevant to the arguments of chapter 8.

Closing our discussion of the pre-modern history of Islamic law, chapter 6 deals with the so-called "Circle of Justice," a long-standing Near Eastern culture of political management that employed the Shari'a not only for the purposes of acquiring political legitimacy by the ruler but also for achieving just rule as the ultimate realization of God's will. Governance according to the Circle of Justice represented one of the highest forms of the rule of law, where the "state" itself was subject to a law not of its own making (unthinkable in our modern state system).

With chapter 7, the book moves on to the modern period, not a chronological measure of time so much as a dramatic transformation in the structure of Islamic law. Hence, the "modern" takes off where and when such transformations occur, in British India, for example, at least half a century earlier than in most other Muslim countries. One of the major themes here is the negative impact brought about by the introduction into the Muslim legal landscape of the modern project of the state, perhaps – together with capitalism – the most powerful institution and feature of modernity. Thus, this chapter offers a historical narrative of legal colonization in key countries: India, Indonesia, the Ottoman Empire, Egypt, Iran and Algeria. The dominant theme throughout this chapter is how the Shari'a was transformed and, eventually, dismantled.

Chapter 8 continues the discussion of this transformation after World War I, focusing on two major themes: first, the methods through which changes in the law were effected at the hands of post-independence nationalist elites; and second, how the Shariʿa was reduced to little more than a set of altered provisions pertaining to family law, and how the coverage of this sphere became a central concern of the state's will-to-power. Precisely because modern family law preserved the semblance of Shariʿa's substantive law (claiming itself to be its faithful successor), it is of particular interest to examine how an oppressive patriarchal system, engineered by the state, came to replace another, arguably milder, form of traditional patriarchy.

This change in the structures and systems of Islamic law is indicative of the drastically different conditions that modernity came to impose on family life and matrimonial relationships, on legal institutions, and on society at large. Coupled with the emergence of oppressive modern states and a deep sense of moral loss, these changes have all combined (together with poverty and much else) to produce a social phenomenon that is predominantly political but also legal and cultural in orientation. This is the Islamist movement, which has been influencing much of what is happening in the Muslim world today. Chapter 9 therefore addresses the complex relationship between the state, Islamists and the traditional religious establishment in a number of key countries – key, in that developments there have deeply affected most other regions in the Muslim world.

Finally, in chapter 10, I summarize some of the salient points of the book, especially those that show how the Shariʿa was a living and lived system of norms and values, a way of life and a malleable practice. This in turn is contrasted with the manner in which the Shariʿa has emerged in the modern world, namely, as a textual entity capable of offering little more than fixed punishments, stringent legal and ritual requirements, and oppressive rules under which women are required to live.

This book constitutes a select abridgment of my longer work *Sharīʿa: Theory, Practice, Transformations*, recently published by Cambridge University Press. Unlike that longer work, intended for advanced readers, this book is not for specialists but rather caters for those who seek a simplified account of Islam and its law. Thus, in abridging the work, I have taken care to eliminate all theoretical and technical discussions and, as much as possible, specialized vocabulary. Those technical terms that I was compelled to retain here are mostly rendered in English – instead of Arabic – and have been wholly CAPITALIZED on first occurrence to indicate that they are defined and explained in the "Glossary of key terms," which the reader will find toward the end of the book. Because it frequently offers added information, and because it cross-references the entries, the Glossary perhaps deserves a reading on its own. In addition to a fairly expansive Chronology, I have also provided a list of "Suggested further reading," to be found at the end of the book as well.

Chapter 1, however, is mostly new, as are several paragraphs in chapter 2 and elsewhere. In the interest of economy of space, and partly because many of the sources I cited in the longer work were in Arabic, I have eliminated here all footnotes excepting those that support direct quotations from other authors. Readers who wish to examine my sources (or fuller arguments) will find them in the chapters of the longer work, corresponding to this book in the following manner: chapter 2 here corresponds to chapter 2 in the longer work; chapter 3 to section 7 of chapter 1; chapter 4 to chapter 3; chapter 5 to chapter 4; chapter 6 to chapter 5; chapter 7 to chapters 14 and 15; chapters 8 and 9 to chapter 16; and chapter 10 to chapter 18.

Part I

Tradition and continuity

1 Who's who in the Shariʿa

In modern legal systems, judges, lawyers and notaries are unquestionably products of the legal profession. They are initially educated in elementary and secondary schools that are regulated by the state, and their education in the law schools from which they eventually graduate is no less subject to such regulation. They study the laws that the state legislates, although in some legal systems they also study the legal decisions of judges who are constrained in good part by the general policies of the state. The point is that the legal profession is heavily regulated by the state and its legal and public policies. It is difficult to think of any legal professional who can go on to practice law without having to pass some sort of exam that is directly or indirectly ordained by the state or its agencies. And when law students become lawyers, and lawyers become judges, their ultimate and almost exclusive reference is to law made by the state.

This situation would have been inconceivable in Muslim lands before the dawn of modernity. The most striking fact about traditional Islamic legal personnel is that they were not subject to the authority of the state, simply because the state as we now know it did not exist (in fact it did not exist in Europe either, its beginnings there going back to no earlier than the sixteenth century). Thus, until the introduction to the Muslim world – during the nineteenth century – of the modern state and its ubiquitous institutions, Muslims lived under a different conception and practice of government. (This is why we must not use the term "state" to refer to that early form of rule under which Muslims lived prior to the nineteenth century. Instead, we will reserve for that kind of authority such terms as "ruler," "rule" or "government.")

Pre-modern Muslim rule was limited in that it did not possess the pervasive powers of the modern state. Bureaucracy and state administration were thin, mostly limited to urban sites, and largely confined to matters such as the army of the ruler, his assistants, tax collection and often land tenure. People were not registered at birth, had no citizenship status, and could travel and move to other lands and regions freely – there being no borders, no passports, no nationalities, and no geographic fixity to residential status. A Cairene family, for instance, could migrate to Baghdad without having to apply for immigration, and without having to show documentation at borders, because, as I said, there were neither borders (not fixed at any rate) nor passports in the first place. And the farther people lived from the center of rule, the less they were affected by the ruler, his armies and his will to impose a certain order or even taxes on them. And the reason for this was simple: in order for the ruler to have complete control over far-away regions, he had to send armies and government officials whose cost of maintenance may not always have been covered by the taxes they levied from the populations under their control.

So, if there was no *state* to regulate society and the problems that arose in it, then how did people manage their affairs? The short answer is: self-rule. Communities, whether living in city quarters or villages, regulated their own affairs. If the civil populations felt it necessary to have a ruler, it was because of the specific need for protection against external enemies, be they raiding tribes, organized highway robbers or foreign armies who might wreak violence on them and play havoc with their lives. But the civil populations did not need the ruler to regulate their own, internal affairs, since such regulations were afforded by a variety of internal mechanisms developed over centuries by their own local communities. Customary law was an obvious source of self-regulation, but the Shar'ia was equally as important.

This is to say that the Shar'ia was not the product of Islamic government (unlike modern law, which is significantly the product of the state). It is true that the Muslim ruler administered justice by appointing and dismissing JUDGES, even defining the limits of their jurisdictions, but he could in no way influence how and what law should apply. So the question before us is: if the Muslim ruler did not create the law of the land, who did?

The answer is that society and its communities produced their own legal experts, persons who were qualified to fulfill a variety of functions that, in totality, made up the Islamic legal system. For now, we will speak – in a limited fashion and by way of an introduction – of four types of legal personnel who played fundamental roles in the construction, elaboration and continued operation of the Shari'a. These are the *MUFTI*, the AUTHOR-JURIST, the judge and the law professor. Of course there were other "players" in the legal system, including the notaries, the court witnesses and even the ruler himself (to be discussed in due course), but their role in the construction of the system and its continuing operation was not "structural" (by which I mean that the system would have remained much the same with or without their participation). But without the fundamental contributions of *mufti*, author-jurist, judge and law professor, the Shari'a would not have had its unique features and would not have developed the way it did. These four players, each in his own way, made the Shari'a what it was.

We begin with the *mufti* because of his central role in the early evolution of Islamic law and his important contribution to its continued flourishing and adaptability throughout the centuries. The *mufti*, performing a central function, was a private legal specialist who was legally and morally responsible to the society in which he lived, not to the ruler and his interests. The *mufti*'s business was to issue a *FATWA*, namely, a legal answer to a question he was asked to address. As a rule, consulting him was free of charge, which means that legal counsel was easily accessible to all people, poor or rich. Questions addressed to the *mufti* were raised by members of the community as well as by judges who found some of the cases brought before their courts difficult to decide. The first legal elaborations that appeared in Islam were the product of this question/answer activity. With time, these answers were brought together, augmented, systematized and eventually transmitted in memory as well as in writing as "law books."

The *mufti* stated what the law was with regard to a particular factual situation. As he was – because of his erudition – considered to have supreme legal authority, his OPINION, though non-binding, nonetheless settled many disputes in the courts of law. Thus regarded as an authoritative statement of law, the *fatwa* was routinely upheld and applied in the courts. A disputant who failed to receive a *fatwa* in his or her favor was not likely to proceed to court, and would instead abandon his or her claim altogether or opt for informal MEDIATION.

*Mufti*s did not always "sit" in court, but this did not change the fact that they were routinely consulted on difficult cases, even if they resided at several days' distance from where the case was being decided. It was not unusual that a judge, say in Cairo, would send a letter containing a question to a *mufti* who lived, for instance, in Muslim Spain.

The authority of the *fatwa* was decisive. When on occasion a *fatwa* was disregarded, it was usually because another *fatwa*, often produced by an opponent, constituted a more convincing and better-reasoned opinion. In other words, and to put it conversely, it was rare for a judge to dismiss a *fatwa* in favor of his own opinion, unless he himself happened to be of a juristic caliber higher than that enjoyed by the *mufti* from whom the *fatwa* was solicited (in which case the judge himself would not seek a *fatwa* in the first place). All this is to say that the *fatwa* is the product of legal expertise and advanced legal knowledge, and the more learned the *mufti*, the more authoritative and acceptable his *fatwa* was to both the court and the public. (The level of a scholar's legal knowledge was determined through practice, not degrees or diplomas. The measure of a leading jurist was, among other things, the quality of his writings and *fatwa*s as well as his ability to win in scholarly debates with distinguished scholars.)

The central role of the *fatwa* in the Muslim court of law explains why the decisions of judges were neither kept nor published in the manner practiced by modern courts. In other words, law was to be found not in precedent established by courts of law (a notion based on the doctrine of *STARE DECISIS*), but rather in a juristic body of writings that originated mostly in the answers given by *mufti*s.

Thus, emanating from the world of legal practice, the *fatwa*s rather than court decisions were collected and published, particularly those among them that contained new law or represented new legal elaborations on older problems that continued to be of recurrent relevance. Such *fatwa*s usually underwent a significant editorial process in which legally irrelevant facts and personal details (e.g., proper names, names of places, dates, etc.) were omitted. Moreover, they were abridged with a view to abstracting their contents into strictly legal formulas, usually of the hypothetical type: "If X does Y under a certain set of conditions, then L (LEGAL NORM) follows." Once edited and abstracted, these *fatwa*s became part and parcel of the authoritative legal literature, to be referred to and applied as the situation required.

The great majority of Islamic legal works, however, were written not by the *mufti*, but rather by the author-jurists who depended in good part on the *fatwa*s of distinguished *mufti*s. The author-jurists' activity extended from writing short but specialized treatises to compiling longer works, which were usually expanded commentaries on the short works. Thus, a short treatise summing up the law in its full range usually came to about two hundred pages, and often elicited commentaries occupying as many as ten, twenty or thirty large volumes. It was these works that afforded the author-jurists the opportunity to articulate, each for his own generation, a modified body of law that reflected both evolving social conditions and the state of the art in the law as a technical discipline. The overriding concern of the author-jurists was the incorporation of points of law (for the most part *fatwa*s) that had become relevant and necessary to the age in which they were writing. This is evidenced in their untiring insistence on the necessity of including in their works "much needed legal issues," deemed to be relevant to contemporary exigencies as well as those issues of "widespread occurrence."[1] On the other hand, cases that had become irrelevant to the community and its needs, and having thus gone out of circulation, were excluded. Many, if not the majority, of the cases retained were

---

[1] Wael Hallaq, *Authority, Continuity and Change in Islamic Law* (Cambridge: Cambridge University Press, 2001), 188–89.

acknowledged as belonging to the "later jurisprudents" who had elaborated them in response to the emerging new problems in the community. Reflecting in their writings the "changing conditions of people and of the age,"[2] the author-jurists opted for later opinions that were often at variance with the doctrines of the early masters. It is also instructive that the *fatwa*s that formed the substance of later doctrine were those that answered contemporary needs and had at once gained currency in practice. On the other hand, those opinions that had ceased to be of use in litigation were excluded as weak or even irregular.

Many of the works written and "published" by the author-jurists served as standard references for judges, who studied them when they were students and consulted them after being appointed to the judiciary. Hence, if the authority of the law resided in the *mufti*'s opinions and the author-jurist's treatises, then the judge – unless he himself was simultaneously a *mufti* and/or an author-jurist – was not expected to possess the same level of expert legal knowledge. This is to say that a person who was a *mufti* or an author-jurist could usually function as a judge, although a judge who was trained only as a judge could serve neither in the capacity of a *mufti* nor in that of an author-jurist.

It is obvious that the business of a judge is to adjudicate disputes, which is indeed the chief task of a modern judge. But this task was only one of many other important duties that the Muslim judge, the *QADI*, had to undertake. The *qadi*, like the *mufti*, was a member of the community he served. In fact, Islamic law itself insists that a *qadi*, to qualify for the position, has to be intimately familiar with the local customs and way of life in the community in which he serves. With the help of his staff, which we will briefly discuss in due course, he was in charge of supervising much in the life of the community. He oversaw the building of mosques, streets, public fountains and bridges. He inspected newly constructed buildings and the operation of hospitals and soup-kitchens, and audited, among other things, the all important CHARITABLE ENDOWMENTS. He looked into the care afforded by guardians to orphans and the poor, and himself acted as guardian in marriages of women who had no male relatives. Moreover, the *qadi* oftentimes played the exclusive role of mediator in cases that were not of a strictly legal nature. Not only did he mediate and arbitrate disputes and effect reconciliations between husbands and wives, but he also listened, for example, to the problems dividing brothers who might need no more than an outsider's opinion.

---

[2] *Ibid.*

Furthermore, the Muslim court was the site in which important trans-actions between individuals were recorded, such as the sale of a house, the details of the estate of a person who had died, or a partnership contract concluded between two merchants. At times a person might approach the court merely to request that it take note of an insult directed at him or her by another, this being equivalent to building a "history" in the event a future dispute erupted with that person.

Equally important was the social site in which the *qadi* and his court functioned. Judges invariably sought to understand the wider social con-text of the litigating parties, often attempting to resolve conflicts in full consideration of the present and future social relationships of the dispu-tants. Like mediators, but unlike modern judges, the *qadi*s tried hard, wherever possible, to prevent the collapse of relationships so as to main-tain a social reality in which the litigating parties, who often came from the same community, could continue to live together amicably. Such a *judicial* act required the *qadi* to be familiar with, and willing to investigate, the history of relations (and relationships) between the disputants.

Finally, we must say a few words about the law professor. The begin-nings of legal education in Islam can in fact be traced back to the *mufti*s who emerged during the last two or three decades of the seventh century as private specialists in the law. They did not have salaries and their interest in the study of law was motivated by piety and religious learning. Around each of these early *mufti*s gathered a number of students – and sometimes the intellectually curious – who were interested in gaining knowledge of the Quran and the biography of the Prophet Muhammad as an exemplary standard of conduct. These gatherings usually took place in the new mosques that were built in the various cities and towns that had come under the rule of Islam. Following the practice of Arab tribal councils when they assembled to discuss important issues, these scholarly gatherings took the form of CIRCLES, where the *mufti*/professor would literally sit on the ground, legs crossed, having students and interested persons sit to his left and right in a circular fashion. (This was also the physical form that court sessions took.) Students did not have to apply formally to study with a professor, although his informal approval to have them join his circle was generally required – as was proper decorum on the part of the student. There were no fees to be paid, except the occasional gift the professor might have received from students or their family members. There were no diplomas or degrees conferred upon graduation, only a license issued by the professor attesting that the student had completed the study of a book that he in turn could transmit or teach to others. The license was personal, having the authority of the professor himself, not that of an impersonal institution (as are the degrees granted by today's universities).

During the first two centuries of Islam, the distinction between a *fatwa* assembly and a teaching circle was not always clear-cut or obvious. In fact, to some extent, this situation continued to obtain even throughout the later centuries when a *mufti* sitting in a circle would announce the end of a *fatwa* session, would open another session for adjudicating cases – thus acting as a judge – and perhaps in the afternoon (at times after sharing a meal with his students) would set up yet another circle for teaching. (We often read in the sources that many JURISTS wrote their legal treatises during the night hours – and in seclusion – thereby acting in the capacity of author-jurists. It must be said that those who acted in all four capacities were usually regarded as among the most accomplished jurists.)

Some *fatwa*s encountered in a *fatwa* session might be discussed in the teaching circle, while some students who participated in the teaching or *fatwa* circle might act as witnesses when the circle was transformed into a court session. Thus, while these three activities or spheres were different from each other, they were interrelated in several ways, at both the level of student participation and that of professor. If a person could act as a *mufti*, then he could teach, and was certainly qualified to perform the duties of a judge (provided, of course, that he had been appointed as *qadi* by the ruler or governor).

Judges, as government appointees, were financially remunerated by the ruler for their work, but not so *mufti*s or professors (with the partial exception of later OTTOMAN practice, which we will discuss in due course). Still, during the first four or five centuries of Islam, even judges did not hold such appointments full-time, and when they did not, had to find, like *mufti*s and professors, other sources of income. This is to say that until the legal profession was institutionalized, the jurists of Islam were not, in terms of gaining a livelihood, full-time legal professionals, however learned and skilled in the law they were. Thus, until the eleventh or twelfth century, the vast majority of jurists held other jobs, with many of them working as tanners, tailors, coppersmiths, copiers of manuscripts, and small merchants and traders. In other words, they generally belonged to what we call today the lower and middle, rather than the upper classes.

2   The Law: how is it found?

Introduction

The question that we need to address briefly at this point is: How did the *mufti*s and author-jurists derive the law from its sources? What, in other words, were the interpretive means and methods of reasoning through which the law was inferred? Before we proceed, however, an important point must be made.

Since the first century of Islam, Muslim legal thinking has had to wrestle with the problem of the extent to which human reason can guide humankind in conducting its material and spiritual affairs. Some philosophers thought that the leading intellectuals might be able to exercise their rational faculties in order to judge what is good and what is bad in the way we deal with each other as social beings, and with the natural world around us. They may know, thanks to their trained intellects, that a certain code of morality or a set of particular laws is *rationally* required for the orderly and civil functioning of society. They may even understand – given that they have all the facts at hand – that the natural environment around us must not be abused and that we are an integral part of this natural order. Damage that and we damage ourselves in the process.

Yet law is not relevant only to intellectuals, since it is essential to society at large, i.e., to the uneducated man or woman as much as to the highly learned. How can ordinary people come to understand the need to abide by certain patterns of conduct if they do not possess the means to think through life's intricate situations or the world's more complex problems? How can even the elite intellectuals determine the exact way in which we should behave properly? Thus, Islamic law and theology posed the central question: Does rational thinking, *on its own*, accomplish the job? Or, to put it differently, is rational thinking – even in its best forms – sufficient for Muslims to know precisely how to conduct themselves in their worldly and religious affairs? (To bring this point into sharp relief, and to continue with the aforementioned example about the natural order, one might consider that our best rational and scientific thinking has led us – during the last century or so – to the virtual destruction of our natural environment.)

The Muslim jurists and most Muslim theologians held the view that rational thinking is a gift from God and that we should fully utilize it – like everything else that He bestowed on us – in as wise and responsible a manner as possible. Just as His material blessings (the wealth some of us have come to possess) must be deployed for good works, our intellects must likewise be exercised for good causes. But what are these good works and causes? What is their *content*? If God granted us precious intellects, by what measure do we think about the world, about its human, material and physical components? In other words, how do we determine what is good and what is evil, what is beneficial and what is harmful in both the short and long runs? In yet other words, it is not only precisely *how* we think but also, and equally important, *what substantive assumptions* must we make when exercising our processes of thought? For example, the content of our modern rationalist thinking about the natural environment may be our immediate concern with material welfare and physical comfort (leading, among other things, to heavy industrialization), but the consequences of this thinking and the ensuing actions could well lead us to an environmental disaster. On the other hand, if the positive content of our rationalist thinking were to be, say, the integrity of the natural order (as, for example, Buddhism teaches), then our conclusions and therefore resultant actions and effects would be entirely different, despite the fact that nothing in our rationalist methods *themselves* has changed. It was precisely this dilemma that Muslims encountered virtually from the beginning of their religion. And their solution was, as it continued to be for centuries, that, however precious, *rationalist thought on its own is insufficient*.

Islamic legal tradition adopted the position that, while our reason is to be exercised to its fullest capacity, the *content* of rational thinking must be predetermined, transcendental and above and beyond what we can infer through our mental faculties. Implied in this thinking was the assumption that humans simply do not understand all the secrets of the world, so that attempting to control it is to be vain and arrogant. God is the One who created the world and therefore the One who knows its secrets. We may exercise our intellects to their fullest capacity, but without His aid, we will overlook and misunderstand much. The content of rationality, in their thinking, must thus be predetermined by the all-knowing God, who has revealed a particular body of knowledge through the Quran and the Prophet. This combination, viewed as a marriage between reason and revelation, was the ultimate source of law. Law, put differently, was the child of this marriage.

Transmission of texts

With this background in mind, Muslim jurists proceeded to articulate a theory of law (*USUL AL-FIQH*) that reflected the concerns and goals of this "marriage." The theory began with the assumption that the Quran is the most sacred source of law, embodying knowledge that God had revealed about human beliefs, about God himself, and about how the believer should conduct himself or herself in this world. This human conduct was the domain of law, and to this end the Quran contained the so-called "legal verses," some five hundred in all (the others being theological, exhortative, etc.).

But God also sent down a prophet, called Muhammad, whose personal conduct was exemplary. Though not, according to Muslim tradition, endowed with divine qualities (as Jesus Christ is said to have been by Christians), Muhammad was God's chosen messenger; he understood God's intentions better than anyone else, and acted upon them in his daily life. Hence the exemplary nature of his biography, which became known in the legal literature as SUNNA – the second major source of law after the Quran. The concrete details of the Sunna – that is, what the Prophet had done or said, or even tacitly approved – took the form of specific narratives that became known as *HADITH* (at once a collective and a singular noun, referring to the body of *hadith* in general and to a single *hadith*, according to context). For example, the Sunna of the Prophet generally promotes the right to private property, but the precise nature of this right was not made clear until the pertinent *hadith*s became known. Thus, we learn in one such *hadith* that when the Prophet once heard that someone had cultivated plants on the land of his neighbor without the latter's knowledge, he said: "He who plants, without permission, in a lot owned by other people cannot own the crops although he is entitled to a wage [for his labor]." In the context of property rights, he also said: "He who unlawfully appropriates as much as one foot of land [from another], God will make seven pieces of land collapse on him when the Day of Judgment arrives." These two *hadith*s, along with many others, give a good idea of what the Prophetic Sunna – as an abstract concept – aims to accomplish in the vital area of property law.

One of the concerns of legal theory was to provide criteria by which the subject matter of the *hadith*s (which, in their entirety, exceeded half a million) might be transmitted from one generation to the next in a reliable manner. The application of these criteria finally resulted in the acceptance of only about 5,000 sound *hadith*s. Thus, a *hadith* that had been passed down via a defective or interrupted chain of transmitters, or by transmitters known to be untrustworthy, was held to lack any legal effect even though its language might be clear and unequivocal. For example, if I know that a *hadith* was transmitted to me from A, B, C, D and F on the authority of the Prophet, but the identity of E is unknown to me or, alternatively, I know him to have been untrustworthy, then I cannot use the *hadith* for reasoning about the law. If the *hadith* passes the test of sound transmission but consists of ambiguous words whose exact meaning I am unable to determine with any precision, then the *hadith* is also rendered useless as the basis of legal reasoning.

Even the Quran contains such ambiguous language, but in terms of transmission it is regarded as *wholly certain*, since the entire community of Muslims was involved in its conveyance from one generation to the next. This position stems from the theory of CONSENSUS, namely, that it is inconceivable for the entire Muslim community to conspire on a false-hood, including forging or distorting the holy Book. Thus, for a text to be deemed credible beyond a shadow of doubt (i.e., to have certainty), it must meet this requirement of multiple transmission, which we will here call RECURRENCE. For recurrence to obtain, three conditions must be met: first, the text must be conveyed from one generation to the next through channels of transmission sufficiently numerous as to preclude any possibility of error or collaboration on a forgery; second, the first class of transmitters must have had sensory perception of what the Prophet said or did; and third, the first two conditions must be met at each stage of transmission, beginning with the first class and ending with the last narrators of the report.

Any text transmitted through channels fewer than those by which the recurrent report is conveyed is termed SOLITARY, although the actual number of channels can be two, three or even more. With the possible exception of a few, the *hadith* reports are generally considered solitary, and, unlike the Quranic text, they do not possess the advantage of recur-rence. In fact, there were far more fabricated, and thus weak, *hadith*s than there were sound ones. But even these latter did not always engender certainty, since most were of the solitary type and therefore yielded only probable knowledge. If all this points to anything about Islamic law, it is its own acknowledgment that, as a practical field, religious law (mostly *hadith*-derivative) does not have to enjoy certainty. Certainty is necessary only when the issue at stake is either the status of one of the law's FOUR SOURCES or a higher order of belief, such as the existence of God himself. As a system of belief and practice, the law on the whole cannot be considered legitimate or meaningful if one or more of its sources rests on probable, and thus uncertain, foundations; or if God himself, the originator of the Law, is not known to exist with certainty.

As we intimated earlier, the trustworthiness of individual transmitters played an important role in the evaluation of *hadith*s. The attribute that was most valued, and in fact deemed indispensable and determinative, was that of being just, i.e., being morally and religiously righteous. A just character also implied the attribute of being truthful, which made one incapable of lying. This requirement was intended to preclude either outright tampering with the wording of the transmitted text, or interpolating it with fabricated material. It also implied that the transmitter could not have lied regarding his sources by fabricating a chain of transmitters, or claiming that he had heard the *hadith* from an authority when in fact he had not. He had also to be fully cognizant of the material he related, so as to transmit it with precision. Finally, he must not have been involved in dubious or "sectarian" religious movements, for if this were the case, he would have been liable to produce heretical material advancing the cause of the movement to which he belonged. This last requirement clearly suggests that the transmitter must have been known to be loyal to Sunnism, to the exclusion of any other community. The TWELVER-SHI'IS had a similar requirement.

Transmitters were also judged by their ability to transmit *hadith*s verbatim, for thematic transmission ran the risk of changing the wording, and thus the original intent, of a particular *hadith*. Furthermore, it was deemed preferable that the *hadith* be transmitted in full, although transmitting one part, thematically unrelated to the rest, was acceptable.

The jurist may encounter more than one *hadith* relevant to the case he is trying to solve, or *hadith*s that may be contradictory or inconsistent with one another. If he cannot reconcile them, he must seek to make one *hadith* preponderant over another by establishing that the former possesses attributes superior to, or lacking in, the latter. The criteria of preponderance depend on the mode of transmission as well as on the subject matter of the *hadith* in question. For example, a *hadith* transmitted by mature persons known for their prodigious ability to retain information is superior to another transmitted by young narrators who may not be particularly known for their memory or precision in reporting. Similarly, a *hadith* whose first transmitter was close to the Prophet and knew him intimately is regarded as superior to another whose first transmitter was not on close terms with the Prophet. The subject matter also determines the comparative strength or weakness of a *hadith*. For instance, a *hadith* that finds thematic corroboration in the Quran would be deemed more weighty than another which finds no such support. But if the procedure of weighing the two *hadith*s does not result in tipping the balance in favor of one against the other, the jurist may also resort to the procedure of ABROGATION, whereby one of the *hadith*s is made to repeal, and thus cancel out the effects of, another.

Abrogation was also unanimously held as one of the key methods of dealing with contradictory Quranic texts. But the theory of Abrogation does not imply that the Quranic passages themselves are actually abrogated – only the legal rulings embedded in these passages.

The fundamental principle of Abrogation is that one text repeals another contradictory text that was revealed prior to it in time. But abrogation may result from a clearer consideration, especially when the text itself stipulates that another should be superseded. An example in point is the Prophet's statement: "I had permitted for you the use of the carrion leather, but upon receipt of this writing [epistle], you are not to utilize it in any manner." Yet another consideration is the consensus of the community as represented by its scholars. If one ruling is adopted in preference to another, then the latter is deemed abrogated, since the community cannot agree on an error.

That the Quran can abrogate *hadith*s is evident, considering its distinguished religious stature and the manner of its transmission. And it is understandable why solitary *hadith*s cannot abrogate Quranic verses (although a tiny minority of jurists permitted this type of abrogation). However, the question that remained controversial was whether or not recurrent *hadith*s could abrogate Quranic verses.

Reasoning

Be that as it may, the language of the Quran and *hadith* was not always clear and unequivocal. That is, some terms lent themselves to more than one interpretation. Metaphorical words and overly general language had to be interpreted to yield specific meanings and, to do so, the jurists developed linguistic rules in order to resolve such problems.

The aim of the reasoning jurist was to establish, for every new case he encountered, a legal norm. The Shari'a recognizes five such norms, intended to order the entire range of human activity and to set human life in good order. The purpose here is not to control or discipline, the two most salient tasks of modern law and the modern state that wields it. Rather, in Muslim thinking, the purpose of the law is to foster living in peace, first with oneself, and second with and in society. The law bids one to do the right thing, to the extent one can and wherever one happens to be. The state permits and forbids, and when it does the latter, it punishes severely upon infraction. It is not in the least interested in what individuals do outside of its spheres of influence and concern. Islamic law, on the other hand, has an all-encompassing interest in human acts. It organizes them into various categories ranging from the moral to the legal, without however making conscious distinctions between the moral and the legal. In fact, there are no words in Arabic, the *lingua franca* of the law, for the different notions of moral/legal.

Thus, all acts are regarded as *shar'i* (i.e., subject to the regulation of the Shari'a *and therefore pronounced as law* – "*law*" being a moral-legal commandment), and are categorized according to five norms. The first of these is the category of the forbidden, which entails punishment upon commission of an act considered prohibited, whilst the second category, that of the obligatory, demands punishment upon omission of an act whose performance is regarded as necessary. Breach of contract and theft are infractions falling within the forbidden category, while prayer and payment of pecuniary debts are instances of the obligatory. Both categories require punishment upon non-compliance.

The three remaining categories are the recommended, neutral and disapproved. Helping the poor, consuming particular lawful foods and unilateral DIVORCE by the husband are, respectively, examples of these three categories. Performing the disapproved and not performing the recommended entail no punishment. But if a person is compliant, i.e., by performing a recommended act or refraining from a disapproved act, then he or she will be rewarded, although the reward is assumed to await one in the Hereafter. Since the category of the neutral prescribes neither permission nor prohibition, then neither reward nor punishment is involved.

Thus, when the reasoning jurist encounters in the Quran and/or the Sunna a word that has an imperative or a prohibitive form (e.g., "Do" or "Do not do"), he must decide to which of the five legal norms they belong. When someone commands another, telling him "Do this," should this command be regarded as falling only within the legal value of the obligatory, or could it also be within that of the recommended and/or the indifferent? The very definition of the imperative was itself open to wide disagreement. Some writers saw it as language demanding of a person that he or she perform a certain act. Others insisted that an element of superiority on the part of the requestor over the person ordered must be present for the expression to qualify as imperative; i.e., an inferior's language by which he commands his superior cannot be taken as imperative. Against the objection that one can command one's equal, they argued that such a command, though it may take the imperative form, is merely a metaphoric usage and should not be treated as a command in the real sense.

These varied interpretive positions do not seem to have offered a satisfactory or consistent solution to the problem of the imperative form. But by the eleventh century, some jurists had succeeded in resolving the issue. They pointed out that the significations of linguistic forms, including the imperative, must be understood in light of what has been established by convention, which is known by means of widespread usage of the language. Through this pervasive usage, which cannot be falsified, we know from past authorities what the convention is with regard to the meaning of a word, or we know that the Lawgiver has accepted and confirmed the meaning as determined by that convention. Such reported usage also informs us of the existence of any consensus in the community on how these words are to be understood or, in the absence of a consensus, how they were understood by scholarly authorities whose erudition, rectitude and integrity would have prevented them from remaining silent when an error in language was committed.

So far, we have discussed the first two sources of the law: the Quran and the Sunna of the Prophet. We now turn to the third source, consensus, which guaranteed not only the infallibility of those legal rulings (or opinions) subject to juristic agreement but also the entire structure of the law. Technically, consensus is defined as the agreement of the community as represented by its highly learned jurists living in a particular age or generation, an agreement that bestows on those rulings or opinions subject to it a conclusive, certain knowledge.

The universal validity of consensus could not be justified by reason, since Muslims held that entire communities or "nations" could go, and indeed had gone, wrong even on important issues. Consensus, therefore, had to be grounded in the Quran and/or the Sunna. But early attempts by theoreticians to articulate a Quranic basis for consensus failed, since the Quran did not offer evidence bearing directly on it. No less disappointing were the recurrent Prophetic reports which contained virtually nothing to this effect. All that were available were solitary reports speaking of the impossibility of the community on the whole ever agreeing on an error. "My community shall never agree on a falsehood" and "He who departs from the community ever so slightly would be considered to have abandoned Islam" are fairly representative of the language employed. While a dozen or more of these reports were considered relevant to the issue of consensus's authority, they gave rise to a problem. Solitary reports are probable and thus cannot prove anything with certainty. Consensus is one of the sources of the law, and must as such be shown to have its basis in nothing short of certain evidence. Otherwise, the whole foundation of the law, and therefore religion, might be subject to doubt.

To solve this quandary, the jurists turned to the reports that are *thematically*, but not verbally, recurrent. Although solitary, these reports not only are numerous but, despite the variation in their wording, possess in common a single theme, namely, that through divine grace the community as a whole is safeguarded against error. The large number of transmissions, coupled with their leitmotif, transforms these reports into the *thematically* recurrent type, thus yielding certain knowledge of an infallible nature.

Conclusively established as a source of law, consensus ratifies as certain any particular rule that may have been based on probable textual evidence. The reasoning advanced in justification of this doctrine is that if consensus on probable evidence is attained, the evidence cannot be subject to error inasmuch as the community cannot err in the first place. Thus, consensus may be reached on rules that were based on inferential methods of reasoning. However, it is important to note that the cases or rules upon which there was consensus are limited, constituting less than 1 percent of the total body of law. Yet because these cases were subject to this extraordinary instrument, they were deemed especially important.

There remains the question of how consensus is determined to have occurred. Much theoretical discussion was devoted to this issue, but in practice knowledge of the existence of consensus on a particular case was determined by looking to the past and by observing that the major jurists were unanimous regarding its solution. And, as we have said, such cases were relatively few.

Knowledge of cases subject to consensus was required in order to ensure that the jurist's reasoning did not lead him to results different from, or contrary to, the established agreement in his school or among the larger community of jurists. The importance of this requirement stems from the fact that consensus bestows certainty upon the cases subject to it, raising them to the level of the unequivocal texts in the Quran and the recurrent *hadith*; thus, reopening such settled cases to new solutions would amount to questioning certainty, including conclusive texts in the Quran and the Sunna. Yet, as already noted, the cases determined to be subject to the certainty of consensus remained numerically insignificant as compared to those subject to juristic disagreement. The point remains, however, that inferential reasoning is legitimate only in two instances, namely, when the case in question had not been subject to consensus (having remained within the genre of juristic disagreement) or when it was entirely new.

The jurists recognized various types of legal reasoning, some subsumed under the general term *QIYAS*, and others dealt with under such headings as *ISTISLAH* (public interest) and *ISTIHSAN* (juristic preference). We begin with *qiyas*, considered the fourth source of law after consensus.

The characterization of this category as a "source of law" need not imply that it was a material source on the *substance* of which a jurist could draw. Instead, it is a source only insofar as it provides a set of methods *through* which the jurist arrives at legal norms. The most common and prominent of these methods is analogy. As the archetype of all legal argument, *qiyas* is seen to consist of four elements, namely: (1) the new case requiring a legal solution (i.e., the application of one of the five norms); (2) the original case that may be found either stated in the revealed texts or sanctioned by consensus; (3) the *RATIO LEGIS*, or the attribute common to both the new and original cases; and (4) the legal norm that is found in the original case and that, owing to the similarity between the two cases, must be transposed to the new case. The archetypal example of legal analogy is the case of wine. If the jurist is faced with a case involving date-wine, requiring him to decide its status, he looks at the revealed texts only to find that grape-wine was explicitly prohibited by the Quran. The common denominator, the *ratio legis*, is the attribute of intoxication, in this case found in both drinks. The jurist concludes that, like grape-wine, date-wine is prohibited owing to its inebriating quality.

Of the four components of *qiyas*, the *ratio legis* occasioned both controversy and extensive analysis, since the claim for similarity between two things is the cornerstone and determinant of inference. Much discussion, therefore, was devoted to the determination of the *ratio*, for although it may be found to be explicitly stated in the texts, more often it is intimated or alluded to. Frequently, the need arose to infer it from the texts. For instance, when the Prophet was questioned about the legality of bartering ripe dates for unripe ones, he queried: "Do unripe dates lose weight upon drying out?" When he was answered in the affirmative, he reportedly remarked that such barter is unlawful. The ratio in this *hadith* was deemed explicit since prohibition was readily understood to be predicated upon the dried dates losing weight; hence, a transaction involving unequal amounts or weights of the same object would constitute USURY, clearly prohibited in Islamic law. In other instances, the *ratio* may be merely intimated. In one *hadith*, the Prophet said: "He who cultivates a barren land acquires ownership of it." Similarly, in 5:6, the Quran declares: "If you rise up for prayer, then you must wash." In these examples, the *ratio* is suggested in the semantic structure of this language, reducible to the conditional sentence "If ..., then ..." The consequent phrase "then ..." indicates that the *ratio* behind washing is prayer, just as the ownership of barren land is confirmed by cultivating it. It is important to realize here that prayer requires washing, not that washing is consistently occasioned by prayer alone. For one can wash oneself without performing prayer, but not the other way round. The same is true of land ownership. A person can possess barren land without cultivating it, but the cultivation of it, and subsequent entitlement to it, is the point.

The *ratio* may consist of more than one attribute, all of which must be considered as "causing" a normative rule to arise from them. For instance, the *ratio* of the theft penalty encompasses five attributes: (1) the object stolen must have been taken away by stealth; (2) it must be of a minimum value; (3) it must in no way be the property of the thief; (4) it must be taken out of custody; and (5) the thief must have full legal capacity. All of these attributes must obtain for an act to qualify as theft, an act punishable by cutting off the hand. All attributes must exist together; no single one by itself suffices to produce the *ratio legis*.

The rationale behind the rule is at times comprehensible: for example, the intoxicating attribute of wine renders it prohibited because intoxication incapacitates the mind and hinders, among other things, the performance of religious duties. In this example, we comprehend the reason for the prohibition. Some properties, however, do not disclose the reason. We do not know, for instance, why the quality of edibility should be the *ratio legis* for the prohibition of usury in the exchange of some goods; all we know is that no object possessing the property of edibility can be the subject of a transaction involving usury.

The *ratio* may also be causally connected with its rule in a less than explicit manner. From Quran 17:23, "Say not 'Fie' to them [parents] neither chide them, but speak to them graciously," the jurists understood that uttering "Fie" before one's parents is prohibited because of the lack of respect the expression entails. If the utterance of "Fie" is prohibited, then striking one's parents is *a fortiori* prohibited. The prohibition of striking is indirectly engendered by the prohibition against uttering "Fie," and is not explicitly stated in the texts. At times, the sequence of events may help unravel the *ratio*, for the sequence may be interpreted causally. The Prophet, for instance, tersely commanded a man to free a slave upon hearing that the man had engaged in sexual intercourse with his wife during the fasting hours of Ramadan. Although the connection between the infraction and the command was not made clear by the Prophet, the sequence of events nonetheless renders them causally so connected. The Prophet would not have behaved in this manner without the occurrence of a particular event that precipitated his particular command.

The *ratio legis* may also be known by consensus. For example, it is the universal agreement of the jurists that the father enjoys a free hand in managing and controlling the property of his minor children. Here, minority is the *ratio* for this unrestricted form of conduct, and property the new case. Thus, the *ratio* may be transposed to yet another new case, such as the unrestricted physical control of a father over his children.

A significant method for discovering and evaluating the *ratio* is that of SUITABILITY (*MUNASABA*). We have noted that the Quran prohibits the consumption of wine because it possesses the attribute of inebriation, leading the intoxicated person to neglect his religious duties. The theorists argued that even if the Quran did not allude to the reason for the prohibition, we would still come to understand that the prohibition was pronounced because of inebriation's harmful consequences. This is reasoning on the basis of suitability, since we, independently of revelation and through our rational faculty, are able to recognize the harmful effects of intoxication and thus the rationale behind certain sorts of prohibition.

However, there are limits to rationality within and without the method of suitability. Since the law cannot always be analyzed and comprehended in (exclusively) rational ways, reason and its products are not always in agreement with the legal premises and their conclusions. Suitability, therefore, may at times be relevant to the law, and irrelevant at others. No *ratio* may be deemed suitable without being relevant, and any irrelevant *ratio* becomes unsuitable, precluding it from further juristic consideration. In the case of divorced women who are of the age of majority, male guardianship is waved by virtue of the life experience that such divorcees have gained. Thus, such divorcees may remarry without the need for a guardian's approval. Logically, this reasoning would apply to divorcees who are minor, but rationally this is inappropriate since it runs counter to the aims of the law in protecting the welfare and interests of minors.

Suitability's goal is to offer "relevant" ways of reasoning that serve the public interest (*MASLAHA*) as defined by the fundamental principles of the law. In other words, interpreting the law in the light of suitability is accomplished independently of the specific revealed texts, since the *ratio* is not, in the first place, textual. Rather, it is rational and seeks to conform to the spirit of the law, which is known to prohibit what is harmful and to promote what is good for this life and for the hereafter. The systematic exclusion of harm and inclusion of benefit are the fundamental aims of the law, and it is to these aims that the rational argument of suitability must conform. Protection of life, religion, private property, mind and offspring are the most salient of these goals. These are known as the indispensable necessities, for without them no society or legal system can meaningfully exist.

Once the *ratio* in analogical *qiyas* is identified and confirmed to be the *relevant* and *complete* common factor between the original and the new cases, very little else is involved in the transference of the legal norm from the former to the latter case. Analogy, however, is not the only method of inference subsumed under *qiyas*. Another important argument, among others, is that of the *a fortiori* type. For example, from Quran 5:3, "Forbidden unto you are carrion, blood, flesh of the pig," the jurists took the last four words to include all types of pork, including that of wild boar, although the original reference was to domestic pigs.

Another type of legal reasoning is *istihsan*, which is an inference that presumably starts from a revealed text but leads to a conclusion that differs from one reached by means of *qiyas*. If a person, for example, forgets what he is doing and eats while he is supposed to be fasting during the month of Ramadan, *qiyas* dictates that his fasting becomes void, since food has entered his body, whether intentionally or not. But *qiyas* in this case was abandoned in favor of a Prophetic *hadith* which pronounced the fasting valid if the act of eating was the result of a mistake. The *qiyas* reasoning here is one that typically falls within a large area of the law where no exceptions are allowed. If fasting during Ramadan is broken on any given day, then *qiyas* requires compensation. Yet, despite the fact that *istihsan* is based on a text, the very choice of this text represents a juristic intention to create an exception to the law. If a mistake does not invalidate fasting, then no atonement or compensation is required.

Some, but by no means all, *istihsan* exceptions were justified by sacred texts. Many were in fact based either on consensus or on the principle of NECESSITY. For instance, to be valid, any contract involving the exchange of commodities requires immediate payment. But some contracts of hire do not fulfill this condition, a fact that would render them void if *qiyas* were to be invoked. The common practice of people over the ages has been to admit these contractual forms in their daily lives, and this is viewed as tantamount to consensus. As an instrument that engenders certainty, consensus becomes tantamount to the revealed texts themselves, thereby bestowing on the reasoning involved here the same force that the Quran or the *hadith* would bestow.

Likewise, necessity often requires the abandonment of conclusions reached by *qiyas* in favor of those generated by *istihsan*. Washing with ritually impure water would, by *qiyas*, invalidate prayer, but not so in *istihsan*. Here, *qiyas* would lead to hardship in view of the fact that fresh, clean water is not always easy to procure. The acceptance of necessity as a principle that legitimizes departure from strict reasoning is seen as deriving from, and sanctioned by, both the Quran and the Sunna, since necessity, when not acknowledged, can cause nothing but hardship.

A third method of inference is *istislah* (public interest), i.e., reasoning that does not appear to be directly based on the revealed texts. We have already taken note of the important role that public interest plays in determining the *ratio*'s suitability in *qiyas*. It is because of this relationship between the *ratio* and suitability that *maslaha* is deemed an extension of *qiyas*. As such, most theorists do not devote to it an independent section or chapter but treat it under the category of suitability. This fact attests to the heavy emphasis that *qiyas* places upon the non-literal extrapolation of rules.

On the basis of a comprehensive study of the law, the jurists came to realize that there are five universal principles that underlie the Shari'a, namely, protection of life, mind, religion, property and offspring.

The reasoning was that the law has come down explicitly to protect and promote these five areas of human life, and that nothing in this law can conceivably run counter to these principles or to any of their implications, however remotely. If the feature of public interest in a case can be shown to be indubitably connected with the five universals, then reasoning must proceed in accordance with *maslaha*. The condition of universality is also intended to ensure that the interests of the Muslim community at large are served.

Legal pluralism

The foregoing interpretive methods constituted the tools of *IJTIHAD*, the processes of reasoning that the jurist employed in order to arrive at the best guess of what he thought might be the law pertaining to a particular case. Except for a relatively few Quranic and Prophetic statements which were unambiguous and which contained clear and specific normative rulings, the rest of the law was the product of *ijtihad*. For unlike the unambiguous textual rulings, which were certain and hence not susceptible to *ijtihad* (because the mind cannot see any other meaning in the language in which they were stated), this latter involved inferences, both linguistic and legal. *Ijtihad*, therefore, was the domain of probability.

Islamic law is therefore overwhelmingly the result of *ijtihad*, a domain of interpretation that rests on probability. Every accomplished jurist could exercise *ijtihad*, and no one knew, except for God, which *MUJTAHID* (the jurist conducting *ijtihad*) was correct. This relativity gave rise to the famous tenet and maxim that "Every *mujtahid* is correct."

Ijtihad also gave Islamic law one of its unique features. For every eventuality or case, and for every particular set of facts, there are anywhere between two and a dozen opinions, if not more, each held by a different jurist. In other words, there is no single legal stipulation that has monopoly or exclusivity, unlike the situation that obtains in the modern state. Islamic law is thus also characterized by legal pluralism, not only because it acknowledges local custom and takes it into serious account, but also because it offers an array of opinions on one and the same set of facts. This pluralism gave Islamic law two of its fundamental features, one being flexibility and adaptability to different societies and regions, and the other an ability to change and develop over time, first by opting for those opinions that have become more suitable than others to a particular circumstance, and second by creating new opinions when the need arose. That Islamic law was accused of rigidity by European colonialism to justify – as we shall see later – the dismantling of the Shariʿa system is therefore not only wrong but highly ironic.

Contents and arrangement of legal subjects

Muslim jurists viewed the Shariʿa as a mandate to regulate all human conduct, from religious rituals and family relations to commerce, crime and much else. The following is an overview of the contents and range of subjects treated in legal works, from short manuals to much longer treatises. These works tended to differ from each other in terms of the organization of their subject matter, although the chapters on ritual in these works always occupied first place and followed a fixed order (i.e., ablution, prayer, alms-tax, fasting and pilgrimage). The differences in the order of treatment of other legal spheres, at times great, can be attributed to the various ways the LEGAL SCHOOLS (to be discussed in chapter 3) conceived of the logical and juristic connections between one area of law and another, which is to say that the most significant organizational variations between and among these works can be attributed to school affiliation and the particular commentarial and interpretive tradition in each of them.

Generally, Muslim jurists gave the main topics of law the title *kitab* ("book"), e.g., the Book of Agency, which, in our modern organizational scheme, we recognize as a chapter. A sub-chapter was termed "*bab*," which would in turn be broken into a number of *fasl*s (sections).

Many jurists conceived of the whole of Islamic law as falling into four major fields, which were called "the four quarters," i.e., "rituals, sales, marriage and injuries." Each of these terms, used in this context metaphorically, stands for a staggering variety of subjects that belong to a single quarter. Thus, the "quarter of sales" would encompass, among many other subjects, partnerships, guaranty, gifts and bequests, while that of "marriage" would cover as varied a field as dissolution of matrimony, foster relationships, custody, and wifely and family support. In the same vein, the "quarter of injuries" includes homicide, the Quranic punishments and the laws of war and peace, among other topics. Works generally ended with what we term procedural law, supplemented by coverage of slave manumission. Other works ended instead with inheritance and bequests.

What follows is a schematic account of legal subject matter. It will be noticed that the main "book" topics are followed by percentages indicating the space typically allocated to the discussion of each topic in legal works. Obviously, works differed from each other in this respect, and so what are given here are rough estimates of space, intended to give a general idea of the quantitative weight of each subject in the overall coverage of the law. However, the legal works had much in common in their proportionate coverage of the law. For example, the Book of Pledge, however short or long it is in various works, can never reach the magnitude of the Book of Prayer or that of Sales.

A. The First Quarter
  1. Book of Purity and Washing (7%)
  2. Book of Prayer (14%)
  3. Book of Alms-Tax (4%)
  4. Book of Fasting (3%)
  5. Book of Pilgrimage (6%)
  6. Book of Food and Drink (less than 1%) [some jurists discuss this and the following Book toward the end of the Third Quarter]
  7. Book of Hunting and Butchering Animals (less than 1%)

B. The Second Quarter

[Some jurists treat these topics in the Third Quarter, with the exception of inheritance and bequests which are generally delayed to the very end of their works.]

  8. Book of Sales (4%)
  9. Book of Pledge (1%)
  10. Book of Insolvency and Interdiction (1%)
  11. Book of Amicable Settlement (less than 1%)
  12. Book of Transfer (less than 1%)
  13. Book of Guaranty (less than 1%)
  14. Book of Partnership (less than 1%)
  15. Book of Agency (1%)
  16. Book of Acknowledgments (1.2%)
  17. Book of Deposit (less than 1%)
  18. Book of Loans (less than 1%)
  19. Book of Unlawful Appropriation (1.5%)
  20. Book of Preemption (1%)
  21. Book of Sleeping Partnership (less than 1%)
  22. Book of Agricultural Lease (less than 1%)
  23. Book of Rent and Hire (2%)
  24. Book of Cultivating Waste Land (less than 1%)
  25. Book of Charitable Trusts (*WAQF*, 1.5%)
  26. Book of Gifts (1%)
  27. Book of Found Property (less than 1%)
  28. Book of Foundling (less than 1%)
  29. Book of Rewards for Returning Escaped Slaves (less than 1%)
  30. Book of Quranic Shares (inheritance, 3.5%)
  31. Book of Bequests (2.5%)

C. The Third Quarter

[Some jurists treat these topics in the Second Quarter.]

32. Book of Marriage (3.5%)
33. Book of Dower (1%)
34. Book of Contractual Dissolution of Marriage (*khul*; less than 1%)
35. Book of Unilateral Dissolution of Marriage by Husband (2%)
36. Book of Re-marriage by the Same Couple (less than 1%)
37. Book of Husband's Oath not to have Sexual Intercourse with his Wife for Four Months (*ila'*; less than 1%)
38. Book of Husband's Oath not to have Sexual Intercourse with his Wife (*zihar*; less than 1%)
39. Book of Husband's Accusing his Wife of Being Unfaithful (less than 1%)
40. Book of Oaths (2%)
41. Book of Waiting Periods (1%)
42. Book of Foster Relationships (less than 1%)
43. Book of Family Support (1.2%)
44. Book of Child Custody (less than 1%)

D. The Fourth Quarter

45. Book of Torts (2%)
46. Book of Blood-Money (less than 2%)
47. Book of Quranically Regulated Infractions (5%)
    a. Sub-chapter on Apostasy
    b. Sub-chapter on Rebels
    c. Sub-chapter on Illicit Sexual Acts
    d. Sub-chapter on Accusing Someone of an Illicit Sexual Act
    e. Sub-chapter on Theft
    f. Sub-chapter on Highway Robbers
    g. Sub-chapter on Drinking Intoxicants
48. Book of Discretionary Punishments (*TA'ZIR*; less than 1%)
49. Book of War and Peace (*JIHAD*, 1.5%) [some jurists place this Book at the end of the First Quarter]
50. Book of Division of Booty (1%)
51. Book of Judges and Judgeship (3%)
52. Book of Suits and Evidence (1%)
53. Book of Testimonies (2%)
54. Book of Manumission (less than 1%)
55. Book of Manumission after Master's Death (less than 1%)
56. Book of Manumission for Payment (less than 1%)
57. Book of Female Slaves who had Children with their Master (less than 1%).

3   The legal schools

One of the most important features of the Shari'a and indeed of Islam as a whole is the pervasive role of the doctrinal legal schools. In Sunni Islam, these schools were four: the HANAFI, MALIKI, SHAFI'I and HANBALI, named after the four MASTER-JURISTS who were assumed to be their founders. (It is worthwhile noting that these schools are entirely different from, and share no characteristics with, the law schools in our universities nowadays.)

The Arabic word for the legal school is *MADHHAB*, a term that has several meanings, all of which are interconnected. Generally, the word means that which is followed and, more specifically, the opinion or idea that one chooses to adopt; hence, a particular opinion of a jurist. Historically, this meaning of the term is of early provenance, probably dating back to the end of the seventh century, but certainly to the middle of the eighth. By the early ninth century, its use had become common.

The term *madhhab* is associated with three other meanings that have emerged out of, and subsequent to, this basic usage, and which reflected the formation of schools. The first of these meanings is a principle defining the conceptual juristic boundaries of a set of cases. For example, an assumption of the Hanafis is that misappropriation, in order to obtain, must involve the unlawful removal of property from its original place, where it had been in the possession of the owner. The Hanbalis, on the other hand, define misappropriation as mere seizure of property, whether or not it is removed from its original place of ownership. Thus, taking possession of a rug by sitting on it (without removing it) is considered misappropriation by the Hanbalis, but not by the Hanafis. In terms of recovery of damages, this basic difference in definition contributed to generating significant differences between the two schools. Whereas the Hanbalis make the wrongdoer liable to the original owner for all growth of, and proceeds from, the misappropriated object, the Hanafis place severe restrictions on the ability of the owner to recover his accruing rights. The reasoning here is that the growth or proceeds of the misappropriated property were not yet in existence when the property was

31

"removed" from the hands of the rightful owner, and since they were not in existence, no liability on the part of the wrongdoer is deemed to arise. This example illustrates a central meaning of the term *madhhab* as a legal doctrine concerning a group of cases – in this instance cases pertaining to the recovery of damages – which are subsumed under a larger principle. And it is in this sense that it can be said that one school's doctrine differs, sometimes significantly, from another's.

The second meaning of *madhhab* is a jurist's individual opinion when this enjoys the highest authority in the school, as distinct from the third associated sense of *madhhab* where it is used to refer to a group of jurists who are loyal to an integral and, most importantly, *collective* legal doctrine attributed to a master-jurist from whom the school is known to have acquired particular, distinctive characteristics. Thus, after the formation of the schools, jurists began to be characterized as Hanafi, Maliki, Shafiʿi or Hanbali, as determined by their *doctrinal* (not personal) loyalty to one school or another. This doctrinal loyalty, it must be emphasized, is to a cumulative body of doctrine constructed by generations of leading jurists, which is to say, conversely, that loyalty is not extended to the individual doctrine of a single master-jurist. By the middle of the tenth century, or shortly thereafter, these meanings were all present, which is to say that by this time the legal schools had come into full maturity.

How and when did the concept of *madhhab* evolve from its basic meaning into its highly developed sense of a doctrinal school? As we have already seen, the early interest in law and legal studies evolved within the environment of the STUDY CIRCLES, where men learned in the Quran and the general principles of Islam began to discuss, among other things, various quasi-legal and often strictly legal issues. By about 730 AD, such learned men had already assumed the role of teachers whose circles often encompassed numerous students interested specifically in religious law. However, by that time, no obvious methodology of law and legal reasoning had yet evolved, so that one teacher's lecture might not have been entirely distinguishable, methodologically and as an *articulated* body of principles, from another's. Even the body of legal doctrine they taught was not yet complete, as can be attested from each teacher's particular interests. Some taught rules of inheritance, while others emphasized the law of ritual, which was a fundamental part of the law. More importantly, we have little reason to believe that the legal topics covered later were all present at this early stage.

During the first half of the eighth century, with SUBSTANTIVE LAW having become more systematic, the jurists had begun to develop their own legal assumptions and methodology. Teaching and intense scholarly debates within study circles must have sharpened the methods by which jurists were doing law, which in turn led them to defend their own, individual conceptions of the law. Each jurist, on adopting a particular method, gathered around him a certain following who learned their jurisprudence and method from him.

Yet, it was rare that a student or a young jurist would restrict himself to one circle or one teacher; indeed, it was not uncommon for young jurists to attend several circles in the same city. During the second half of the eighth century, aspiring jurists did not confine themselves to circles within one city, but traveled near and far in search of reputable teachers (one of the notable characteristics of learning in pre-modern Islam). Each prominent teacher attracted students who "took law" from him. A judge who had studied law under a teacher was likely to apply the teacher's doctrine in his court, although, again, loyalty was not exclusive to a single doctrine. If he proved to be a sufficiently promising and qualified jurist, he might "sit" as a professor in his own turn, transmitting to his students the legal knowledge he gained from his teachers, but seldom without his own reconstruction of this knowledge. The legal doctrines that Abu Hanifa, Malik and Shafi'i, among many others, taught to their students were largely a transmission from their own teachers. None of these, however, despite the fact that they were held up as school founders, constructed his own doctrine in its entirety, as later Islamic history would have us believe. Rather, all of them were in fact as much indebted to their teachers as these latter were indebted to their own.

During the eighth century, therefore, the term *madhhab* meant a group of students, LEGISTS, judges and jurists who had adopted the doctrine of a particular leading jurist, such as Abu Hanifa – a phenomenon that I call here a "personal school." Those who adopted or followed a jurist's doctrine were known as associates, namely, those who studied with or were scholarly companions of a jurist. Most leading jurists had such associates, a term that also meant "followers." Thus, all master-jurists were linked with a *madhhab*, namely, a personal school revolving around both his circle and personal legal doctrine.

Nonetheless, doctrinal loyalty was not yet in order. As we noted, it was not unusual for a legist to shift from one doctrine to another or simultaneously adopt a combination of doctrines belonging to two or more leading jurists. This became inconceivable once the doctrinal schools emerged.

Indeed, as it came to pass, the standard reference of the technical term "*madhhab*" was to the doctrinal school, which featured several characteristics lacking in its personal counterpart. First, the personal school comprised the substantive legal doctrine of a single leading jurist, and, at times, his doctrine as transmitted by one of his students. The doctrinal school, on the other hand, possessed a cumulative doctrine of substantive law in which the legal opinions of the leading jurist, now the assumed "founder," were only the first among equals; that is, equal to the rest of the opinions and doctrines held by various other jurists, also considered leaders *within* the school. In other words, the doctrinal school was a collective and authoritative entity, whereas the personal school remained limited to the individual doctrine of a single jurist.

The second characteristic was that the doctrinal school constituted as much a methodological entity as a substantive, doctrinal one. In other words, what distinguished a particular doctrinal school from another was largely its legal methodology and the substantive principles it adopted in dealing with its own law. Methodological awareness on this level had not yet developed in the personal schools, although it was on the increase from the middle of the eighth century.

Third, a doctrinal school was defined by its substantive boundaries, namely, by a certain body of law and methodological principles that clearly identified the outer limits of the school as a collective entity. The personal schools, on the other hand, had no such well-defined boundaries, and departure from these boundaries in favor of other legal doctrines and principles was a common practice.

The fourth characteristic, issuing from the third, was loyalty, for departure from legal doctrine and methodological principles amounted to abandoning the school, a major event in the life of a jurist. Doctrinal loyalty, in other words, was barely present in the personal schools, whereas in the later doctrinal schools it was a defining feature of both the school itself and the careers of its members.

How, then, did the doctrinal schools emerge? A central feature of the doctrinal school – yet a fifth characteristic distinguishing it from the personal school – was the creation of an axis of authority around which an entire methodology of law was constructed. This axis was the figure of the one who came to be known as the founder, the leading master-jurist, in whose name the cumulative, collective principles of the school were propounded. Of all the leaders of the personal schools – and they were many – only the four we mentioned above were raised to the level of "founder" of a doctrinal school. The rest did not advance to this stage, with the result that their personal schools did not long survive their deaths.

The so-called founder, the eponym of the school, thus became the axis of authority construction. As bearer of this authority, he was called the IMAM, and was characterized as an absolute master-jurist who was responsible for having created the school's methodology on the basis of which its precepts and law were constructed. Furthermore, his doctrine laid claim to originality not only because it derived directly from the revealed texts, but also, and equally importantly, because it was gleaned systematically from the texts by means of clearly identifiable interpretive principles. Its systematic character was seen as the product of a unified and cohesive methodology that only the founding imam could have forged; but a methodology itself inspired and dictated by revelation. To explain all of this epistemic competence, the imam was viewed as having been endowed with exceptional personal character and virtuosity. The embodiment of pure virtue, piety, modesty, mild asceticism and the best of ethical values, he represented the ultimate source of legal knowledge and moral authority.

What made a *madhhab* (as a doctrinal school) a *madhhab* is therefore this feature of authoritative doctrine whose ultimate fount is presumed to have been the absolute master-jurist, the founder, not the mere congregation of jurists under the name of a titular eponym. This congregation would have been meaningless without the centripetal effect of an authoritative, substantive and methodological doctrine constructed in the name of a founder.

Finally, we must ask the question: why did the doctrinal schools come into being in the first place? Wholly native to Islamic soil, the *madhhabs'* gestation was entirely occasioned by internal needs. We have noted that the embryonic formation of the schools started sometime during the last decades of the seventh century, taking the form of study circles in which pious scholars debated religious issues and taught interested students. The knowledge and production of legal doctrine began in these circles – nowhere else. Legal authority, therefore, became epistemic (i.e., knowledge-based) rather than political, social or even religious. That epistemic authority is *the* defining feature of Islamic law need not be doubted, although piety and morality played important supporting roles. A masterly knowledge of the law was the sole criterion in deciding where legal authority resided; and it resided with the scholars, not with the political rulers or any other source. This was as much true of the last decades of the seventh century as it was of the eighth century and thereafter. If a CALIPH actively participated in legal life, it was by virtue of his recognized personal knowledge of the law, not so much by virtue of his political office or military power. Thus, legal authority in Islam was personal and private; it was in the persons of the individual jurists (be they laymen or, on occasion, caliphs) that authority resided, and it was this competence in religious legal knowledge that was later to be known as *ijtihad* – a cornerstone of Islamic law.

Devolving as it did upon the individual jurists who were active in study circles, legal authority did not reside in the government or ruler, and this was a prime factor in the rise of the *madhhab*. Whereas law – as a legislated system – was often "state"-based in other imperial and complex civilizations, in Islam the ruling powers had, until the dawn of modernity, almost nothing to do with the production and promulgation of legal knowledge or law. Therefore, in Islam, the need arose to anchor law in a system of authority that was not political, especially since the ruling political institutions were, as we shall see, deemed highly suspect. The study circles, which consisted of no more than groups of legal scholars and interested students, lacked the ability to produce a unified legal doctrine that would provide an axis of legal authority. For while every region possessed its own distinct, practice-based legal system, there was nevertheless a multiplicity of study circles in each, and within each circle scholars disagreed on a wide variety of opinions.

The personal schools afforded the first step toward providing an axis of legal authority, since the application (in courts and *fatwas*) and the teaching of a single, unified doctrine – that is, the doctrine of a leading jurist around whom a personal school had formed – permitted a measure of doctrinal unity. Yet, the large number of personal schools was only slightly more effective than the multiplicity of study circles, so an axis of authority was still needed. The personal schools, forming around all the major scholars, were doctrinally divergent and still very numerous, numbering perhaps as many as two dozen. Furthermore, the leader's doctrine (which was little more than a body of legal opinions) was not always applied integrally, being subjected, as it were, to the discretion or even reformulation of the judge or jurisconsult applying it. Doctrinal and juristic loyalty was also still needed.

The eighth-century community of jurists not only formulated law but also administered it in the name of the ruling dynasty. In other words, this community was – juristically speaking – largely independent, having the competence to steer a course that would fulfill its mission as it saw fit. Yet, while maintaining juristic and largely judicial independence, this community did serve as the ruler's link to the masses, aiding him in his bid for legitimacy. As long as the ruler benefited from this legitimizing agency, the legal community profited from financial support and an easily acquired independence.

Rallying around a single juristic doctrine was probably the only means for a personal school to gain loyal followers and thus attract political/financial support. Such support was not limited to direct financial favors bestowed by the ruling elite, but extended to prestigious judicial appointments that guaranteed not only handsome pay but also political and social influence. These considerations alone can explain the need to rally around outstanding figures whose legal authority as absolute *mujtahid*-imams or master-jurists had to be constructed in order to raise their personal schools to doctrinal entities. This construction was a way to anchor law in a source of authority that constituted an alternative to the authority of the body-politic; or, to put it more accurately, it came to fill a gap left untouched by Muslim rulers. Thus, whereas in other cultures the ruling dynasty promulgated the law, enforced it and constituted the locus of legal authority (or legal power), in Islam it was the doctrinal legal school that produced law and afforded its axis of authority. In other words, legal authority resided in the collective, juristic doctrinal enterprise of the school, not in the ruler or in the doctrine of a single jurist.

The legal schools represent a fundamental feature of the Shariʿa. Once they were formed, and until they were dissipated by modern reform, no jurist could operate independently of them. Although lay persons were free to follow any of these schools for a particular transaction or way of conduct (e.g., rituals), each school tended to have influence in particular regions. The Hanafi school started in Iraq but quickly extended its influence eastward, to Iran (until about 1500), Central Asia and the Indian Sub-Continent. Later on, it was adopted as the school of choice of the Ottoman Empire. Today, traditionally Hanafi populations include those in Bangladesh, Pakistan, India, Central Asia, Iraq, Syria, Jordan, Palestine and Turkey.

The Maliki school started in the Hejaz but immediately spread to Egypt and, extensively, to Muslim Spain (until the fifteenth century) and North Africa, where it has continued to hold unrivaled sway until now. With the main exceptions of South Africa, Zanzibar and some parts of Egypt, the populations of the African continent have been traditionally of Maliki persuasion.

The Shafiʿi school began essentially in Egypt, but later spread to Syria (which gradually became mostly Hanafi after the sixteenth or seventeenth century), Lower Egypt, some parts of the Yemen, Malaysia and Indonesia. The Hanbali school, the smallest of the four, was strong in the city of Baghdad between the tenth and thirteenth centuries, but now has a wide following in Saudi Arabia.

While the Zaydi Shiʿi school is predominant in the Yemen, its Twelver (Jaʿfari) counterpart has been strong in Iran (after c. 1500), Bahrain, southern Iraq, southern Lebanon and Azerbaijan.

4   Jurists, legal education and politics

Introduction

With the background provided in the previous chapter, we now turn to discuss how the class of legists perpetuated itself and how its evolution intertwined with the interests of the ruler. During the first two or three centuries of Islam, education was largely and deliberately disconnected from politics, being limited to private scholarship which the rulers sought to influence without much success. The story of this chapter is that of the transformation of legal scholarship from a highly independent enterprise to a markedly subordinate system that came to serve the ruler and his administration. However, as we have already intimated, this eventual subordination did not mean that the content of the law and its application was compromised by any political accommodation. In fact, it was the ruler who – from the beginning of Islam until the middle of the nineteenth century – consistently had to bow to the dictates of the Shariʿa and its representatives in governing the populace. As a moral force, and without the coercive tools of a state, the law stood supreme for over a millennium.

Sometime during the late tenth century, the law college, known in Islamic languages as the *MADRASA*, came into being, exhibiting a tendency to superimpose itself over the study circle, and in the long run changing some if its features. The circle differed from the *madrasa* in one crucial respect: it was largely a free scholarly gathering of a professor and his students, for the most part without political interference and unfettered by financial patronage. The *madrasa*, on the other hand, was as much, if not more, a financial and a political phenomenon as it was an educational one, and it subjected legal education to increasingly systematic control by rulers. It was established as a charitable trust through the law of *WAQF*, whereby a mosque would be dedicated to the teaching of law, and the professor and students provided with, among other things, stipends, food, a library and dormitories. While ordinary men and women founded many such *madrasas*, these remained limited educational projects usually having no effect or influence beyond the local neighborhood.

What gave rise to the complex relationship between law and politics was the important fact that those who founded the largest, most affluent and most prestigious *madrasa*s were the rulers and their immediate entourage (viziers, commanders, mothers, wives, brothers and daughters). Legal education and the informal circle could not, in other words, escape the effects of political control. An account of the development of pre-modern Muslim education is therefore important not only for its own sake, but also, as we shall later see, for explaining the foundational and dramatic changes that befell Islamic law during the modern period.

To understand the historical evolution of Islamic legal education, a number of threads must be brought together. First, we must trace the dynamics of the early relationship between the legal scholars and the caliphate, for in these dynamics lie the seeds of the political elite's interest in the jurists, judges and their law; second, a brief account of legal education within the circle is in order, for it was this forum of legal scholarship that remained, until the nineteenth century, the most enduring mechanism of transmitting knowledge in Islam; third, we need to describe the rise of the *madrasa* and its patronage, a line of enquiry that can hardly be separated from the law of *waqf*, which was in turn vital to the *madrasa*'s very establishment; and finally, we will return to the relationship that obtained in pre-modern times between the legal profession and the ruling elite.

Law and government in the formative period

During most of the first century of Islam, the main representatives of the law were the proto-*qadi*s who, to all intents and purposes, were not only government employees and administrators of sorts but also laymen who – despite their experience in adjudication and knowledge of customary law – had no formal legal training of the sort that came to prevail later. Their appointments as *qadi*s were most often combined with other functions, including posts as provincial secretaries and story-tellers who transmitted biblical stories, Quranic narratives and details from the biography of the Prophet. In these capacities, they functioned as the provincial governor's assistants, if not – on rare occasions – as governors-cum-*qadi*s. In the near absence of a class of private, legal specialists at this time, these proto-*qadi*s constituted the bulk of what may roughly be termed a legal profession, and as such they were an integral part of the ruling class.

Despite the inseparability of the proto-*qadi*'s office from that of government administration, the government in this early period rarely, if ever, interfered in determining what law was applied. The caliphate was by no means a distinct or a comprehensive source of law. No edicts regulating law are known to have come down from caliphs; there were no constitutions, and certainly no legal codes of any kind. Even when no class of legal specialists had yet appeared, neither the caliphs nor their viziers or provincial governors made any effort to control or appropriate the sphere of law, which was largely customary and Quranic.

The legal role of the caliph was one of *occasional* legislative intervention, coming into play when called for or when special needs arose. But this intervention must be understood to have been harmonious with those laws and rules propounded by the proto-*qadi*s, for the caliphs drew on the same sources. The caliphal legislative function was thus minimal, falling well short of the role of exemplary religious and political leader. In this latter role, some – but by no means all – caliphs were seen by the proto- and later *qadi*s as providing a good example to follow, but this was not because of royal edicts or intrusive policy. The occasional invocation of a caliph's ruling was an entirely private act, the free choice of a *qadi* or a scholar. On the other hand, caliphal orders enjoining a judge to issue a particular ruling were a rare occurrence and ephemeral. Such orders did not represent "secular" or "royal" law as opposed to religious law, but rather a different interpretation of the same sources of authority. In such cases, caliphs were themselves pronouncing on law as jurist-*qadi*s or acting on the advice of legal specialists or *qadi*s sitting in assembly with them. Thus, the proto-*qadi* was principally a government administrator who acted largely according to his normative understanding of how disputes should be resolved – guided, as he was, by the force of social custom, Quranic values and the established ways of the forebears.

The early caliphs saw themselves as equally subject to the law, and acted within the consensual framework of a distinct and largely binding social and legal fabric. Like their predecessors – the Arab tribal leaders and even Muhammad himself – they viewed themselves as part not only of their communities but also, and primarily, of the social and political customs that had come down to them across the generations and from which they could not have dissociated themselves. The proto-*qadi*s' relative judicial independence was therefore due to the fact that social, customary and evolving religious values governed all, but were no more known to, or incumbent upon, the caliph than his judges. If the judges queried the caliphs with regard to difficult cases, it was also true that the caliphs queried the judges. That knowledge of the law – or legal authority – was a two-way street in the first century or two is abundantly clear; the caliph of Islam was far from an exclusive source of law, and not even a distinct one.

The emergence, around 700 AD, of a class of private legal specialists signaled a new phase in Islamic history, one characterized by the spreading in Muslim societies of a new religious impulse accompanied by an ascetic piety that became the hallmark of the learned religious elite in general and of the jurists and later mystics in particular. The importance of this piety in Muslim culture cannot be over-emphasized, either at this early time or in the centuries that followed. If anything, its increasing force was to contribute significantly to later developments. Yet, even in this early period, ascetic piety took many forms, from dietary abstinence to abhorrence of indulgent lifestyles (with which the later caliphs were, with some exceptions, partly associated). Above all, this piety called for justice and equality before God – the very emblem of Islam itself.

By the end of the first century and the beginning of the second, it had become clear that a wedge existed between the ruling elite and the emerging legal class. This wedge made itself evident with two concurrent developments, the first of which was the spread of a new religious ethic among the ranks of the legal specialists, who increasingly insisted upon ideal human conduct driven by piety. In fact, it is nearly impossible to distinguish this ethic from the social category of legal scholars, since the scholars' constitution was, as we have said, entirely defined by this ethic of piety, mild asceticism and knowledge of the law and religion. The second wedge was the increasing power and institutionalization of the ruling elite, who began to depart from the egalitarian forms of tribal leadership known to the early caliphs and according to which they had conducted themselves. The later caliphs began to live in palaces, wield coercive powers, and gradually but increasingly distance themselves from the people they ruled. This gap was further increased by the growth in size of Muslim populations, especially in the larger cities throughout the Muslim lands. Thus, while earlier, smaller communities were easily accessed by the ruler, the later communities were large enough to prevent him from forging personal alliances and ties at a local level.

These religious feelings, enriched by ethical and idealistic values and inspired by the extensive religious narratives of the story-tellers and TRADITIONISTS (those who recorded and transmitted exemplary Prophetic biography), began to equate government and political power with vice and corruption. This attitude originated sometime around the end of the seventh century, and was reflected in the many accounts and biographical details speaking of appointments to the office of judgeship. As of this time, and continuing for nearly a millennium thereafter, the theme of judicial appointment as an adversity, even a calamity, for those so designated became a recurring detail of biographical narrative (amply recorded in the countless biographical works the jurists have written about themselves). Jurists are reported to have wept – sometimes together with family members – upon hearing the news of their appointment;

others went into hiding, or preferred to be whipped rather than accept office.

Suspicion of political power and of those associated with it was so pervasive that the traditionists – and probably the story-tellers amongst them – managed to find a number of Prophetic traditions that condemned judges and rulers alike, placing both ranks in diametrical moral and eschatological opposition to the learned, pious jurists. On the Day of Judgment, one tradition pronounces typically, the judges will be lumped together with the sultans in Hellfire, while the pious jurists will join the Prophets in Paradise. Yet, this profound suspicion of association with the political did not mean that the legists predominantly refused judgeships, nor even that they did not desire them. In fact, by and large, they accepted appointment and many junior legists must even have viewed it as a high point in their careers. At the same time, the ruling elite could not dispense with the jurists. Religion and, by definition, legal knowledge had now become the exclusive domain of the jurist, the private scholar. It is precisely because of this quality of learning and knowledge that the ruling elite needed the legists to fulfill the Empire's legal needs, despite its profound apprehension that the legists' loyalties were not to the government but to the civil populations and to their own law and its requirements, which frequently conflicted with the views of the ruling class. However, the fact remained that each side needed the other, and thus both learned to cooperate with each other.

Many legists were often paid handsome salaries when appointed to a judgeship, but they also often received generous grants as private scholars. Throughout the eighth century, the remuneration for judicial appointments was steadily on the increase, reaching by the end of the period levels of income that made judgeships in large cities highly coveted. The *qadi*s, however, were not alone in benefiting from government subsidies. The leading private scholars were no less dependent on the government's financial favors, and this, as we shall see, was for a good reason.

The rulers, on the other hand, were in dire need of legitimization, which they found in the circles of the legal profession. The latter served as an effective tool for reaching the masses from whose ranks they had emerged and whose interests they represented and protected. As we noted, the jurists and judges emerged as the civic leaders who, though themselves a product of the masses, found themselves, by the nature of their profession, involved in the day-to-day running of civic affairs. Jurists and judges felt responsibility toward the common man and woman, and on their own frequently initiated action on behalf of the oppressed without any formal petition being made. As a product of their own social environment, the legists' fate and worldview were inextricably intertwined with the interests of their societies.

Hence the religious scholars in general and the legists in particular were often called upon to express the will and aspirations of those belonging to the non-elite classes. They not only interceded on their behalf at the higher reaches of power, but also represented for the masses the ideal of piety, rectitude and fine education. Their very profession as Guardians of Religion, experts in religious law and exemplars of the virtuous Muslim lifestyle made them not only the most genuine representatives of the masses but also the true "heirs of the Prophet," as one Prophetic report came to attest. They were the locus of legitimacy and of religious and moral authority. The later caliphs realized that brute power could not yield legitimacy, which they were striving to attain. Legitimacy lay in the preserve of religion, erudition, ascetic piety and moral rectitude; in short, in the *persons* of those men who had profound knowledge of, and fashioned their lives after, the example of the Prophet and the exemplary forefathers. Thus, these caliphs understood that, inasmuch as the pious scholars needed their financial resources, they in turn needed the scholars' cooperation, for the latter were the ruler's only source of political legitimacy.

Increasing Islamization among the masses throughout the first two centuries of Islam left the caliphs no option but to endorse the religious law as interpreted by the legal scholars. Those who had mastered this science (of jurisprudence) were the jurists, and it was they and their ability to determine the law that set restrictions on the absolute powers of the rulers, be they caliphs or provincial governors. The caliph and the entire political hierarchy that he commanded were subject to the law of God, like anyone else. No exceptions could be made. The very reason for the caliphate itself was to enforce the religious law, not to make it. If the caliph occasionally involved himself in resolving legal problems, he did so on a par with the legists, and not as one superior to them in their roles as judges and jurists. His engagement was an integral part of, and no more than a supplement to, the legists' interpretive activities. The result then was not a struggle over religious authority, where the caliphs competed with the legal scholars, for the caliphs did not challenge the legal scholars in their own domain of competence. Rather, caliphal engagement in the law represented an effort to gain political legitimacy through a demonstration of juristic competence that the jurists and the early caliphs (who were set up as models to be emulated) possessed.

As caliphs increasingly grew detached from what had become a specialized field of legal knowledge, they were expected to surround themselves with competent jurists who would assist them in addressing difficult legal matters. This, being conducive to their legitimacy, they duly observed in practice. So, whereas the earliest caliphs could acquire legitimacy by virtue of their own knowledge of the law, it later became necessary to supplement the caliphal office with jurists who routinely sat in royal courts and who, in effect, constituted the legitimacy that the caliphs (and later all sultans and emirs) needed. In these royal–juristic assemblies, not only were matters of religion, law and literature discussed, but scholarly disputations were held between major jurists. Almost every caliph of the eighth, ninth and tenth centuries was known to have befriended the legists, and later emirs and sultans did much the same.

The privileges and favors the jurists acquired not only brought them easy access to the royal court and to the circles of the political elite, but also rendered them highly influential in government policy as it affected legal matters, and perhaps in other matters of state. Beginning in the middle of the eighth century, almost all major judicial appointments were made on the recommendation of the CHIEF JUSTICE at the royal court or the assembly of jurists gathered by the caliph, or both. And when the provincial governor wished to find a qualified judge, he too sought the advice of jurists. Some jurists, throughout Islamic history, were immeasurably influential in legal as well as political matters.

However, there remained points of friction between political power and religious law. The relationship between the two was constantly negotiated, and it was never devoid of sporadic challenges mounted by the ruling elite, not against the law, but against its application by its representatives. And while such challenges seem to have occurred mostly in the provinces and on the periphery, the caliphs themselves also appear, on rare occasions, to have interfered in the judiciary and the judicial process. Yet, it remains true that the caliphal office was thought to uphold the highest standards of justice according to the holy law, and the caliphs themselves felt such responsibility, generally conducting themselves in accordance with these expectations. Inasmuch as the law in and of itself possessed authority, the caliph and his office were seen not only as another locus of the holy law, but also as its guarantor and enforcer. As a rule, the caliphs and their provincial representatives upheld court decisions and normally did not intervene in the judicial process.

From the first centuries of Islam until the later Ottomans (who ruled vast areas from the sixteenth to the twentieth century), Islamic political culture displayed a particular, if not unique, pattern of governance. As a rule, monarchs and their lieutenants acted with remarkable fairness and justice when arbitrating disputes and conflicts to which they were not parties. Their occasional infringements were usually associated with, and limited to, cases in which their own interests were involved. Although this in no way means that encroachment occurred whenever such interests were present, it does suggest that whenever rulers staked their interest in the judicial process, they had to weigh their overall gains and losses. To have accomplished their ends through coercion would have meant that their legitimacy had failed the test. On the other hand, total compliance with the law at times meant that their quest for material gain or will to power would be frustrated. It was this equation that they attempted to work out and balance carefully, at times succeeding but at others not. The POST-FORMATIVE centuries of Islamic history suggest that rulers generally preferred to maintain an equation in favor of compliance with the religious law, since compliance was the means by which the ruling elite could garner the sympathies, or at least tacit approval, of the populace.

Yet, compliance with the law was a relatively passive act, insufficient on its own to promote and augment the much coveted goal of political legitimacy. As it happened, the sphere of legal education proved to be fertile ground, allowing the ruling dynasties not only to garner legitimacy but also to implement, during the nineteenth century, fundamental and ever-lasting changes in the legal system. It is to legal education then that we now turn.

The informal financial patronage offered to the legists during the early period was in due course to be systematized and institutionalized. It so happened that the law college, the *madrasa*, became the chief means by which the legists were coopted by the ruling elites. The fairly sudden appearance of the *madrasa* on the scene and its rapid diffusion make it impossible to imagine the legal and educational history of Islam without the presence of this institution. Similarly, it is impossible to make sense of the demise of Islamic law during the modern period without taking into account this educational institution. Yet, as a legal and educational institution, the *madrasa* continued to operate in ways thoroughly rooted in the pedagogical tradition that had existed prior to its appearance. This tradition was represented in the study circle we earlier discussed, at once an educational, legal and sociological phenomenon. The circle was in effect the engine that ran legal education; indeed, the *madrasa* would not have been viable had it not been for the existence of the circle.

The circle manifested a certain hierarchy, where the professor would be flanked by his senior students who themselves would soon become teachers or legal specialists of some sort. At times, they were accomplished scholars in other fields, attending the circle in order to gain knowledge or mastery in law. These advanced students also functioned as teaching assistants. A remarkable feature of this circular hierarchy was the perfect continuity between teacher and students. The teacher was the most learned, the advanced students his immediate subordinates, and the less advanced students the subordinates of the latter.

Until about the fourteenth century, the circle exhibited an intimate relationship between professor and students, especially advanced ones. The professor was not merely a teacher of a technical science, as modern university professors are. He was an educator, a companion, a supporter and a moral mentor. Instilling a deep sense of morality based on the concept of rectitude was as much part of the curriculum as any "formal" subject (if there was ever a curriculum in our sense of the word). As we shall see later, the application of law presupposed a system of social morality, a system upon which the efficacy of law depended and from which it could not be separated. The professor, among others, cultivated in the student the elements of this moral system. The professor–student relationship was often akin to that of father and son, and many students not only resided in, and dined at, the homes of their professors but married their daughters as well. And it was precisely this institution of marriage that fostered close ties between the legal class in one city or region and between and among them in distant locales.

Each professor was free to teach the treatises of his choice, a freedom later mildly restricted by the appearance of authorized texts of law. Although any type of treatise could be taught, abridgments were generally preferred after the eleventh century when they became abundant. Some of these abridgments were specifically produced by professors for teaching purposes, their intent being to sum up legal doctrine by invoking legal principles and alluding to "cases" that supported these principles. The professor explained the terse statements of the abridgment by appealing to the large compendia and *fatwa* collections on which these abridgments were based. The students had to memorize the abridgment, not for its own sake but as an outline of the law embedded in the comprehensive and extensive works. The professor's function in the circle was to make the abridgment intelligible and comprehensible. Repetition and further explanation of the day's lesson were performed by the teaching assistant after the professor had left the circle. The teaching assistant also listened to the students recite what they had learned, his task being to ensure that the lesson was understood before the next session was held.

The teaching was manifestly oral. The student did not read the work for himself in silence but listened to the professor, who would recite the work for all to hear. This reading was inevitably accompanied by commentary, the true contribution of the teacher. Learning was also conducted on the initiative of the student: he read the work out loud before the professor, who queried him on difficult points. The two processes of instruction were at times combined. A professor might teach his students a text he had authored himself, and the students would write down the lectures, thereby producing a copy of the book. Reading the copied text back to the professor constituted a process of certification that ensured that the work conformed in every detail to the demands of the professor. While this process constituted an integral part of the activity of publishing (namely, making hand-written copies of an author's work accessible to the public), it was often an important ingredient in advanced legal education. The last stage of this education was the writing of the dissertation or "commentary" that showed the mastery of the student in a specialized field of law. Some of these dissertations were, and continue to be, considered impressive treatises on legal scholarship.

For centuries, therefore, the circle – serving as the locus of the educational, social and moral relationships between professors and students – defined Muslim education. It was and remained until the nineteenth century the only Islamic form of imparting and receiving knowledge, despite the introduction of the *madrasa*. The latter, it must be emphasized, did not constitute a new form of education but rather bestowed on the study circle an external legal framework that allowed educational activity to be conducted under the auspices of endowments. The *madrasa*, in other words, affected neither the curriculum of the circle nor its method of transmitting knowledge. It was the professor, not the *madrasa*, who decided the curriculum, and it was he who continued to enjoy an exclusive monopoly over the granting of licenses. The pre-modern *madrasas*, as "institutions" that possessed no juristic personality, bestowed not a single diploma or license.

The role of endowments

The basic features of the *madrasa* appear to have developed toward the end of the eighth century, when provisions and salaries began to be made in favor of the staff of certain mosques, including the professors who taught law there. Soon thereafter, some mosques were enlarged to include dormitories for transient students and even for the professors themselves. Eventually, the salaries and food and shelter for students and professors were paid by endowments (*waqf*). The *madrasa*, the last stage of this development, came to meet all the other essential needs of professors and students, and this included an endowed, fully furnished building for the meeting of study circles, sleeping quarters for staff and students, food, a library, paper, ink, and much else.

The founding in Baghdad of eleven imposing *madrasas* during the second half of the eleventh century by the Saljuq vizier Nizam al-Mulk (1063–92) was a significant event that brought the *madrasa* onto the center stage of Islamic history. By the end of the century, the *madrasa* had spread to lands west of Baghdad, including Cairo, Damascus and, later, Istanbul, the capital of the Ottoman Empire. By the time the Mamluks came to power in the middle of the thirteenth century, Cairo had thirty-two *madrasa*s, and Alexandria could claim several more. According to one count, Cairo would increase its *madrasa*s to seventy-three by the early fifteenth century, and by 1869 the active *madrasa*s of Istanbul alone had reached, by the lowest estimate, 166, with no fewer than 5,370 students.

The significance of this astounding proliferation of *madrasa*s will be addressed later. But in order to appreciate fully the meaning and ramifications of this increase, especially in light of modern reforms, it would be better to dwell further on the nature and constitution of the *madrasa*. Physically, the *madrasa* was constituted of a building that at times was the mosque itself, but at others was a special structure built as an annex to a mosque. Inns were also built in the vicinity of the mosque, separate from the *madrasa*, but at times they constituted a part of the annex that was the *madrasa*. Yet all this, even the wealth that was needed to sustain it, was not enough for "raising up" a *madrasa*. There was something else needed to bring all these ingredients to operate in a particular way, and this was the monumental law and practice of *waqf*, a defining and enormously important aspect of the culture and material civilization of Islam.

The law of *waqf*, therefore, represented the glue that could bind the human, physical and monetary elements together. Essentially, *waqf* was a thoroughly religious and pious concept, and as a material institution it was meant to be a charitable act of the first order. One gave up one's property "for the sake of God," a philanthropic act which meant offering aid and support to the needy (this latter defined in a broad sense). The promotion of education, especially of religious legal education, represented one of the best forms of promoting religion itself. A considerable proportion of charitable trusts were thus directed at *madrasa*s, although *waqf* provided significant contributions toward building mosques, Sufi orders, hospitals, public fountains, soup kitchens, travelers' lodges, and a variety of public works, notably bridges. A substantial part of the budget intended for such philanthropic enterprises was dedicated to the maintenance, daily operational costs and renovation of *waqf* properties. A typical *waqf* consisted of a mosque and rental property (e.g., shops), the rent from which supported the operation and maintenance of the mosque.

Once the founder alienated his or her property as a *waqf*, the act was legally deemed irrevocable, entailing as it did the complete transfer of the right to ownership from the hands of the founder to those of God. Once alienated, the property could not be bought, sold, inherited, gifted, mortgaged or transferred in any other manner. The only exception was when the property ceased to serve its intended purposes. Only then was it permissible to sell it in order to purchase another, usually equivalent, property that would serve the same purpose. The property was usually immovable, but some movables, such as books, were at times the object of *waqf*s. Thus libraries constituted an essential part of endowed *madrasa*s.

The founder appointed trustees to manage the property, designated beneficiaries, and determined the ratio of benefit for each beneficiary. He could appoint himself or a member of his family as the trustee of the *waqf* and could stipulate that he and/or one or more of his descendants could alter, in the face of changing circumstances, the terms of the *waqf* deed. However, once the deed was certified and witnessed (usually before a judge), the founder could no longer effect any substantive changes to its stipulations. The judge had the ultimate power to supervise and oversee the *waqf*'s administration, budget and operation, and he intervened whenever a situation not covered by the deed arose or whenever he felt his intervention was necessary or called for.

The trustee administered the *waqf* in accordance with duties, responsibilities and powers specified in the deed. He could appoint assistants or deputies to help him in the dispensation of these responsibilities, the most important of which were: maintenance of the *waqf* properties; appointing and dismissing staff whose duties included cleaning and repairing; leasing property and collecting rent for the sake of the beneficiaries and for payment of salaries; farming land and selling its produce to generate supporting income; and resolving disputes and representing the endowment's interests in any litigation.

The charitable nature of the *waqf* dictated that the rich could not benefit from charitable endowments, and this was the understanding of the majority of jurists. A minority of later jurists, however, came to approve of establishing endowments for the benefit of the well-to-do, a modification of doctrine that appears to have reflected the practice on the ground.

The average Muslim individual founded mainly the smaller, local and less significant endowments. On the other hand, it was almost a universal pattern that the founders of those major endowments that supported, among other things, *madrasa*s and Sufi orders were the rich and powerful, in particular the ruling elite and their retinue. Their endowments dwarfed not only all other endowments, but even the large public buildings in Muslim cities. A case in point is the *madrasa* of the Mamluk sultan Hasan, built in Cairo at the end of the fourteenth century. Of colossal dimensions, it features a spacious inner courtyard, flanked by four large halls that hosted the study circles of four professors, each representing one of the legal schools of Sunni Islam. Multistoried edifices lying between these halls supported other *madrasa*s, with each *madrasa* offering its students separate accommodation and a mosque. The endowment's student population exceeded five hundred, and all but about a hundred of these studied law. Those who did not specialize in law studied, among other things, Quranic exegesis, Prophetic reports, language, logic, mathematics and medicine. Several imams led prayers in the various mosques of the college, and over a hundred Quran readers maintained an uninterrupted recitation of the Quran. All building and personnel expenses were paid by endowed revenues, as were the costs of construction itself. Typically, all major *madrasa*s included such facilities, not to mention other features such as primary schools and a tomb chamber for the founder and his family.

These towering and awe-inspiring royal buildings outlived the more modest *waqf*s and, more importantly, projected the ruler's munificence and political power. This projection is a nearly universal characteristic of rulers, and as such it must have been partly on the mind of the sultans, emirs and their political dependants when they embarked on establishing these endowments. Yet, this consideration was not the prime motive behind their seemingly auspicious acts. Uppermost in their minds was their crucial (even desperate) need to find a group or an entity that could represent their rule to the masses and represent the masses before their rule. If the latter part of the equation was important, it was so because it served the imperatives of the former, which at the end of the day amounted to little more than an anxious search for legitimacy.

The question that inevitably arises here is: why this search? The answer lies partly in the universal nature of pre-modern government, and partly in the specific circumstances of the Muslim context – in contradistinction, for instance, to those of China and Europe. Pre-modern governments typically exercised their power through small ruling elites, with a limited sphere of direct influence. As we noted earlier, they could not penetrate the societies they ruled, nor could they regulate the internal affairs of their subject populations.

More importantly, rulers failed to have *systemic* control over the societies they governed because they lacked the mechanisms necessary to administer the smallest units of which these societies were made. This is another way of saying that the pre-modern state lacked the bureaucratic organization that provided the tools for establishing particular relations of power, relations that are the cornerstone of all modern political regimes. Once firmly rooted in a society, impersonal bureaucracy tends to replace personal rule. Unlike bureaucratic rule, therefore, pre-modern forms of governance depended upon personal loyalty rather than upon obedience to abstract, impersonal regulations.

The absence of pervasive bureaucracies from such pre-modern forms of governance meant that the ruler was navigating at the surface of the societies he ruled. Even if he had a staff that could be hierarchically deployed to reach the lowest social strata, loyalty to him progressively dissipated as it moved away from the center. In other words, in the absence of the modern rule of bureaucracy (with all its attendant props, including nationalism and surveillance), the farther the pre-modern official found himself from the center of power, the less loyalty he had to the ruler, and, in turn, the more loyalty he had to the social group from which he hailed. Thus, the ruler could neither penetrate nor control or integrate these societies. He merely sat atop a pyramid of "self-reliant" groups consisting of linguistic and religious communities, guilds, clans, village assemblies, city councils and literate elites whose internal ties of loyalty were unsurpassable, and whose daily lives were barely touched by whatever administrative machinery the ruler could muster.

In the specifically Islamic context, there were at least three features in the exercise of political power that further intensified the gap between the ruling elite and the populace. First, the rulers and dynasties of the Islamic world, at least from Transoxiana and India to Egypt (but to a certain extent also in South East Asia), were not native to the territories they ruled. In general, they and their armies neither shared the cultures of the populations they governed nor spoke their languages. Arguably, this alone was a formidable obstacle. Second, until the thirteenth century, Islamic dynasties did not last long enough to establish genuine roots among the subject populations, in terms either of creating a "rule of bureaucracy" (as had been achieved in Europe) or of building institutionalized mechanisms that tied them in a particular relationship of power to these populations. Owing to the fluid nature of political loyalty, no policy that may have aimed at creating such mechanisms could have outlasted a ruler's death, for loyalty was to the person, not to a policy enshrined in "corporate" governance. Third, and despite the ancient secretarial traditions of the Near East, Islamic rulers could never command powerful and intrusive bureaucracies such as those developed in Europe or Sung China. With the partial exception of the Ottomans (a semi-European empire), the Muslim ruling elites saw no need to develop the surveillance–bureaucratic mechanisms which Europe later excelled at producing.

Thus, the dynastic rulers who governed Muslim lands after the ninth century (and who eclipsed the caliphate) could not administer their domains directly, having constantly to appeal to the legal profession that served as representatives of the "self-reliant" groups referred to above. This appeal, as we saw earlier, was also characteristic of the caliphate, although the latter differed from the warlords in one important respect: it possessed the politico-religious authority to speak and act in the name of Islam, whereas the later foreign rulers did not, for they were mostly foreigners and, as if this were not enough to alienate them from the populace, they were in want of authority as well as legitimacy. Accordingly, they stood in dire need of local, indigenous support. It was the legal profession that provided this support, but not readily and not without much reluctance, for a substantial investment had first to be made on the part of these rulers in order to successfully coopt this profession.

Among the first major dynastic warlords to sweep through Iran and the Middle East were the Saljuqs (r. 1055–1157), committed Sunnis who defeated the Buyids (r. 934–1055), but otherwise lacked both religious authority and political legitimacy. Toward solving this problem, the Saljuqs set in motion a pattern of governance that was to be emulated and reinforced until the nineteenth century. Their first experiment was in the province of Khurasan, where they turned to a policy of establishing *madrasa*s.

Deriving their moral authority and social standing from the religious law, the legists were the only civilian elite that could represent the foreign ruler and the indigenous subjects to each other. By the eleventh century, the social backgrounds of the legists had become varied, representing all segments of society. They hailed as much from the lowest strata of tradesmen and farmers as from affluent merchant families and the politically influential secretarial classes. Their socio-economic connections – deeply embedded in their own societies but also in relative proximity to the ruling classes – thus allowed them to fulfill a variety of functions in mediating the relationship between the government and the subject population.

These *madrasa*s were effectively used to recruit the loyalties of the major jurists in the larger cities. Probably the first to exploit so skillfully the minutiae of the law of *waqf* for political gains, the Saljuq vizier Nizam al-Mulk personally took charge of appointing, with handsome pay, well-known jurists and law professors. He retained exclusive powers over appointment and dismissal, for this guaranteed his leverage to bestow *personal* favors and thus acquire the loyalty of the legal profession. As political loyalty was not institutional, Nizam al-Mulk's personal involvement was indispensable. With the partial exception of the later Ottomans, this personal involvement was invariably the rule. It was the sultan, emir, vizier or (often) influential female members of the ruling elite who founded *madrasa*s, named them after themselves, and took a personal interest in how they were run and who taught in them. It was in this way that the foreign rulers and military commanders, who characterized the political scene in the Muslim world for centuries, could insert themselves into social networks, thereby fitting their political strategies into the populations they ruled.

By the end of the eleventh century, a substantial segment of the legal elite was in the pay of government. With the incorporation of the professors into the *madrasa* system, the political domain encroached further into the terrain of the law, subordinating a considerable segment – even the elite – of the professorial profession and contributing to the increasing diminution of the "moral community" of the legists. Some of the best professors were now in the company of viziers and sultans. This was why many jurists refused to accept teaching posts, just as many others had refused judgeships. The money that paid the judges' salaries came from the same coffer as that which built the towering *madrasa*s and which hired the most accomplished professor-jurists. But the coffer was generally regarded as suspect, having been filled through dubious means. No wonder then that, like the honorable jurists who refused judgeships, professors who did likewise were lauded and praised.

Yet, the legal elite ultimately succumbed to moral compromise, and increasingly so. By the seventeenth century, most legists were in the employ of the government, and the professors and author-jurists who held out had to function within a diminishing "moral community" created by the financial and material dependence of their less independent peers on the ruling powers. The *madrasa*, now widespread, quickly became a means of recruiting the *sharī'a* specialists into government service.

On the whole, an equilibrium did exist between the men of the sword and those of the law: the ruling elite received the cooperation of the scholars and their promotion of its legitimacy, while the scholars received a salary, protection, and the full right to apply the law as they saw fit. The office of the judge was, and continued to be, the prototype of what was becoming an increasingly complex and interdependent relationship: the government appointed, dismissed and paid the judge, but the judge applied the religious law as the author-jurists and *mufti*s required. If there was one constant in this relationship between rulers and legists, it was that the religious law and its application to the population were not compromised.

The *madrasa*s, we have said, created for the legists abundant career opportunities. Enterprising students from modest economic and social backgrounds found in the endowed and subsidized colleges auspicious opportunities to pursue their education that in turn opened the door to professional and social mobility. The advanced student soon became an assistant to his professor, then perhaps moved on to work as a court scribe or a court witness. These steps could be immediately followed by an appointment to a judgeship that could in turn culminate in a chief magistracy if the candidate had sufficiently extensive credentials and, at times, connections. Yet, such a career path did not necessarily preclude the

student's concomitant engagement in the more complex and sophisticated fields of legal scholarship that would lead him, usually somewhat
later in life, to the two highest ranks in the profession, namely, those of
mufti and/or author-jurist. While both areas of expertise were the most
prestigious in the legal profession, they did not guarantee economic or
material privileges. By the eleventh century, only the *qadi* and his court
subordinates – the scribe and witness – had routinized incomes. Studying
and teaching in the *madrasa* was to become part of this routinization.

Yet, the *madrasa* had no monopoly over legal education, and many
legists who served as judges did not acquire their education in a *madrasa*.
Furthermore, a minority of *madrasa* graduates ended in government
service, mainly as administrative secretaries or viziers, which leads us to
the conclusion that the *madrasa* was neither intended nor perceived as a
tool for training government administrators and bureaucrats, but rather
instituted in order to generate and augment political legitimacy. The
madrasa's function of training bureaucrats was only to be introduced in
later centuries, as we will see in due course.

Professionalization of the legists

The *madrasa*'s proliferation after the eleventh century created another
venue of income. Now, not only could students benefit from free and
subsidized education, but so could jurists gain paid employment as professors. The more *madrasa*s that were founded, the more teaching jobs
became available and, in turn, the larger the number of legists who
benefited from them. The growth in these numbers also meant a dramatic
increase in competition among the legists. The competition intensified
particularly where the major *madrasa*s (founded by sultans and grand
viziers) were involved, as professorial salaries offered there were usually
higher than anywhere else.

The accrual of income from judgeships and professorships – not to
mention scribal and witnessing functions – allowed a class of legists to
make service in the law a full-time, life-long career. By the sixteenth or
seventeenth century, especially in the Ottoman Empire, a majority of
legists secured most or all their incomes from a judgeship or a *madrasa*-
professorship. And they did what everyone else did at the time, be he
professor, carpenter, janitor or jeweler: he passed on the profession to his
male children.

Whereas the pursuit of knowledge in the earliest centuries was, generally speaking, done for its own sake, or, more accurately, for the sake of
epistemic and social prestige (and no doubt propelled by a deep sense of
religiosity), it had now come to pass that knowledge was being acquired

for the sake of a competitive edge, which in part led back to the acquisition of social prestige. This is to say that the increasing professionalization of the legal profession rendered it – in unprecedented fashion – a venue for garnering political, economic and social capital. Furthermore, once knowledge itself became (as a source of income) commodified, its stand-ards were manipulated as the need arose. And the more posts became available, the more commodified the entire profession appeared to be. In every corner of the Islamic world, the rise and spread of the *madrasa* was causally accompanied by this process of "familial professionalization."

Between the thirteenth and seventeenth centuries, this process of pro-fessionalization grew steadily, but the legist families could not achieve a complete monopoly over the social background of the legal profession. Conversely, while these families were able to increase their numbers in the legal profession, merchant and other families continued to have access to it, albeit gradually less so. A complete monopoly by the legist families over the profession had to await the early eighteenth century, when in the Ottoman Empire not a single legist from a merchant background occu-pied high office.

The legists' family-centered monopoly over the legal profession, and especially over prominent governmental posts, was the result of a delib-erate and systematic centralization policy that the Ottomans had begun to pursue as early as the sixteenth century. Whereas Nizam al-Mulk founded two or three dozen *madrasas* throughout the Saljuq Empire, the Ottomans built a *madrasa* in every city and town they conquered; indeed, the larger the population conquered, the bigger the *madrasa*. But the largest and most prestigious colleges were reserved for Istanbul, where a succession of sultans – as well as other influential men and women – poured much of their wealth into these colossal foundations. More important is the crucial fact that, whereas provincial and smaller *madrasas* within and without Istanbul continued to train students and produce legists and scholars of all sorts, the men of law who ran the Empire were consistently graduates of the Istanbul sultanic *madrasas*. In other words, entry into government service was predicated upon completing the required course of study in these imperial *madrasas*, which were increasingly staffed by the children of the legist families. Smaller, non-imperial and provincial *madrasas* contin-ued to train students, but their graduates never came to be part of the professional hierarchy that regulated society and, in certain respects, government.

The absorption of legal education into the political and bureaucratic structure of government was nowhere more manifest than in the legal hierarchy that the Ottomans constructed as part of their general policy of governance. One of the striking facts about this hierarchy is that, from the end of the fifteenth century, the SHAYKH AL-ISLAM (Chief Mufti) became the supreme religious figure in the Empire; he alone was responsible for appointing and dismissing provincial judges, and for a long time possessed the de facto power to depose sultans. Until the seventeenth century, he enjoyed life appointment, and could not be dismissed even by the sultan himself. He at times adjudicated disputes upon appeal from litigants before provincial Shariʿa courts, but more often ordered judges to conform to the religious law, which he usually stated for them.

The functions of the Ottoman Shaykh al-Islam were not entirely consistent with the earlier judicial history of Islam, where the chief justice, a *qadi* himself, was the official who would appoint and dismiss provincial *qadi*s and who would hear judicial appeals. Nor were they consistent with the earliest phases of Ottoman legal history itself, as the two highest judicial positions in the Empire were the two *QADI-ʿASKAR*S who controlled, respectively, the European and Asian jurisdictions of the Empire. The explanation for the Shaykh al-Islam's enhanced role appears, however, to have been closely connected with an evolving policy that had vague beginnings during the Saljuq period in Transoxiana and that eventually culminated with the Ottomans – a policy developed specifically to increase the ruling elite's control over legal education. From the initial stages of the Saljuq state of Rum (r. 1077–1307), the forerunner of the Ottoman Empire, a Shaykh al-Islam was appointed as head of the scholarly group involved in legal education in each city. Professors and colleges fell under his supervision. He was a *mufti*, but he had neither monopoly nor preeminence in this field, for his real powers lay in his office as supervisor of the colleges and their professors. While he would be the only Shaykh al-Islam in the city, he might be only one among several *mufti*s and legal scholars. Thus, in their bid to make of Istanbul a centralizing and centralized capital, the Ottomans did with the Shaykh al-Islam what they had done with regard to creating a monopoly of sultanic *madrasas*: they made the Shaykh al-Islam of Istanbul the supreme head directly responsible for the provinces. This step in the policy of centralization was not only as decisive as that which led to the creation of sultanic *madrasas*, but was also in fact an integral part of the overall policy to appropriate into the political realm the legal profession, utilizing it in the administration of the Empire. And that is precisely what the Ottomans managed to accomplish. Yet, in doing so, they also resolved once and for all the problem of legitimacy. In the nineteenth century, as we will see, the Ottomans were to multiply their gains, since the absorption of the legal profession into an Istanbul-centered hierarchy allowed them to decapitate it, and decapitate it they did.

5   Shari'a's society

Mediation

Whereas the great majority of disputes in industrial societies are nowadays resolved by state-instituted courts of law or arbitration regulated by state law, typically pre-industrial societies, and certainly those of Islam, were only marginally subject to government intervention. To put it slightly differently, in pre-modern Islamic societies, disputes were resolved with a minimum of legislative guidance, the determining factors being informal arbitration and, equally, informal law courts.

Furthermore, it appears to be a consistent pattern that, wherever mediation and law are involved in conflict resolution, morality and social ethics are intertwined, as they certainly were in the case of Islam in the pre-industrial era. By contrast, where they are absent, as they are in the legal culture of Western and, increasingly, non-Western modern nation-states, morality and social ethics are strangers. Morality, especially its religious variety, thus provided a more effective and pervasive mechanism of self-rule and did not require the marked presence of coercive and disciplinarian state agencies, the emblem of the modern body-politic.

In speaking of the "legal system," it would be neither sufficient nor even correct to dwell on the law court as the exclusive vehicle of conflict resolution. In any system, what goes on both outside the court and prior to bringing litigation before it are stages of conflict resolution that are just as significant to the operation of the legal system as any court process. This is particularly true in closely knit social structures, such as traditional Islamic societies, where groups tended to manage conflicts before they were brought before a wider public forum, mainly the law court. It was within these groups, from Malaya to Morocco, that the initial operation of the legal system began, and it was through the continued involvement of such groups that the Muslim court was able to accomplish its task of conflict resolution. For, as we shall see, it was inconceivable for the Muslim court in particular to process claims regarding disputes without due consideration of the moral sensibilities and communal complexities of the social site from within which a dispute had arisen.

Disputes occurring prior to and outside the court's involvement thus centered in the various small communities which made up Muslim societies. The extended family, the clan and the tribe constituted the core and kernel of social existence, even when they happened to be intersected by other social orderings. Small villages predominantly consisted of these units, but in towns and cities other units of social coherence shared the demographic landscape. The neighborhood, an important unit of social organization, constituted a sort of corporate group that was at times based on kinship, but at others on religious or other unifying ties. The neighborhoods of the Christians, Jews, immigrant communities (Armenians, Maghrebites, Franks), as well as the guilds of the tanners, soap-makers, porters, physicians, copper merchants and the like, were fixed presences in Muslim cities. Each neighborhood consisted of dozens, even hundreds, of families and houses, with shops, public facilities, a house of worship, a school, a public bath, a public fountain, and several small streets or alleys connected to a main road. The neighborhood was usually contained within walls, with guarded gates at the points leading to the main roads of the city.

It was the extended family that constituted the unshakable foundation of social existence and, as such, its members always stood in a relationship of solidarity with each other. The family not only constituted an economic unit of production, but provided lifetime security for its members. The family, in other words, defined much of human relationships, and made an investment not only in the well-being of its individual members but also in ensuring their moral and legal compliance; for "it was commonly accepted that they could suffer when a member of the group offended ... In the words of a Malay text, 'Parents and children, brothers and sisters, share the same family fortune and the family repute. If one suffers, all suffer.'"[1]

Even before the appearance of corporate professional guilds under the Ottomans of the fifteenth and sixteenth centuries (guilds which further enhanced the inner groups' dynamics of mediation and conflict resolution), the extended family, clan, religious communities, neighborhoods and the various loosely organized professions all provided extensive social networks for informal conflict resolution. Many private disputes, such as spousal discord and disagreements over joint family property, were often

---

[1] M. Peletz, *Islamic Modern: Religious Courts and Cultural Politics in Malaysia* (Princeton, NJ: Princeton University Press, 2002), 30.

mediated by the head of the household or an authoritative figure in the clan or neighborhood. Village imams, as well as the elders of nomadic, semi-nomadic and settled tribes, commonly appear in court records as having intervened as arbitrators in disputes prior to the arrival of the case before the judge. As much under the Ottomans as under the Malayan Laws of 1667 (Dato Sri Paduka Tuan), village elders were to report to authorities any and all crimes that might disrupt public order or the life of the community. But these elders also played a crucial role in mediation and conflict resolution. Indeed, many court cases in which the claimants' evidence was inconclusive were resolved (often at the recommendation of the judge) by such mediators during the process of litigation, and before the judge passed sentence. At times, the "PEACEMAKERS" would be relatives of the claimant and/or defendant or simply residents of the same neighborhood. At others, these peacemakers were officials of the court, specifically appointed to carry out this particular task. Cases were often dismissed by the judge when mediators from within or without the court were successful in settling the dispute.

The legal maxim "AMICABLE SETTLEMENT is the best verdict" represents a long-standing tradition in Islam and Islamic law, reflecting the deep-rooted perception, both legal and social, not only that arbitration and mediation are integral to the legal system and the legal process but that they even stand paramount over court litigation, which was usually seen as the last resort. In a society that viewed as sacrosanct all family relations and affairs, disputes involving intimate and private matters were kept away from the public eye and scrutiny. For every case that went to court – and these were countless – many more were informally resolved at the local level, with the intervention of the elders, the imam, the household matriarch, or others of equal prestige and authority. Informal mediation was also necessary in order to avoid the escalation of conflict. In communities that heavily depended on group solidarity and in which the individual was defined by his or her affiliation to larger group-units, private disputes had great potential for becoming "expandable into political disputes between competing groups."[2] If the sanctity of family was paramount, it was so also because it constituted an integral part of a larger consideration, namely, the maintenance of social harmony. Attending to and eliminating disputes at the most local level preempted the escalation of disputes that might have disrupted such harmony.

[2] June Starr, "A Pre-Law Stage in Rural Turkish Disputes Negotiations," in P. H. Gulliver, ed., *Cross-Examinations: Essays in Memory of Max Gluckman* (Leiden: E. J. Brill, 1978), 130.

The court

In chapter 1, we noted the role Muslim judges played in resolving disputes through informal arbitration and through the court process. Like arbitration, the court process was never remote from the social world of the disputants. It was embedded in a social fabric that demanded a moral logic of social equity rather than a logic of winner-takes-all resolutions. Restoring parties to the social roles they enjoyed before appearing in court required social and moral compromise, where each party was allowed to claim at least a partial gain. Total loss was avoided wherever possible, and was usually only countenanced when a litigant had caused an irreparable or serious breach of social harmony and the moral code.

In this system, judges cared less for the application of a logically consistent legal doctrine or principle than for the creation of a compromise that left the disputants able to resume their previous relationships in the community and/or their lives as these had been led before the dispute began. But even when this was not possible, and even when the victim recovered all damages, the wrongdoer was also usually allowed a partial recovery of his moral personhood, for, by the informal nature of the Muslim court, the parties and their relatives, neighbors and friends were allowed to air their views in full and without constraint, defending the honor and reputation of one litigant or the other.

Such a collective and public expression permitted even the loser to retain some moral dignity, for this defense explained and *justified* the compelling circumstances under which wrongdoing had taken place. This amounted to a moral exoneration that could, in the community's imagination, border on the legal. For although the actual legal punishment here may have been inevitable, the circumstantial compulsion under which the wrongdoing occurred left the loser and, particularly, his relations (who were both the moral extension and moral predicate of the culprit and who would have to leave the court to resume their communal lives) able to retain sufficient dignity to allow them to function in the normative and morally structured social world. The moral foundations of such a reinstatement constituted the means by which the court – with its socially oriented structure – fulfilled one of its chief tasks, namely, the preservation of social order and harmony.

Social equity, which was a major concern of the Muslim court, was defined in moral terms, and it demanded that the morality of the weak and underprivileged be accorded no less attention than that attributed to the rich and mighty. As the former undoubtedly saw themselves (and were seen) as equal members of the moral community, the court had to afford them the same kind of treatment it did the latter, if not even more attentively. It was particularly the court's informal and open format that permitted the individual and defenders from within his or her micro-community to argue their cases and special circumstances from a moral perspective. But it was also the commitment to universal principles of law and justice that created a legal culture wherein everyone expected that injustices against the weak would be redressed and the wrongdoing of the powerful curbed. This was an expectation based on a centuries-long proven practice where peasants almost always won cases against their oppressive overlords, and where Jews and Christians often prevailed in court not only over Muslim business partners and neighbors but also against no less powerful figures than the provincial governor himself.

The Muslim court thus afforded a sort of public arena for anyone who chose to utilize that space for his or her defense. The highly formalized processes of the modern court and its structure of legal representation (costly and tending to suppress the individual voice of the litigants, let alone their sense of morality) were unknown to Islam. So were lawyers and the excessive costs of litigation that prevent the weak and the poor from pressing their rights. The Muslim court succeeded precisely where the modern court fails, namely, in being a sanctified refuge within whose domain the weak and poor could win against the mighty and affluent. A case in point was women. Considerable recent research has shown that this group received not only fair treatment in the Muslim court but also even greater protection than other groups. Taking advantage of largely unrestricted access to the court in litigating pecuniary and other trans-actions, women asserted themselves in the legal arena in large numbers and, once there, they argued as vehemently and "volubly" as men, if not more so.[3] Protected by a moral sense of honor and sanctity, they asserted their rights and privileges within the court as well as outside it. And when legal doctrine proved restrictive toward them – as it sometimes did – they developed strategies in response that were recognized and accommodated in the law court.

That the court was embedded in both society and social morality is attested to by the nature of the court's social constitution, on the one hand, and by the legal-mindedness of the very society the court was designed to serve, on the other. The *qadi* himself was typically a creature of the culture in which he adjudicated disputes. Embedded in the moral fabric of social relations, he could have no better interest than to preserve

---

[3] Leslie Peirce, *Morality Tales: Law and Gender in the Ottoman Court of Aintab* (Berkeley: University of California Press, 2003), 176; A. Marcus, *The Middle East on the Eve of Modernity: Aleppo in the Eighteenth Century* (New York: Columbia University Press, 1989), 106.

these relations. If mediation and arbitration sought to achieve social equity and to preserve the individual's sense of morality, the *qadi* had to absorb these imperatives into his court and accommodate them within a normative legal framework. Every case was considered on its own terms, and defined by its own social context. Litigants were treated not as cogs in the legal process, but as integral parts of larger social units, structures and relations that informed and were informed by each party to a case.

The *qadi*'s accommodation of litigants-as-part-of-a-larger-social-relationship was neither the purely customary mode of negotiation (prevailing in the pre-trial stage) nor the black-and-white, all-or-nothing approach (mostly prevailing in systems where the judge is socially remote from the disputants). Rather, the *qadi* mediated a dialectic between, on the one hand, the social and moral imperatives – of which he was an integral part – and, on the other, the demands of legal doctrine which in turn recognized the supremacy of the unwritten codes of morality and morally grounded social relations.

Yet the *qadi* was not the only socially linked official in the court. All other functionaries, most notably the witnesses and the court officials, shared the same social and moral landscape. Much of the work of the court related not only to the investigation of events but also, and perhaps more importantly, to that of the moral integrity of the persons involved in litigation or in these events.

One of the *qadi*'s primary duties was to recruit court officials (called CERTIFYING-WITNESSES) who possessed moral integrity and who themselves were in turn charged with the task of assessing the moral worth of people involved in a particular litigation, primarily situation-witnesses appearing on behalf of the litigants. The function of certifying-witnesses, who were fixtures of the court (unlike situation-witnesses), would have been rendered impossible without local knowledge of existing customs, moral values and social ties. Impossible not only because the knowledge of others would be inadequate and insufficient but, more importantly, because the credibility of the testimony itself – the bedrock of adjudication – would cease to be both testable and demonstrable. For moral trustworthiness – the foundations of testimony – constituted a personal moral investment in social ties. To lie meant in effect to risk these ties and, in turn, to lose social prestige, honor and all that was productive of life's networks of social obligations.

Each case was inscribed into the minutes of the court, and attested at the end of the minute by certifying-witnesses whose number ranged from two to several. Although these witnesses, retained and paid by the court, hailed usually from the higher social classes – some of them being prominent jurists and provincial magnates – other witnesses who accompanied the litigants obviously represented the entire spectrum of social classes in the wider population, particularly the lower strata. Their attestation at the end of each record summing up the case amounted not only to a communal approval of, and a check on, court proceedings in each and every case heard by the court, but also a depository of communal memory that guaranteed present and future public access to the history of the case. In many ways, therefore, these witnesses functioned as community inspectors of the court's business, ensuring the moral integrity of its procedures, just as their counterparts, the court's legal experts (usually *muftis*), ensured the soundness of the application of law.

Like judges and certifying-witnesses, the scribe of the court (who wrote down the minutes of court proceedings) was also a member of the local community and himself a jurist of some sort. His ties to the community enhanced the already strong connections between the court and the society which the court was designed to serve. The scribe was instrumental in preserving social and legal continuity between court and society (and it was oftentimes the case that senior scribes were appointed as deputy-*qadi*s).

Litigants and consumers of the law appeared before the *qadi* without ceremony and presented their cases without needing professional mediation, for Islamic law had no lawyers. The litigants spoke informally, unhampered by anything resembling the discipline of the modern court. They presented their cases in the way they knew how, without technical jargon. This was possible because in the Islamic system of justice no noticeable gulf existed between the court as a legal institution and the consumers of the law, however economically impoverished or educationally disadvantaged the latter might be. Yet, it was not entirely the virtue of the court and *qadi* alone that made this gap virtually nonexistent, for some credit must equally be given to these very consumers. Unlike modern society, which has become estranged from the legal profession in multiple ways, traditional Muslim society was as much engaged in the Shar'i system of values as the court was embedded in the moral universe of society. It is a salient feature of that society that it *lived* legal ethics and legal morality, for these constituted the religious foundations and codes of social praxis. To say that law in pre-modern Muslim societies was a living and lived tradition is merely to state the obvious.

If law was a lived and living tradition, then people knew what the law was. In other words, legal knowledge was widespread and accessible, thanks to the *mufti* and other legists who were willing to impart legal knowledge free of charge, and nearly at any time someone wished to have it. The social underdogs thus knew their rights before approaching the court, a fact that in part explains why they won the great majority of cases in which they happened to be plaintiffs. Their counsels were neither lawyers who spoke a different, incomprehensible language, nor higher-class professionals who exacted exorbitant fees that often made litigation and recovery of rights as expensive as the litigated object.

But the spread of the legal ethic and legal knowledge in the social order was also the function of a cumulative tradition, transmitted from one generation to the next, and enhanced at every turn by the vibrant partic-ipation of aspiring law students, the greater and lesser *mufti*s and the imams, and by the occasional advice that the judge and other learned persons dispensed while visiting acquaintances, walking in the street or shopping in the market. Thus when the common folk appeared before the court, they spoke a "legal" language as perfectly comprehensible to the judge as the judge's vernacular "moral" language was comprehensible to them. Legal norms and social morality were largely inseparable, one feeding on and, at the same time, sustaining the other. As much a social as a legal institution, the Muslim court was eminently the product of the very community which it served and in the bosom of which it functioned.

Women

Before we conclude this chapter, we must say something more about women and law. Our sources, which largely consist of court records, tell us little about the social background of the women involved in court proceedings, how they were viewed by the individual members of their social group, how they were perceived and positioned in the larger group making up their immediate communities, and, more importantly, how influential and disadvantaged women differed from each other in reaping the benefits of the law. It is clear, however, that personal rectitude played a decisive role in legal proceedings, a fact that translated into decisions and injunctions in favor of women who themselves were of such a character or supported by female witnesses seen to have an equally elevated moral character. If judicial evidence is the thread by which justice hangs, then rectitude and moral character are the filaments from which the thread is made. And rectitude and morality were no less the province of women than they were of men.

The pervasive legal conviction that women possessed full legal person-ality largely explains the fact that women enjoyed as much access to the Muslim courts as did their male counterparts. Like men, they approached the courts not only with prior knowledge of their rights, but with the apparent conviction that the courts were fair and sympathetic, and oper-ated with the distinct inclination to enforce their rights. They often represented themselves in person, but when not – and this being typically in the case of women (and many men) of the higher classes, including non-Muslim women – they normally had a male relative, a servant or their business manager represent them. By all indications, when they approached the court in person, they did so on the same terms as did men, and asserted themselves freely, firmly and emphatically. The courts allowed for a wide margin of understanding when women were assertively forthright, giving them ample space to defend their reputation, honor, status and material interests. They approached the court as both plaintiffs and defendants, suing men but also other women. Muslim women sued Christian and Jewish men and women, and these latter sued them in turn (though litigation between religious denominations appears to have been substantially less frequent than within each respective denomination). Manumitted female slaves took their former masters to court as often as they sued others for defaulting on a debt owed to them, or for a breach of pecuniary or other contracts. Women sued for civil damages, for dissolution of their marriages, for alimony, for child custody plus expenses, for remedies against defamation, and brought to trial other women on charges of insolvency and physical assault. But women were also sued by men on charges of physical abuse.

It is certainly true that Islamic law, reflecting the social make-up of the great majority of Islamic communities, promoted gendered social and legal structures. Equally true, as some historians have observed, is the fact that "the court language privileged the social status of men and Muslims over women and non-Muslims."[4] But nothing in this language or in the court itself could diminish the rights of women or even discourage them from approaching the court, much less take away from them the full rights of property ownership, of juridico-moral rectitude or of suing whomever they pleased. This was equally true of non-Muslim women, who, in the language of the court, were doubly underprivileged by the facts of being women and non-Muslims. Yet their rights, as well as their actual legal and social powers, were no more disadvantaged than their Muslim counterparts.

It is also true that in legal doctrine a woman's testimony, in most areas of the law, carried half the weight of that of a man. However, we have few data on the actual effects that such juristic discrimination had on the actual lives and experiences of women. How, in other words, did this evidentiary rule affect their marital, familial and property rights – among

---

[4] F. Göçek and M. D. Baer, "Social Boundaries of Ottoman Women's Experience in Eighteenth-Century Galata Court Records," in M. C. Zilfi, ed., *Women in the Ottoman Empire: Middle Eastern Modern Women in the Early Modern Era* (Leiden and New York: Brill, 1997), 63.

others – and, equally important, how were these effects perceived and interpreted by Muslim women themselves? Judging by the available evidence, the overall and relative effect of such discriminatory evidentiary rules certainly compares not unfavorably to the experience of their contemporary European counterparts.

Evidence of the innocuousness involved in women's diminished evidentiary value is the glaring fact that women appeared in court as plaintiffs or defendants in every sphere of legal activity, ranging from criminality to civil litigation. Although the majority of cases bringing them to the court (admittedly not the only province of law) were economic in nature, they were active on several other fronts. It may even be said that courts often preferred women as guardians of minors, asking (and paying) them to manage the orphans' financial affairs and the wealth they inherited. They were no less hesitant to sue on behalf of these minors than they were with regard to their own farms, agricultural tools, weaving equipment, livestock and slaves.

Much litigation about property related to lapsed divorce payments and inheritance settlements. In either case, the common presence of women in court, mostly as plaintiffs, attested to the relatively advantageous positions in which they stood. Divorce, as the jurists understood very well, and as legal practice testifies, was a very costly financial enterprise for the husband, let alone that in many cases it was effectively ruinous (a fact which may also explain the rarity of polygamy). Upon divorce, the ex-wife was entitled to maintenance for at least three months, delayed dower, children's maintenance, any debts the husband incurred to her during the marriage (a relatively frequent occurrence), and if the children were young, a fee for nursing. And if the husband had not been consistent in paying for marital obligations (also a relatively frequent occurrence), he would owe the total sum due upon the initiation of divorce.

In this context, it must be clear that when women entered marriage, they frequently did so with a fair amount of capital, which explains why they were a source of lending for many husbands and why so many of them engaged in the business of money-lending in the first place. In addition to the immediate dower and the financial and material guarantees for her livelihood, the wife secured a postponed payment, but one that she could retrieve at any time she wished (unless otherwise stipulated in the contract). But equally significant was the trousseau that she received from her parents, customarily consisting of her share of her natal family's inheritance paid in the form of furniture, clothing, jewelry and at times cash.

Many women, before or during marriage, were also endowed with a *waqf* portion, giving them further income. Whatever the form of the trousseau and the total wealth they could accumulate, women were entirely aware of their exclusive right to this wealth, and understood well that they were under no obligation to spend any portion of it on others or even on themselves. They apparently spent their own money on themselves only if they chose to do so, since such expenses as pertained to sustenance, shelter and clothing (in the expansive meaning of these terms if the husband was prosperous) were entirely his responsibility, not hers. In other words, unlike that of husbands, the property of wives was not subject to the chipping effect of expenditure, but could instead be saved, invested and augmented.

Considering the unassailability over the centuries of these rights – which on balance availed women of property accumulation – it is not surprising that, in the historical record, unilateral divorce by the husband appears to be less common than *KHUL'*, the contractual dissolution of marriage (where the wife surrenders some of her financial rights in exchange for divorce). The relative frequency of *khul'* in Istanbul, Anatolia, Syria, Muslim Cyprus, Egypt and Palestine has been duly noted by historians. It is a phenomenon that explains – in this context – three significant features of Muslim dissolution of marriage. First, while the husband could divorce unilaterally, there was also a "price" that he paid for this prerogative. In other words, the average husband was constrained by hefty financial deterrents, coupled with legal and moral deterrents installed by the law as well. Second, the husband's unilateral divorce in effect also amounted to a one-way transfer of property from the husband to the wife, beyond and above all that he was – for the duration of the marriage – obliged to provide his wife by default. In fact, an important effect of this transfer was the fact that many repudiated women purchased the husband's share in the matrimonial house, funneling the divorce payment due to them toward such a purchase. Third, *khul'*, within the economic equation of Muslim marriages, was in a sense less of a depletion of the woman's property because the payment by the wife was usually the delayed dower her husband owed her, plus her waiting period allowance. This was so typical that the juristic manuals reflected this practice as a normative doctrine. The point, however, remains that it was the very financial promise made by the groom that was used as the bargaining chip for *khul'*.

Khul', a means by which a woman could exit an unhappy marriage, provides an excellent context to assess domestic violence against women and other causes of their marital discord. Because they had fairly easy access to the courts, unhappy wives had the option of addressing themselves to the *qadi*, who would assign officials of the court to investigate the abuse or other harm that made these women's marriage unbearable. If abuse was proven, the court had the power to dissolve the marriage, as it often did. The law also allowed the woman the right to self-defense, including, under certain circumstances, the killing of an abusive husband. But if the husband was not at fault, a wife who found her marriage unbearable could at least dissolve it by *khul*.

The formal legal aspect of such situations might well be augmented by another social aspect. Obviously, the ties of the wife/woman with her original family were not, upon marriage, severed, and her parents, brothers and sisters continued to watch closely as the marriage of their daughter/sister unfolded. It was, after all, the parents of the wife who had usually arranged the marriage, and who were at least to some extent responsible for it as well as for the well-being of their daughter. If the marriage failed, they not only had to deal with such a failure in the public space, but also had to "take back" their daughter, with all the economic and other consequences this "taking back" might entail. Their interest in the success of their daughter's marriage explains the close scrutiny many families exercised (and still do) to prevent abuse by the husband of their daughter (including such measures as the beating of the abusive husband by the wife's brothers). Unlike the present situation of many women who, in the nuclear family of today, must fend for themselves, women in earlier Islamic societies continued to have the psychological and social – and when necessary economic – backing of their original families. This obviously did not prevent abuse in all cases, but it did contribute significantly to its reduction. However, when all attempts had failed, the wife's original family, often with the collaboration of the husband's own family, would exercise the necessary pressures to bring the marriage to an end, before the *qadi* or not.

Finally, a few words about women and property rights are in order. Making up about 40 percent of the real estate dealers in some cities, women regularly approached the court to register their sales and purchases, recording in this way the fact that they were heavily involved in transactions related to house transfers. As court litigation and registries show, women owned both residential and commercial properties, mainly rent-earning shops. They often owned their own houses, and frequently jointly purchased houses with their husbands, during, but also before, the marriage. As already mentioned, when they were repudiated by their husbands, they often bought the latter's share in their matrimonial house with the very money their husbands owed them as a result of divorce.

Women were also participants in one of the most powerful economies in Muslim lands, namely, the real property dedicated as *waqf*, which, by the dawn of European colonialism, constituted between 40 and 60 percent of all real property. Except for the largest endowments, usually established by sultans, kings, viziers and emirs, many of the founders of medium-size and smaller *waqf*s were women. They often founded and managed endowments alone, and to a lesser extent they were also co-founders, along with males and other females. A relatively impressive number of *waqf*s were established by manumitted female slaves associated with the political and military elites, and these too established *waqf*s independently as well as with their (former) masters (a fact that attests to the financial, and even political, power of female slaves). *Waqf*s of modest range appear to have been established by men and women in equal numbers. Their participation in the important *waqf* economy began early on, and steadily increased throughout the centuries. By the eighteenth century, women constituted between 30 and 50 percent of *waqf* founders. In some places, there were more women establishing endowments than men. In certain cities, a significant number, and at times more than half, of the endowments established by women were public, dedicated to religious and educational purposes or to caring for and feeding the poor. And like men, most women creating endowments purchased their properties for this purpose.

It is only reasonable to assume that more women benefited from *waqf* endowments as beneficiaries than there were women who founded such endowments. Quantitative evidence of the proportions of men and women who were *waqf* beneficiaries has still to be tabulated, but the general evidence thus far points to well-nigh equal numbers. The theory that the juridical instrument of *waqf* was used to deprive females of their entitlements to inheritance no longer stands, for it appears, to the contrary, that the *waqf* was resorted to in order to create a sort of matrilineal system of property devolution. Equally important, however, was the crucial factor of avoiding the partition of family property (which Quranic inheritance tended to do), this frequently having harmful economic effects that were curbed by having recourse to the *waqf* instrument. It should therefore not be surprising to find many *waqf* deeds that allocate to the beneficiaries the same proportional entitlement to the estate as the Quranic shares.

One historian has found that in eighteenth- and nineteenth-century Aleppo women were disadvantaged as inheritors in less than 1 percent of the 468 *waqf* deeds she examined.[5] Women generally designated more females than males as beneficiaries, while some 85 percent of men designated their wives and/or daughters, a situation that obtained in

[5] M. Meriwether, "Women and Waqf Revisited: The Case of Aleppo, 1770–1840," in Madeline C. Zilfi, ed., *Women in the Ottoman Empire: Middle Eastern Women* (Leiden and New York: Brill, 1997), 138.

sixteenth-century Istanbul as well. The same pattern occurs with regard to rights of residency in the family dwelling of the founder. The great majority of *waqf* deeds – in Aleppo, Istanbul and elsewhere – did not discriminate against females, nor did they limit their rights in any way. But when they did, the restriction did not preclude the right to live in the house until marriage, or to return to it when they became orphaned or divorced. Nor did preclusion apply to female descendants, a fact that "left the door open for married women and their spouses and their offspring to claim their rights to live in the house."[6]

Women were also deemed to be as qualified as men in their capacity as managers of endowments, an influential administrative and financial position. Although there were more men than women performing this function, a large number of women appear as administrators of *waqf*s established by their fathers, mothers, grandparents and distant relatives. In the eyes of the court too, women manifestly had precedence over younger males as administrators. And like men, women reserved for themselves the right to be the first administrators of their own endowments. They also reserved and used the right to sue against infringements of *waqf* rights, on behalf of themselves as well as others.

In sum, Muslim women were full participants in the life of the law. As one historian has put it with regard to Ottoman women, they "used their right of access to the courts to promote their interests, in which a manumitted slave could restrict the claim of her past master to her estate, where a farm woman could challenge the claim of a creditor upon the expensive livestock she had purchased, where a widow could assert her priority right to buy her husband's share in real property, and where a woman traveling alone from one village to another could charge a police officer with obstructing her path."[7] But if the law depended, in its proper functioning, on the moral community, then women – just as much as men – were the full bearers of the very morality that the law and the court demanded. And as moral denizens, or denizens who aspired to the power that was generated by moral character, they engaged in the law, losing and winning on the way. As participants in the legal system, they developed their own strategies, and drew on the moral and social resources available to them. They no doubt lived in a patriarchy, but the inner

---

[6] *Ibid.*, 138–39.
[7] Yvonne Seng, "Standing at the Gates of Justice: Women in the Law Courts of Early Sixteenth-Century Isküdar, Istanbul," in Susan Hirsch and M. Lazarus-Black, eds., *Contested States: Law, Hegemony and Resistance* (New York: Routledge, 1994), 202.

dynamics of this patriarchy afforded them plenty of agency that allowed them a great deal of latitude. That "Islamic modernity" has often proven to be oppressive of women, as we shall see in chapter 8, cannot take away from the fact that for a millennium before the dawn of modernity they compared favorably with their counterparts in many parts of the globe, particularly in Europe.

6   Pre-modern governance: the Circle of Justice

The Ottomans, the longest-ruling dynasty in Islam, governed vast territories extending from Arabia to Eastern Europe to North Africa. The history and practices of the Empire are documented in modern scholarship more extensively and better than those of any other Islamic dynasty. As in the foregoing two chapters, here too we will pay special attention to the legal and judicial practices of this Empire, attempting to uncover that which is new and unique to it, while bringing out those practices that represented a continuation of earlier forms of Islamic justice. This focus is all the more important because Ottoman judicial innovations, brought about during the sixteenth and seventeenth centuries, proved to be instrumental to the fundamental modern transformations effected during the nineteenth century and thereafter.

By 1517, the three holiest cities of Islam – Mecca, Medina and Jerusalem – had fallen under Ottoman rule, while at the same time the surviving 'Abbasid caliph in Egypt had been moved to Istanbul to lend the regime a semblance of legitimacy. In a strictly Shari'a-minded sense, Ottoman rule had begun with Bayazid I (r. 1389–1401) who, more than any of his predecessors, sponsored the religious elite, especially the jurists. His patronage differed somewhat from that of Nizam al-Mulk and the dozens of Muslim rulers who had come and gone in the interval. For Bayazid invited the legists to assist him and, in effect, to enter into an active ruling partnership with him. As it happened, his venture became an entrenched paradigm of governance for the two centuries after his death, and continued to have a marked, though less significant, influence on the style of Ottoman rule until the end of the Empire.

Engaging the legists in the administration of justice within the body-politic was a model of governance that answered the political exigencies that arose after the decline of the 'Abbasid caliphate. In the Muslim worldview, kingship represented a morally repugnant form of political governance that Islam had originally come to replace. The Arabic language reserves the terms *malik* and *mulk* to designate, respectively, "king" and "kingship," while retaining their original sense of "possessor" and "possession." To be a king is to possess that over which one rules. Yet, the foundational Quranic language and the Shariʿa assign categorical possession exclusively to God who is recognized as, and given the name, Owner of the Universe in both of its spheres, the here and the hereafter. Any human claim to earthly possession must thus be either metaphorical or a plain usurpation of the divine Kingdom. For a man to rule without incriminating himself in the irredeemable sin of usurpation, he must act as the guardian and administrator of the Law, just as the caliphs had done earlier. They claimed to possess nothing of God's world, and stood as administrators of, and thus beneath, His Law.

This perception of divine sovereignty lay at the foundations of the relationship between the ruling dynasties and the civilian populations they came to rule. As we saw in chapter 4, gaining and holding on to legitimacy was the prime challenge that every ruler and dynasty had to face. The imperative of upholding justice as embodied in the Shariʿa thus had to be reconciled with the demands and expediency of political rule, for it was widely recognized that the latter's failure would be assured without the backing of the former. Yet, it was equally and fully acknowledged that, without the sovereign's juridico-political administration (SIYASA SHARʿIYYA), the Shariʿa would also become a hollow system. The Shariʿa thus defined the substance and form of legal norms, while the sovereign ensured their enforcement. Hence the formula – adopted by both the Sunnis and the Shiʿis – that the *qadi*s were appointed and dismissed by the ruler, and their independent judgments enforced by him, but without any interference on his part in the substantive law that was applied.

From the perspective of the rulers, the desideratum of governance was the maintenance of their own sovereignty and its tool, legitimacy. The religious law, long established and impossible to expunge, constituted not only an efficient tool of governance but an effective means through which sovereignty and legitimacy were achieved. It would be a mistake, therefore, to assume that Muslim rulers merely tolerated the Shariʿa and its servants, for the latter, in the absence of a state machinery of bureaucracy and surveillance, *were indispensable to any form of political rule*.

The notion of the Circle of Justice begins with the idea that no political sovereignty can be attained without the military; yet no military can be sustained without financial resources. These resources furthermore can be raised only through levying taxes, which presupposes continuous economic productivity on the part of the subjects; but to maintain a level of prosperity that can sustain taxable income, justice needs to be ensured, and this in part means controlling the excesses of provincial officials whose vision of justice may be overshadowed by personal power and rapacity. Thus, to be attained, justice requires public order, all-important social harmony, and control of abusive and greedy government servants. To achieve all this, the Shari'a, clearly the axis of governance, points the way. But the Shari'a cannot be implemented without political sovereignty, and this cannot be attained without the military. Here, the Circle is joined.

From the perspective of the legists, on the other hand, this version of the Circle – while accepted as entirely valid – conceptually begins at the wrong point, since the emphasis is placed on the sovereignty of the ruler and his authoritative and military standing, rather than on the Law. The legists would instead advocate the highest goal to be the attainment of justice through implementation of the Shari'a, which in turn requires public order and social harmony. In their conception, the sovereign's function is to ensure stability and prevent internal fractiousness at any cost, and to this end he raises legally prescribed taxes to support his regime and implements *siyasa shar'iyya*, that is, political rule according to the pre-scriptions of Shari'a.

Siyasa shar'iyya represented the discretionary legal powers of the ruler to enforce the *qadi*'s judgments and to supplement the religious law with administrative regulations that mostly pertained to the regime's machinery of governance, including powers to limit jurisdiction to certain areas of the law or to particular types of cases, as well as to curb and discipline abuses by government officials. (This latter function came to be identified in both Sunnism and Shi'ism with the courts of grievances, known as *MAZALIM*.) The dilemma that regimes faced was their inability, due to distance from the center, to control the abuses of provincial governors and their men who often extorted illegal taxes from the population. In addition to tax regulations, *siyasa shar'iyya* normally dealt with matters related to public order, land use, and at times criminal law and some aspects of public morality that could affect social harmony. The qualifi-cation "*shar'iyya*" in this compound expression was intended to convey the notion that exercise of the powers of *siyasa* was not only permitted, but in fact mandated by Shari'a juristic theory and judicial practice. Such powers not only were consistent with the dictates of religious law, but could in no way constitute an infringement thereof if properly exercised. (Many Muslims nowadays view the modern state as operating within this mandate, thereby missing in this evaluation the crucial fact that, in the functioning of pre-modern *siyasa*, the political regimes were subordinated to independent Shari'a, whereas in modernity the state has come to sit on top of a largely dismantled Shari'a.)

Toward the end of the sixteenth century, the Ottomans introduced an important change to their method of governance – they unified admin-istrative and legal powers within the jurisdiction of the Shari'a judge. The *qadi* became the only government official empowered to hear cases and to adjudicate them, and more importantly, to decide on the legality of conduct of the highest provincial officials, including provincial governors. It was the *qadi* who supervised the transfer of the governor's office: he was the one who called on the outgoing governor to surrender his documents, weapons, gunpowder, and everything else related to his office; he was the one who confirmed the new governor and his subordinates, such as guards, tax-farmers, canal janitors, etc. In fact, in order to ensure the compliance of the governor, the lines of communication between Istanbul and provincial *qadi*s were kept open, unconstrained by any intermediate official. Obviously, curbing the abusive powers of the provincial governors depended, at the end of the day, on Istanbul's military might, as evidenced by its failure to control provincial separatism in the late eighteenth century.

The *qadi* under the Ottomans often overtook many of the *MUHTASIB*'s functions as well. The *muhtasib*, a centuries-old institution, heard disputes mainly in three domains: (1) foul play with respect to weights and measures in the marketplace; (2) fraud in the sale and pricing of merchandise; and (3) refusal to pay back debts when the debtor was solvent. But in fewer instances he was also charged with other functions, including bringing government officials to court on charges of corruption or abuse of the powers delegated to them by the sultan, although it was the *qadi* who alone could pass verdict on such infractions. The *muhtasib* was also assigned the duty to urge neighborhood residents to attend Friday prayers, and generally to conform to good conduct. Yet, he had the competence neither to pass a judicial decision nor to imprison any person on the charge of non-payment of a debt. And herein lies another difference between the *qadi*'s and the *muhtasib*'s duties: the *qadi* was passive in that he presided in his *MAJLIS*, awaiting litigants to appear before him, whereas the *muhtasib*'s function was proactive, in that he could suddenly appear on site, reining in malpractice while it was being committed. Insofar as executive competence was concerned, the *muhtasib* ranked lower than the *qadi*, just as the *qadi* ranked lower than the judge presiding over *mazalim* tribunals. This ranking, it must be clear, was a matter of normative practice, sanctioned by no formal hierarchy.

That the *qadi* at times took over the *muhtasib*'s inspectorial functions in the area of tax collecting underscores a fundamental policy of the Ottomans, namely, that in fulfillment of the philosophy embedded in the Circle of Justice, the power of government officials was to be curbed and checked at every point. Until the very end of the eighteenth century, the system worked, and worked well, because a number of factors combined to produce these curbing effects.

First, the civilian population was subject to the law of the Shari'a, an unwavering standard of justice. The people thus enjoyed immunity from the sovereign's crude power whether with regard to life or property. The government's servants, by contrast, were subject to a less merciful code, which may aptly be called sultanic. We have here a unique feature of justice in the lands of Islam, for while no man or woman, Muslim, Christian or Jew, in the civilian population could be punished without a Shari'a court trial – largely independent of the sovereign's will – the sultanic code was absolute with regard to the sovereign himself and his men.

The sovereign himself was expected to observe not only his own code but, more importantly, the law of the Shari'a. Forbearance, mercy and near infinite forgiveness were expected, standards of governance that, when violated, could result in his dismissal or even assassination, a frequent event in later Ottoman times. For political power to acquire any legitimacy, it had to meet these standards, and conduct itself in a morally and legally responsible way. Even highly unsympathetic European observers of the Islamic legal system felt compelled to acknowledge this feature. For example, the eighteenth-century English scholar Alexander Dow observed that the Shari'a "circumscribed the will of the Prince" who "observed [the law]; and the practice of ages had rendered some ancient usages and edicts so sacred in the eyes of the people, that no prudent monarch would choose to violate either by a wanton act of power."[1]

Therefore, ruling in accordance with *siyasa shar'iyya* was in no way the unfettered power of political governance but in a fundamental way the exercise of wisdom, forbearance and prudence by a prince in ruling his subjects. In the case of the civilian population, these qualities manifested themselves in the recognition of the *qadi* as the final judge and as representative of the religious law, for in each and every case referred by the sultan to the *qadi*, it came with the unwavering sultanic command that the *qadi* apply the law. While the imperial servants, on the other hand, also frequently benefited from the sultanic virtue of forgiveness – especially upon first or less grave infractions – they were ultimately subject to the sultanic code that was absolute, swift and harsh. The right of summary judgment was reserved for the sultan against his own men and, by extension, their official representatives, all of whom owed complete allegiance to him. For, after all, these men, who were brought up from childhood as the servants of the state, literally belonged to the *saltana* (sultan-ship). They themselves, and all the wealth that they would accumulate in their

---

[1] Cited in John Strawson, "Islamic Law and English Texts," *Law and Critique*, 6, 1 (1995): 35.

lives, were the property of the *saltana*; and this property was to revert to whence it came at the discretion of the sultan.

Government employees, including *qadi*s, thus represented the sultan who, as the overlord, was responsible for any commission of injustice by his servants. With the virtual abolition of the *mazalim*, the Ottomans augmented the powers of the *qadi*, making him the judge of these servants' conduct and affirming the supremacy of the Shari'a's jurisdiction. But the function itself continued at the same time to operate through means that were now more direct than before. Misconduct of government servants and of *qadi*s could be referred directly to the sultan or the Office of Complaints in Istanbul. What is remarkable about this conception and practice of governance is that, far from depending on an ethic of desirable and fair conduct of institutions (or constitutions), it was grounded in a different ethic seen as indispensable for political legitimacy and for the well-being of "state" and society. In other words, it was a culture. For the sultan himself and his Imperial Council and Office of Complaints were all as accessible to the peasant as to the urban elite. It was thus by design that a line of communication was always left open between the tax-paying subjects and the imperial order. The symbiotic existence of government and society fulfilled the requirements of a Shari'a-based political community, without which the aims of the Circle of Justice could not be accomplished.

Second, the imperial officials working on the ground were themselves members of the very communities to whom they were appointed as the ruler's representatives, or as the representatives of his regional representative, the governor. The local officials were the only administrative staff who knew their environment, since the highly frequent reshuffling of provincial governors – which, in the first place, was intended precisely as insurance against establishing local connections and a power-base – rendered them incapable of intimately understanding, and therefore dealing with, the local population. This is also why the governor's assembly, which met regularly to discuss local problems, included the *qadi*s, the tax-collectors, the notables, the leading *mufti*s, the neighborhood representatives, and a host of other figures from the populace.

These local officials were therefore subject to intersecting interests whereby the loyalties they may have otherwise shown to the sultan and the Empire would be mitigated and counterbalanced by the local stakes they had in maintaining their own social, economic and moral networks. Indeed, the local *qadi*s, *mufti*s, representatives of neighborhoods and of professional guilds and even tax-farmers sat in the assembly as defenders of their communities' interests, which latter had justified their appointment to that assembly in the first place.

Third, and hardly dissociated from the two foregoing considerations, the loyalty of government servants to the sovereign was itself enshrined in the imperatives of the Circle of Justice. Yet, in order to realize these imperatives, *siyasa* required that a supplement be made to the Shariʿa in what was known as the *QANUN*, the sultan's edicts and decrees. Often, the *qanun* merely asserted the provisions of religious law in an effort not only to place emphasis on such provisions but also to depict the sultanic will as Shariʿa-minded. In these instances, the bid for legitimacy is unmistakable. But the *qanun* did add to the religious law, especially in areas having to do with public order, the bedrock of any successful regime. Among the most important of these areas were highway robbery, theft, bodily injury, homicide, adultery and fornication (and accusation thereof), usury, taxation, land tenure, and categorically all disturbance of order and peace. With a view toward a strict enforcement of these religious and sultanic laws, the *qanun* permitted torture (mainly to extract confession from thieves) and the execution of highway robbers by the sultan's executive authority.

Legalized usury, extra-judicial taxes and torture were perhaps the most objectionable pieces of legislation in the view of the jurists. The latter, along with several Shaykh al-Islams, often militated against the *qanun*, and particularly, it seems, against the latter two provisions. The jurists' objections notwithstanding, the *qanun* – in its thin but diverse substance – was mostly seen, and accepted, as an integral part of the legal culture, and as an extra-judicial element that was required – after all – by the *siyasa sharʿiyya* itself.

The Shariʿa and the *qanun* had far more in common than they differed upon. True, substantive *qanun* transgressions upon the Shariʿa did occur, but they were limited to narrow spheres and the *qadi*s and *mufti*s ignored them whenever they could. More remarkable, however, were the similarities between the two. The *qanun* and Hanafi law recognized, each in its own sphere but also mutually, a cumulative tradition: the later school texts (and in particular those of the Hanafi school, adopted as the official law of the Ottomans) never abrogated the earlier ones, and the founding fathers' doctrines continued to be enmeshed in the much later *fatwa* literature and author-jurist compilations. The *qanun* too was a cumulative discourse, each sultan propounding his own decrees while largely maintaining the sultanic laws of his predecessors.

To be sustainable, it was in the nature of these cumulative legal traditions to integrate into their structure the viability and necessity of juridical difference. The concept of individual *ijtihad* in the legal schools constituted an analogue to the individual sultanic will that produced different *qanun*s at different times and places. The internal differences exhibited by the two traditions were clearly intended to accommodate the local and regional differences throughout the Empire. Just as the Shariʿa insisted on local custom as a guiding principle in the application of the law, the *qanun*, in its various compilations, catered to the needs of particular towns, districts and provinces.

*Qanunname*s – the written records bearing the *qanun*s – were issued at each of these levels, as well as at the universal level of the Empire. And like the Shariʿa law, the *qanun* developed structural mechanisms to accommodate change and to respond to diachronic and synchronic geographical variations. Finally, and no less importantly, both systems viewed their own laws as a "statement of the limits of the tolerable rather than a set of inflexible rules to be imposed regardless of circumstances."[2]

What is striking about the *qanun*, and consistent with the Ottoman policy of allowing the widest scope for Shariʿa justice, is the fact that the *qadi* stood as the exclusive agent of the *qanun*'s enforcement. On the ground, he was the ultimate administrator and final interpreter of the *qanun*, which was unwavering in reiterating the decree that no punishment could be meted out without a trial by a *qadi*; and indeed, evidence from court records overwhelmingly shows that the decision to punish was exclusively the *qadi*'s, and that the meting out of penalties was normally the province of executive authority.

The *qanun*'s decrees, frequently restated in the *qanunname*s of several succeeding sultans, in effect constituted a direct prohibition against conduct by government servants that might lead to injustice being inflicted upon the civilian population. The *qanun* of Sulayman the Lawgiver (r. 1520–66), for example, states that the "executive officials shall not imprison nor injure any person without the cognizance of the [Shariʿa] judge. And they shall collect a fine according to [the nature of] a person's offense and they shall take no more [than is due]. If they do, the judge shall rule on the amount of the excess and restore it [to the victim]."[3] The *qanun* therefore upheld the Shariʿa by enhancing and supplementing its position and provisions, while the Shariʿa, on the other hand, required the intervention of sultanic justice. This complementary duality was endlessly expressed in various decrees and letters in the judicial discourse of the Ottoman authorities, be they sultans, Shaykh al-Islams, viziers or *qadis*: justice had always to be carried out "according to the Sharʿ and *qanun*."[4]

---

[2] Leslie Peirce, *Morality Tales: Law and Gender in the Ottoman Court of Aintab* (Berkeley: University of California Press, 2003), 122.

[3] *Ibid.*, 119, 327.

[4] R. C. Jennings, "Limitations of the Judicial Powers of the Kadi in 17th C. Ottoman Kayseri," *Studia Islamica*, 50 (1979): 166, 168; Peirce, *Morality Tales*, 119.

We have already said that one of the central changes effected by the Ottomans was their adoption of the Hanafi school as the official law of the Empire. The other schools never vanished, of course, and they retained followers – albeit decreasingly – in the population as well as in the judiciary. The farther a province lay from Istanbul, and the less strategic it was, the less influenced it was by this policy. But provinces and regions adjacent to the capital were affected significantly. Every major city or provincial capital in the Empire was headed by a Hanafi *qadi al-qudat*, a chief justice, who appointed deputies in several quarters of the city as well as throughout the province (appointment of such deputy-judges by the chief *qadi* of the city or region was a common practice). Some of these deputy-judges were non-Hanafis who held court in neighborhoods and large villages whose inhabitants were either Shafi'i, Hanbali or Maliki. But the official system and government apparatus were Hanafi to the core, and any advancement in a government legal career (under the Ottomans the most prestigious and powerful of all legal arenas) presupposed Hanafi legal education as well as membership in the Hanafi school.

If the chief *qadi*s appointed from Istanbul were all Hanafi, it was because the legists who ran the judiciary were products of the exclusively Hanafi royal *madrasa*s of Istanbul. And in order to rise to the highest levels of judicial and government careers, they had to stay Hanafi through and through. The effects of this policy were clear: the legal profession, law students and legists of non-Hanafi persuasion were encouraged to, and indeed did, migrate to the Hanafi school in search of career opportunities. For instance, in Greater Syria, the majority of the population in general and the population of the legists in particular were Shafi'is at the time of the Ottoman conquests in 1516–17, whereas by the end of the nineteenth century only a tiny minority of Shafi'is remained in that region, the rest having become Hanafis.

Such effects constituted the culmination of a deliberate effort to create uniformity in the subject populations, and to streamline the administration of justice throughout the Empire if possible, but certainly throughout each of its main provinces. The age of uniformity had begun, in the Ottoman Empire no less than in Europe. Uniformity, in other words, entailed low costs of governing, management and control, for, after all, economic efficiency in domination was a desideratum of any form of rule.

An indirect effect of adopting Hanafism as the official school of the Empire was the considerable marginalization of legists from the Arabic-speaking provinces, for they had little, if any, role to play in the administrative bureaucracy centered in Istanbul. The same appears to have been true of the Balkans. Not only were the high-ranking administrators in the capital all "Turks" (known as Rum), raised by the Istanbul elites and educated in the royal *madrasa*s of the same city, but so was virtually every chief *qadi* appointed to run the judicial affairs of the Arab provinces, including Syria and Egypt. Syrian and Egyptian *mufti*s and *qadi*s received their education locally, particularly in Egypt. These *mufti*s, while enjoying local prestige by virtue of their erudition and religious–social standing, remained outside the pale of officialdom, just as the locally trained *qadi*s could aspire to no higher position than that of deputy-*qadi* under the "Turkish" chief justice.

Placing the administration of the Empire's affairs in the hands of "Turks" was not a nationalist act, however. Of distinctly European origin, nationalism was not on the minds of Ottomans before the second half of the nineteenth century. Rather, the Turkification of Ottoman adminis-tration aimed at creating a unified and centralized bureaucracy that could efficiently manage a diverse Empire with multiple ethnicities, religious denominations, languages and cultures and an endless variety of sub-cultures. On the one hand, the "universal" *qanun*s aimed to create an overarching unity within the Empire as a whole, while those *qanun*s issued for cities or even specific courts were intended to impose law and order while showing great sensitivity to the cultural uniqueness of the recipients. On the other hand, the provincial *qanun*s represented a middle stage between the two, striving to balance both the local context of the city and that of the Empire as a whole. Just as the universal *qanun*s operated in conjunction with the Istanbul-based legal education (both emitting cen-tralized values of "Turkish" administration), the regional–local *qanun*s and the indigenous deputy-*qadi*s represented Istanbul's awareness of, and attention to, regional differences and local variety.

Centralized bureaucracy, judicial administration and legal education in the capital were momentous developments that served the Ottomans well during the first three centuries of their rule and they had a considerable effect on the course of events leading to the Empire's encounter with the modern West. We shall deal with the impact in the next chapter, but here we need only stress the newness and tenacity of Ottoman centralization at all levels of judicial administration.

The Ottomans were the first in Islamic history to commit the court to a particular residence, a courthouse so to speak. *Qadi*s could no longer hold their *majlis* in the yards of mosques, in *madrasa*s or in their residences. Existing "public" buildings were modified for this purpose, and the number of courts was increased significantly when compared to the pre-Ottoman period. Whereas it was typical before the Ottomans to have in or around the commercial city-center a total of four courts, each represent-ing one of the four schools, the Ottomans had several around the city, usually in large neighborhoods. The Ottomans were also the first, it seems, to bestow on the court register a public status. The *qadi*s could no longer keep these registers in their private custody, but had to surrender them to a government department.

Fixing the physical site of the court was an administrative act of the first order. The court had become at one and the same time the smallest unit and the core of the Empire's administration. For it was the court that became the destination of sultanic *qanun*s, and it was from the court that these decrees were promulgated in the name of the sovereign. The court was also the locus of fiscal administration, where taxes paid and taxes due were recorded and monitored. And in order to commit the provincial court system to a regularized contact with the capital – a centralizing act – the provincial chief justice not only was an Istanbul man and a "Turk," but also was rotated every one to three years to work in various cities, including the capital. This policy ensured that the top provincial judge was nearly always from Istanbul or, at the very least, thoroughly inculcated in its political and legal culture, and thus loyal to the dynasty that ruled from it. This structured practice was unprecedented, having been made possible by another unusual process, namely, coopting the legal training of the Empire's judicial servants from the private sphere of the jurists and concentrating it in a permanent, affluent, powerful and ever-growing capital.

Furthermore, the court became, probably for the first time, financially independent and a source of income for the imperial treasury. Whereas pre-Ottoman *qadi*s received salaries from the government, as well as public stipends which they disbursed to the officials who staffed the courts, the Ottoman judges depended on fees that were paid directly by court users, including, probably, litigants. Most probably for the first time in Islamic history, *qadi*s were forbidden from hearing cases that did not involve formal petitioning of the court, the purpose being that fees had first to be paid and a formal record of the case maintained. Also for the first time, at least in Egypt (and almost certainly in most other provinces), all marriages were to be recorded in court, and a fee was to be levied. At work here was a double-pronged policy of introducing writing as a means of control, and of regularly replenishing the central treasury.

Part II

Modernity and ruptures

The British in India

Until the eighteenth century in India, and the early nineteenth century in the Ottoman Empire, Islamic law and local customs reigned supreme, both having long been a way of life. But during the 1600s, Britain began its penetration of India through the agency of the East India Company (EIC), whose sole goal was commercial profit. For about a century and a half, the EIC tried gradually to increase its political and military influence, but it was not until 1757 that it asserted its almost total military dominance, henceforth embarking upon the massive project of colonizing India, both economically and juridically. In the eyes of the British, economic and commercial ambitions were intimately connected with the particular vision of a legal system structured and geared in such a manner as to accommodate an "open" economic market. The legal system was, and continued to be, the sphere that determined and set the tone of economic domination. But most importantly for the British, the avid desire to reduce the economic costs of controlling the country led them to maximize the role of law. Law was simply more financially rewarding than brute power.

And so it was not until the appointment of Warren Hastings as Governor of Bengal in 1772 that a new stage in the British legal redesign of India got underway. The appointment ushered in the so-called Hastings Plan, to be implemented first in Bengal. The Plan conceived a multi-tiered system that required exclusively British administrators at the top, seconded by a tier of British judges who would consult with local *qadi*s and *mufti*s regarding issues governed by Islamic law. On the lowest rung of judicial administration stood the run-of-the-mill Muslim judges who administered law in the civil courts of Bengal, Madras and Bombay. The plan also rested on the assumption that local customs and norms could be incorporated into a British institutional structure of justice that was regulated by "universal" (read: British) ideals of law.

Hastings' tax-collectors also doubled as chief justices who applied Islamic law to Muslims and Hindu law to Hindus. These British magistrates are said to have been struck by both the staggering variety of opinion and the pliability of Islamic (and Hindu) law – features that led the British to phase out the indigenous experts whose loyalty was, in any event, considered suspect.

In order to deal with what was seen as an uncontrollable and corrupted mass of individual juristic opinion, the Oxford classicist and foremost Orientalist Sir William Jones (1746–94) proposed to Hastings the creation of codes or what he termed a "complete digest of Hindu and Mussulman law."[1] The justification for the creation of such an alien system within Islamic law rested on the claim that this law was unsystematic, inconsistent and mostly arbitrary. The challenge thus represented itself in the question of how to understand and legally manage native society in an economically efficient manner, which in part shaped Jones' ambition of constructing a system that offered "a complete check on the native interpreters of the several codes."[2]

Hastings was impressed by Jones' proposal. Before long, he commissioned the translation of a handful of classical Islamic legal texts into English, the immediate purpose of which was to make Islamic law directly accessible to British judges who deeply mistrusted the native Muslim legists advising them on points of law. Furthermore, the British thought that reliance on these few texts would reduce the likelihood of juristic disagreement, for them the source of much detested legal pluralism. The texts were concise enough to qualify as codes.

As it happened, these translations largely succeeded in codifying Islamic law – for the first time in its history. Through this act of translation (and codification), the texts were also severed from their Arabicate interpretive and commentarial tradition, which meant that they ceased to function in the way they had done until then. There were at least three dimensions to this process. First, through this act, the British in effect disposed of the Muslim jurists and *muftis* who had served in the system and who were its backbone. Second, Islamic law was slowly transformed into a state law, where the legal and judicial independence of the socially grounded legal profession was displaced by the corporate and extra-social agency of the modern state. And third, the law was simultaneously being changed to resemble, if not to be, English law.

---

[1] B. Cohn, *Colonialism and its Forms of Knowledge: The British in India* (Princeton: Princeton University Press, 1996), 69.

[2] Cited in *ibid.*, 69. See also Michael Anderson, "Legal Scholarship and the Politics of Islam in British India," in R. S. Khare, ed., *Perspectives on Islamic Law, Justice, and Society* (Lanham, MD: Rowman & Littlefield, 1999), 74.

Yet another consequence of undertaking the translations was the suppression of customary law, whose elimination was intended to streamline (or homogenize) the otherwise complex and complicated legal forms with which the British had to deal. At the same time, Islamic law was deprived of one of its mainstays: the communal and customary laws that were entwined with the Shariʿa on the level of application. Thus the *very act* of translation uprooted Islamic law from its interpretive-linguistic soil, and, at one and the same time, from the native social matrix in which it was embedded, and on which its successful operation depended.

The law that emerged out of the application by British judges of these translated laws became known as Anglo-Muhammadan law, a designation that reflected a heavily distorted English legal perspective on Islamic law as administered to Muslim individuals. It may even be argued that Anglo-Muhammadan law at times involved the forceful application of English legal precepts as Islamic law, such as the highly subjective notions of "justice, equity and good conscience."

Furthermore, Anglo-Muhammadan law was no less affected by British perceptions of governance, themselves heavily derived from the intractable connections between law and the modern state. For instance, Governors Hastings and Cornwallis (1786–93) both rejected, as did their British counterparts elsewhere, the entire tenor of the Shariʿa law of homicide on the grounds that this law granted private, extra-judicial privileges to the victim's next of kin, who had the power to decide on meting or not meting out punishment (ranging from retaliation, to payment of blood money, to pardon) as they saw fit. This right, they held, was the exclusive preserve of the state which, by definition, had the "legitimate" right to exercise violence. Reflecting an entrenched state-culture of monopoly over violence, Cornwallis further argued that too often criminals escaped punishment under the rule of Islamic law, a situation that would not be allowed to obtain under what he must have seen as an efficient state discipline. His voice echoed Hastings' complaint that Islamic law was irregular, lacking in efficacy and "founded on the most lenient principles and on an abhorrence of bloodshed."[3] (Ironically, these colonial perceptions of Islamic law have been diametrically reversed since the 1970s.)

Thus between 1790 and 1861 Islamic criminal law was gradually replaced by its British counterpart, so that by the latter year no trace of Islamic criminal law was being applied. As one historian perceptively noted,

[3] Nicholas Dirks, *The Scandal of Empire: India and the Creation of Imperial Britain* (Cambridge, MA.: Belknap Press, 2006), 221.

British justice [in India] turned out to be far more draconian – in practice as well as in principle – than Islamic justice had been, resorting much more frequently to capital punishment, and much less often to community-based methods of enforcement and reconciliation … [The EIC] was far more concerned with public order, and with the specific use of the law to protect its own trade and commerce as well as authority, than was the old regime.[4]

Another fundamental change caused by the creation of Anglo-Muhammadan law and its translated texts was the rigidification of Islamic law as a whole, a rigidification intensified by the adoption of the doctrine of *stare decisis* (the obligation of courts to follow the uncontroversial previous judicial decisions of higher courts). This doctrine could have evolved in Islam, but for a good reason did not. The Shari'a assigned legal expertise and, more importantly, *ijtihad*ic authority to the *mufti* and author-jurist, not to the *qadi* who, while possessing more or less the same amount of legal knowledge as did his British counterpart, was deemed insufficiently qualified to "make" law. Linguistic and legal interpretation was the very feature that distinguished Islamic law from modern codified legal systems, a feature that permitted this law to reign supreme in, and accommodate, such varied and diverse cultures, sub-cultures, local moralities and customary practices as those which flourished in Java, Malabar, Madagascar, Syria and Morocco. But insofar as judicial practice was concerned, the bindingness of a ruling according to the specifically British doctrine of precedent deprived the *qadi* of the formerly wider array of opinions to choose from in light of the facts presented in the case. Once a determination of law in a specific case was made binding, as would happen in a British court, the otherwise unceasing interpretive activities of the Muslim *mufti* and author-jurist were rendered pointless, both in law and in the life of the community.

Enshrining in Anglo-Muhammadan law a doctrine of *stare decisis* in effect transformed the sources of legal authority altogether. Instead of calling upon the school principles and the juristic authorities whose props were the dialectics of textual sources and context-specific social and moral exigencies, the Anglo-Muhammadan lawyer and judge were forced to look to the higher courts, and the higher courts in turn to the Privy Council, which sat in London, not Delhi or Bombay. The Council was remote not only geographically but also from the real concerns of the colonized natives.

Be that as it may, during the second half of the nineteenth century a major displacement of Anglo-Muhammadan law was effected, especially after the transforming effects of the 1857 Rebellion. The 1860s and 1870s

[4] *Ibid.*

witnessed the abolition of slavery, as well as the Islamic laws of procedure, criminal law and evidence. All these were superseded by British laws enacted by statute. By the end of the century, and with the exception of family law and certain elements of property transactions, all indigenous laws had been supplanted by British law. But all this was introduced piecemeal, answering, in an ad hoc and generally incremental manner, the growing anxiety of the British to exercise control over their Indian subjects, especially after the events of 1857 and in a world where London ruled directly, rather than through the EIC (dissolved that year). In this picture, Anglo-Muhammadan law represented no more than the middle stage in a process of colonial consolidation of economic, political and legal power.

The Dutch in Indonesia

The Dutch began their occupation of Java in 1596. Owing to the fact that they could not bring all or even most of the Indonesian Archipelago under their control until the second decade of the twentieth century, and partly because their interests were largely focused on commercial profit, the Dutch did not significantly interfere in native legal affairs until about the middle of the nineteenth century. As D. Lev has aptly put it, the Dutch East India Company from the outset "resolved to respect local law – another way of saying that, by and large, they could not have cared less – except where commercial interests were at stake."[5]

As "law and order" constituted the backbone of colonialist administration, the Dutch, after some failed efforts, finally succeeded in promulgating a penal code for natives in 1873, a code whose implementation remained exclusively in their hands. Since the native district courts, as well as the Shari'a and *ADAT* (customary) courts, were allowed to handle only minor and non-monetary cases, all criminal cases and major offenses were tried at the next level, namely, at the *Landraden* courts, which also handled important civil cases pertaining to the natives. For example, all matters of *waqf* and the all-important area of inheritance fell within the jurisdiction of these courts. Until the 1920s, the chairmen of the latter were exclusively Dutch. But ultimate authority did not lie even in the hands of these chairmen, for appeals were heard at the High Courts (numbering six in total), whose jurisdiction was presumably confined to the Dutch colonial settlers alone.

---

[5] Daniel Lev, "Colonial Law and the Genesis of the Indonesian State," *Indonesia*, 40 (October 1985): 58.

In 1882, the Dutch reorganized the Islamic courts (now called "priest-courts," *Priesterraden*), creating a collegial system whereby the Shari'a bench would consist of three magistrates (at times more). Serious criticism of these reforms forced the Dutch to create, in the 1930s, the Islamic High Court to hear appeals from all the religious courts of Java. A parallel system was established also in Madura and Kalimantan.

As the British did in India, the Dutch colonial administration of Indonesia called upon Orientalist scholars for assistance. One such Orientalist was L. W. C. van den Berg, who published, in 1882, a trans-lation of a key Islamic legal text. This translation had an effect somewhat similar to those we have discussed in the context of British India, but the translation itself also implied a bias on the part of van den Berg himself. The Indonesian Archipelago had a dual, but mutually supportive, system of laws: Islamic law and the *adat*, the customary laws of the islands. Van den Berg's project essentially declared enthusiastic support for the posi-tion that the Shari'a, not *adat*, was the paradigmatic law of these islands.

Adat law had originally existed in oral form, and, despite the fact that it was in small part recorded, this orality remained one of its hallmarks. But orality had and still has – even in so-called "simple" societies of the present day – a function. Orality requires communal participation in, and under-standing of, customary law. Knowledge in this environment does not lie with a specialized class of people, such as *mufti*s or modern lawyers. Instead, it is knowledge of common behavior, perceived as such in relative terms by those upon whom it is incumbent to conduct themselves in a particular way. All in all, legal knowledge of this sort does not reside in an elite but rather is diffused in the community, although some, especially the elders, may know it better than others. If no writing is required, then no commentaries are needed; thus, no commentators or jurists can become the locus of either legal or epistemic authority. The preclusion of writing therefore entails the exclusion of codification, an essential tool of a cen-tralized state authority. The structure and constitution – or more catego-rically, the nature – of the *adat* depends on the crucial fact of its being in a state of orality, a state of fluidity. In its original form, then, the *adat* as a whole constitutes a state of affairs, a practice, a state of mind, a moral code and a way of seeing the world, but can scarcely be reduced to our modern notions of law, operating as the legal organ of a coercive state or even as that of a loving God.

Much like Islamic law, *adat* was not intended to apply to the letter, but represented a guide to proper conduct or a maximal limit to what could be tolerated by a particular, local community. The writing down of some *adat* practices did not considerably affect their fluidity, for the record remained both partial and unofficial. It could no more, at any rate, have represented an official law than any given Islamic legal manual. And so, under Dutch colonization, *adat* began to metamorphose, acquiring in the process different and unprecedented characteristics. Chief among these was an elision into rigidity. Yet, it is not difficult to understand why the Dutch insisted on capturing *adat* in written form. Coming from the Continental legal tradition, the Dutch could not conceive of any unwritten law as law properly speaking, and if *adat* was to have any force it would have to be endorsed by the written law. Thus, to be so sanctioned, *adat* law had first to be identified and set down in writing.

Where India had its Sir William Jones, Indonesia boasted Cornelius van Vollenhoven, an influential Dutch Orientalist specializing in "*adat*-law" – or what was by his time called "*adatrecht*." Coined by the other stellar Dutch Orientalist Christian Snouck Hurgronje, this field of study confirmed the legal duality that had been "discovered" by the Dutch. There is no indication that this duality was construed by the Malay peoples in oppositional terms; nor was the relationship between one and the other problematized. Rather, before the end of the nineteenth century, *adat* and Shari'a appear to have been viewed as complementary and intertwined. But Snouck's "discovery" of *adat*, and van Vollenhoven's elevation of the study of this discovery into a "science," in effect opened a Pandora's box within the political and legal life of Indonesia that has not been closed to this day.

Hailing from a pedigree of Dutch scholars who viewed Islam as a threat (very much in the same vein as the French saw this religion and its law in Algeria), van Vollenhoven vehemently espoused the position that *adat*, not the Shari'a, should be employed to govern the pluralistic societies of the Netherlands Indies. Criticizing the proponents of Shari'a, he argued that *adat* exercised such a wide sway over the Archipelago's population that Islamic law stood in comparison as both thin on the ground and virtually irrelevant. (Remarkably, all this knowledge he managed to garner from two, rather brief, visits to the colony.) He also espoused the view that any attempt at weakening *adat* was nothing less than an invitation to open the floodgates to Islam, a religion seen by van Vollenhoven and many of his compatriots not only as a native political tool of unification, but as the very religion that had threatened Christendom for centuries. Furthermore, to side with *adat* was to promote secularism, the new religion of Europe. Among other initiatives, he compiled an extensive work in which he committed to writing the otherwise oral *adat*, identifying eighteen versions of it, when in fact the archipelago consisted of over a thousand islands, each with its own version (or versions) of *adat*. The writing down of *adat* "violated a primary principle of *adat* law theory, that the *adat* lived in local tradition. Now, written, it lived in books, which

Dutch judges, and Indonesian judges half a century later, used as if they were codes."[6]

Thus, when in 1927 the Dutch government declared that *adat*, not the Shari'a, constituted the normative law, institutional changes began to take effect, and further scholarship aimed at systematizing *adat* (especially by Bernard Ter Haar) came to bolster that policy with renewed vigor. Henceforth, Dutch scholars and their native students – who hailed mainly from the Javanese aristocracy – as well as colonialist advisors and administrators were officially trained in *adatrecht* as the paradigmatic law. The confluence of the Dutch and native elites' interests ensured the relegation of the Shari'a to a largely secondary status, where it would be accepted only insofar as it was provisionally allowed to modify *adat* in a particular locale (this having been termed "reception theory").

Concurrent with these later judicial and legal developments was the gradual introduction to Java and Madura of the Dutch educational system that proved itself – here as in the Ottoman Empire and elsewhere – instrumental not only in facilitating the legal transformation but also in accelerating the latter's dissemination and extending its cultural roots deeper in the new Muslim soil. Put differently, the introduction of Western-style schools, wittingly or not, tended to produce a number of effects besides the obvious Westernization of education in Muslim lands. In the Ottoman Empire, by the end of the nineteenth century, European forms of education facilitated the ousting of Shari'a legists through the ready supply of a new Westernized elite in whose interests it was to promote the Western institutions upon which it depended. But more importantly, Western education was both the prerequisite to, and the means of, naturalizing the new imperial culture without which no hegemony would be viable.

No system of *madrasas* could be established in Indonesia on any scale similar to that which had existed in the Ottoman Empire, and thus the Dutch schools (which numbered more than a thousand by 1910 and which were quickly imitated by the native population) did not have the same effect. Their primary effect lay in affording to the local population an opportunity to rise in the Western system, which was the locus of government and power. It gave the Javanese and other elites the means of education that prepared them to pursue their legal studies in Western institutions, whether these were located in Batavia or Leiden. And it was from amongst this elite that students of the *adatrecht*, many of whom advocated the reception theory, emerged.

---

[6] *Ibid.*, 66.

On the other hand, and as happened in Malaysia earlier, the Islamic impulse grew as colonial power consolidated its grip over the colony. Just as the legal transformations in the Ottoman Empire and Egypt informed each other, so too were the religious movements of South East Asia influenced by the Hejazi–Egyptian world of Muslim legal scholarship and religious thought. By the early decades of the twentieth century, the European steamship became the dominant mode of transportation in the Indian Ocean, a phenomenon that promptly brought with it a tremendous increase in the number of Javanese scholars studying in the Hejaz and at Cairo's AZHAR University. The overall result was an increase in Islamic consciousness, both as a marker of cultural identity and as a prop for a counter-movement that generated resistance not only to the secularized national elite but to the centuries-old and venerable *adat* as well.

The Ottoman Empire under pressure

By the end of the sixteenth century, the Ottomans had built the largest and most powerful empire in the Muslim world. However, by 1812, they began to experience major military defeats at the hands of the Russians, losing on the way their control of the northern shores of the Black Sea and the Crimea. By this time, Arabia and Egypt had defected, the former taken by the Wahhabites and the latter by Muhammad 'Ali. The Empire appeared on the verge of crumbling.

The rise during the eighteenth century of European and Russian military power meant dramatic and in effect unprecedented corollary increases in military expenditure for the Ottomans. The financial resources needed to remedy the military weakness of the Ottoman center lay in the provinces which, in order to produce the necessary income, in turn needed central military control. That a strong army was needed to raise money, and that money could not be raised efficiently without a strong army, constituted the most fundamental dilemma for the Ottomans during the second half of the eighteenth century. This dilemma had always existed, and was, as a rule, managed relatively successfully. But during that century, European military technology was too extensive and too rapidly developing for the Ottomans – as well as for all Afro-Asian dynasties – to be able to adjust to the swiftly changing realities. Add to this a high level of inflation which brought with it not only higher prices but countless popular riots. Just when the demand on financial and material resources was at its highest, not to mention unprecedented, provincial income was on the decline. The consequences were devastating.

With the weakening of central power and authority, provincial governors, the Janissaries, tax-collectors and local magnates lacked the restraints and the checks and balances that had been characteristic of the sixteenth and seventeenth centuries. The provincial officials began to act with a free hand, not only against the local populations but also in defiance of the courts and law of the land. Extortion, harsh taxation and violent punishment of civilians began to occur with increasing frequency and without the option of recourse to higher courts of justice. Toward the end of the eighteenth century, governors, who were not trained judges, began to adjudicate civil cases, hitherto the distinct purview of the Shariʿa court. Punishments were at times corporal, going beyond the Shariʿa prescriptions, but they were almost always sure to include pecuniary penalty, constituting another source of income for the ruling provincial elite. The level of intimidation dramatically increased, and on-the-spot punishments without trial became ever more frequent.

With the Empire in near disarray and its armies defeated by the Russians and Europeans, the Sublime Porte realized that reform had become imperative. In 1826, the traditional army units (the Janissaries) were eliminated, and because they were also guildsmen who engaged in crafts and the manufacture of goods – and therefore advocated economic protectionism – their disappearance from the scene opened the door to economic liberalism. Thus, a dozen years after the extinction of the Janissaries, the ground had been adequately prepared to impose on the Empire a "reform" program that would open its population and markets to European exploitation.

The 1838 Treaty of Balta Limanı between Istanbul and the British not only confirmed all previous capitulatory privileges (which gave to European subjects more extensive rights in the Empire than its own subjects), but now ensured the final removal of any form of monopoly that could protect Ottoman manufacturers against European competition. In effect, it abolished all restrictions on foreigners' movement within the Empire, thereby exposing the hitherto protected and surviving Ottoman economic sectors to the annihilating competition of the European market. Thus, the famous reformist 1839 Gülhane Decree came to confirm and sanction trends that had begun earlier, but it also formalized a state of affairs that was taken for granted when further reforms were imposed in the future. This Decree, in effect an Ottoman payment to the superpowers (Britain, Austria, Prussia and Russia) for their aid against the separatist Egyptian Muhammad ʿAli, rejected traditional economic forms and declared material wealth a desideratum. All indigenous impediments to economic development were to be removed, and the model of change would become European culture, science and capital.

Opening Ottoman markets to European capitalism was only a part of what the Gülhane Decree was intended to accomplish, though it was perhaps the most important goal. Another, better-known, aspect of the Decree was to grant equality to all subjects of the Empire, irrespective of their religion. The new distributive freedoms had of course little to do with any intrinsic democratic interest that Europe had in the religious minorities of the Ottoman Empire, and much more with increasing European interests among segments of Ottoman populations that might act as middlemen, in both the economic and political spheres. Having secured the Ottoman economic market as a source of raw materials and having ensured the political cooperation of the sultanate, the European powers found it unnecessary to break up the Empire, now the so-called "sick man of Europe." Keeping the sick man alive was also dictated by the rival interests of Russia, Britain and France, whose potential disagreement over how the Empire might be divided amongst them kept such a division a remote possibility, at least until the middle of World War I. That the Empire was "sick" became, by virtue of European military and economic superiority, a self-evident reality; that it had been "of Europe," being all but directly colonized by it, was an undeniable truth.

Similar developments occurred in Qajar Iran (1779–1924). Within four decades of their coming to power, the Qajars had suffered crushing military defeats at the hands of the Russians and, just as in the Ottoman Empire, by 1828 Iran had lost much of its territory in the Caucasus as well as all rights to navigate the Caspian Sea. The 1828 Treaty of Turcomanchay, and the Persian–British treaty of 1836, placed foreign subjects and their property outside Persian jurisdiction, and created special tribunals to adjudicate cases involving foreigners and Persians. As happened in the Ottoman Empire, no judicial decision of these courts could be deemed valid or binding without the final approval, not of Persian courts, but of the consul or ambassador. In addition to this political subjugation, wars with Russia and the Ottomans had a devastating effect on Iran's economy and reduced the populations of its major cities to half their usual size. Identical effects began to show themselves in the independent Muslim principalities in Transoxiana, Afghanistan and North Africa. The Khanate of Khiva and the Mangits lost their continental trade and were reduced to no more than local, small-time merchants. The usurpation by Europeans of the sea trade and the unprecedented efficiency and militarization of European navigation significantly detracted from the importance of land routes, the backbone of Irano-Transoxianan commerce. By the middle of the nineteenth century, it was a rare Muslim country that had escaped surrendering its political and juridical powers to foreign nationals and, particularly, in favor of European states.

The Ottoman reforms, however, started in earnest as early as 1826. It was in that year, and for the first time in Islamic history, that the *waqf*s supervised by the Shaykh al-Islam, the Grand Vizier and a number of important others were placed under the control of a new Imperial Ministry of Endowments, thus depriving these particular statesmen of an independent economic base. Shortly thereafter, the incomes of more substantial *waqf*s were claimed by the Ministry, and within less than a decade the incomes of all major *waqf*s in the Empire were seized. This process led to the creation of salaried posts for local notables who would administer the endowments on behalf of Istanbul.

The Ministry further seized the Water Works Administration, since public fountains and the public water supply were largely constituted as *waqf* endowments. But the most striking fact about these appropriations was the volume of property involved. At the beginning of the nineteenth century, it is estimated, more than half of real property in the Empire was consecrated as *waqf*. The government's economic and political gains were thus enormous: economically, it had become the "middleman" who secured considerable profits in the process of collecting the revenues of the endowments and then paying out salaries for the minimal upkeep and operation of the *waqf*-foundations. In part due to the government's diverting of funds to military and other projects, and in part due to corruption within the ranks of the Ministry, this back-payment of salaries to the educational and other public endowments progressively declined, reaching zero point by the middle of the century. The central *waqf* administration was charged with financing and supervising, at its own expense and obviously from endowment money, military and public projects, such as the building of tramways in Istanbul and of yarn factories for the production of military uniforms – all of which were intended to, and did indeed, strengthen the emerging modern state, but at the expense of the traditional recipients of *waqf* revenues.

The mosques, and the *madrasa*s along with them, appeared to many observers to stand on the brink of total collapse. Politically, the absorption of the *waqf*s into the central imperial administration weakened the allies of the now vanished Janissaries, i.e., the ULAMA and the *SOFTAS* (law students) who had shown some resistance to the early reforms. Thus, the reorganization of *waqf* administration, which reflected the rise of an aggressive new form of bureaucratization, delivered, together with the abolition of the Janissaries, the first major blow to the strong position of the traditional legal profession in the Empire. (The Iranian experience also attests to an overarching transformation that led to an *étatist* administration of *waqf*. In 1854, the Ministry of Pensions and Awqaf [pl. of *waqf*] was created, and a decade later it became mandatory for every *waqf*-foundation and administrator to register with the Ministry all assets under his/her control.)

The salarization of *waqf* administration constituted the first step toward the salarization of the entire legal profession, which was to take effect in the wake of the 1839 Gülhane Decree. During this period, there was a series of minor, but important, judicial reforms aimed at instituting new policies for judicial appointments, including entry exams, and the replacement of court fees as funding for the judiciary – a hallmark of Ottoman practice – by salaries. Like all other civil servants, the *qadi*s were now prohibited from collecting dues on inheritance division or for issuing deeds or court documents. Their monthly salary was to be paid directly by a salaried imperial comptroller who had now himself been charged with collecting all court revenues. Furthermore, in an effort to create a clear distinction between the judicial and executive spheres, the provincial governors as well as the grand vizier were deprived of their tribunals, thus becoming an integral part of the steadily centralized court system.

These fundamental changes were made to be concomitant with institutional restructuring. Already in 1838, Mahmud II had created the so-called Supreme Council of Judicial Ordinances, a body that not only prepared the ground for the later New Courts (Nizamiyye; Ar. Nizamiyya) but also signaled the removal of the judiciary from the Shari'a domain to that of the state. The Supreme Council set itself up as the highest court in the land, controlling and supervising the activities of all courts as well as all quasi-judicial assemblies of provincial governors.

In 1840, and in the spirit of the 1839 Decree, a modern-style penal code that was yet grounded in Islamic criminal precepts was promulgated. Furthermore, new local councils began to be formed of civil notables, a *qadi*, a *mufti*, and representatives of the local communities, including non-Muslims. These councils were, much as before the reforms, responsible for civil, judicial and financial matters, but their new organization and formal constitution were intended to mark a departure from the traditional, *qadi*-centered administration. Whereas the *qadi* had been the leading judicial and administrative officer in the pre-reform councils, he was now relegated to a secondary position, or at least to that of one among many others of equal importance. The new leaders were the government employees, the administrators and those who were soon to become bureaucrats. It was these persons, together with the notables representing segments of the community, who were in charge of hearing the major suits brought before the *qadi*'s court. Whereas before the reform the "court assembly" assisting the *qadi* in *legal matters* consisted of the learned scholars (mainly *mufti*s), now they were non-Shar'i figures who represented the interests of the community in an official, state-determined capacity. These officials emerged, as before, from within the community, but it was now the central government, not the community and its immediate representatives, that decided how, when and under what conditions they should serve.

However, aside from installing a modern system aimed at improving the method of tax collection, the most serious change that came in the wake of the Gülhane Decree was the gradual rise of the Nizamiyye courts, named after the so-called New Order. This latter administration, which produced new courts, new laws, a new judicial process and – by the end of the century – a new legal culture, operated at the nominal orders of the sultan who, for the first time in the history of the Empire (and of Islam as a whole), placed himself as well as his bureaucratic legislative council above the Shari'a. His power to legislate the *qanun*s (government regulations), which had complemented and supplemented, but had never overridden the Shari'a and its law, now became overarching and universal.

The sultan's reforms – in effect representing the political will of a Westernizing and secularizing Istanbul elite – also reflected the enormous European and Russian pressures on the Empire. For example, under these pressures a commercial Nizamiyye court was first established in Istanbul with a jurisdiction pertaining to disputes between and among Ottoman subjects and European nationals. A criminal court, with the same jurisdiction between various nationals, was created in 1847. In these courts, foreign consuls and consular representatives of European states enjoyed the right to veto the decisions of the court against their respective nationals, thus in effect holding powers that entitled them to entirely neutralize court verdicts at will. (The severity of such intrusions can only be imagined if we were to assume that China had the right today to veto and neutralize the decisions of US courts in cases where Chinese nationals were convicted for criminal activity in the United States.)

Under clear French influence, the first Westernized commercial code was promulgated in 1850. A second penal code was introduced the next year, defining, with more specific details, the jurisdictional boundaries between the Shari'a courts and the new criminal courts. In 1854, the Supreme Council was transformed into the Supreme Council of the Tanzimat, one of whose first acts was the promulgation of a new criminal code that showed the greatest dependence yet, this time on the French penal code of 1810. The new name of the Supreme Council epitomized the worldview of the Ottoman modernizers who saw in their reforms a means to accomplish "order," "regularity" and "law," all of which stood in diametrical opposition to the steadily diminishing Shari'a culture that was perceived as lacking on these counts. The Tanzimat (literally meaning "ordering") constituted a regimenting practice, and reflected highly modern notions of discipline, law, inspection and incarceration. Indeed, these notions found expression not only in the evolving judicial structures and

codes (as well as reporting, statistics, centralized supervision and surveillance), but also in the significant fact that the Nizamiyye legal order
generated – along with a distinctive legal culture of its own – an unprecedented and colossal prison system that was part of this culture and that
could accommodate inmates for up to twenty years. This is to be contrasted with the fact that such prison terms and prison systems were
entirely unknown to the Shari'a.

With the conclusion of the Crimean Wars of 1853–56, the Ottomans
incurred further debts to France and Britain, both politically (for their
military support against the Russians) and financially (for the major loans
the British made to Istanbul). These debts translated into further, intense
hegemonic pressures on Istanbul, resulting in another series of concessions embodied in the Humayun Decree of 1856. Unlike its 1839 pred-
ecessor, which was compiled by Ottoman senior statesmen, the 1856
Decree was drafted after intensive consultation with the French, British
and Austrian ambassadors. It moved further away from the Islamic principles of governance, not mentioning the Quran or the Shari'a once, for
instance. It emphasized European-style representative government, and
furthermore gave non-Muslim minorities formal rights (again, defined by
Western conceptions of governance) equal to those enjoyed by the
Muslim subjects of the Empire. This was not only a European imposition,
but an Ottoman strategy that aimed at appeasing and absorbing the
nationalist sentiments that were making themselves known in the provinces. The constitution of the new Nizamiyye courts reflected this new
reality no less than did the structural changes in the laws of evidence and
procedure.

The new wave of reforms led to the adoption of the Penal Code of 1858
and the Land Law of the same year. Likewise, a series of French-inspired
commercial codes, including a maritime commercial code, were promulgated for the benefit of the New Courts. Similarly, the Land Law of 1858
required the cultivators of state land to register their lots under their
names, a step intended to secure direct payment of taxes to the central
government, thus eliminating the intermediaries who traditionally
claimed a percentage of the revenue. In Egypt, the process had started
earlier, but in all cases the land code, in both of its varieties, was also
designed to implement a policy aimed at binding the peasants to the land.
Although it was purported that these modernizing codes were conceived
as a contribution to the emergence of private property, their effects on
peasants (a large segment of the population) were disastrous in more
ways than one. Fearing conscription and excessive taxes, they registered
the lands they cultivated in the names of deceased family members,
city magnates or rural notables. The end result was the conversion of

their position from controllers of land to tenants who could be evicted at will.

The new land code (in both the Ottoman Empire and Egypt) had the remarkable effect of producing, toward the end of the century, a landed class that rivaled the religious elite in terms of political and material power. The families who profited from the changes brought about by the new land and other codes, and by the emerging bureaucratic and administrative structures, were secular in orientation. Yet, some religious families also held large tracts of land, continued to hold on to their positions of power, and managed to partake in the advantages these land codes had created for members of the upper social strata. And in order to compete in the market of new economic realities, they inserted themselves in the secular bureaucracies of the state, gradually changing their "specialization" and identity as members of a privileged religious establishment. By the end of the century, the children of these families, both secular and originally religious, were largely integrated into the state bureaucratic machinery and politics at the district, provincial and national levels. This social transformation of the religious elite explains, at least in good measure, why the upper ulama class did not mount any serious resistance to the major transformations that took place, inter alia, in the legal system.

In the midst of these foundational and structural changes, European pressures on Istanbul continued to increase dramatically. Deeply in debt after the Crimean Wars, the Ottomans secured, in 1860, substantial loans from Britain, but not without the latter attaching to the loan-agreement certain political and economic strings. As if the capitulations and concessions in favor of foreign nationals were not enough, the British demanded and secured further allowances pertaining to the purchase of real property in the Empire. The introduction of the land codes, which had essentially privatized real property, was one step in this direction. But in order to maximize the opportunity for profit, they also demanded, and received the promise, that the *waqf* system – which barred much real property from entering the open market – would be abolished.

Over the next two decades, the pressure was renewed with added vigor by both the British and the French, whose scholars – doubling as colonial officers – were already propounding the idea not only that *waqf*s reflected a primitive mode of existence and belonged to the decadent history of the now maligned "church," but also that they impeded economic development and thus the much desired "progress." These pressures, coupled with Istanbul's conviction as to the superiority of Western culture, created a mood among the reformist bureaucrats that translated into a massive ideological campaign portraying *waqf* as a cause of cultural malaise and material decline. In 1909 the reformers moved aggressively against the *waqf*, thus initiating a process which led eventually to its abolition in the Turkish Republic and elsewhere. But the ideological preparation for this move had been underway since as early as the middle of the preceding century.

Beginning in 1864, there were also attempts to reorganize and restructure the judiciary at the provincial level. On the benches of appeal courts there presided, in equal numbers, Shari‘a judges and elected members of the civil service, signaling a yet further step in formalizing the process by which civil officers and technocrats had now come to share the judicial powers of the *qadi*s. Conversely, installing Shari‘a judges in the New Courts suggests that there was a confluence between the traditional and new legal professions, one that prevents us from drawing neat lines of separation between the two systems. This concourse was further augmented by the fact that the Shari‘a courts themselves also underwent a modernizing administrative and procedural reorganization, even as their jurisdiction was becoming increasingly limited to the spheres of personal status and the diminishing *waqf*.

As a part of these centralizing policies, all Shari‘a – and Nizamiyye – personnel were appointed by Istanbul, and the age-long principle of judicial delegation ceased for good. This administrative act, together with the payment of salaries directly from Istanbul, further consolidated centralized control, and transformed the Shari‘a court into an official arm of the state. Judicial centralization was manifested in the creation, as part of the Nizamiyye courts, of the COURT OF CASSATION, whose seat was in Istanbul, comprising both civil and criminal sections. And for the benefit of supervision by the Istanbul Ministry of Justice, all courts were ordered to report the cases they adjudicated once every three months.

The transposition of Islamic law from the fairly independent and informal terrain of the jurists to that of the highly formalized and centralized agency of the state found manifestation in the compendium entitled *Majallat al-Ahkam al-‘Adliyya* (henceforth: Majalla). Between 1870 and 1877, the sixteen books making up the Majalla (containing 1,851 articles in the Turkish language) were published, all dealing with civil law and procedure to the exclusion of marriage and divorce. One of the aims of the Majalla was to provide, in the manner of a code, a clear and systematic statement of the law for the benefit of *both* the Shari‘a and the Nizamiyye courts, a statement that was geared to a professional elite that had lost touch with the tradition of Arabic juristic interpretation. Yet, the source of this codification was the *corpus juris* of the Hanafi school, especially those opinions within it that seemed to the drafters to offer a modernized version of Islamic law.

The Majalla was to be implemented in the Nizamiyye courts, whose staff were increasingly being trained in non-Shariʿa law. But since no juristic opinion was truly binding on any judge without the sovereign's intervention, the Majalla, after its complete publication, was promulgated as a sultanic code (a momentous act sanctioning, once and for all, the supreme authority of the state, and demoting that of the Shariʿa). Yet, while in structure and appearance the Majalla was code-like, it did not really function as codes do, enjoying unrivaled, exclusive authority. In practice, it continued to coexist with the books of the jurists, or whatever was left of them on the benches of the slowly vanishing qadis. And it was soon to have a fierce rival in the 1880 Code of Civil Procedure, modeled, again, after the French example. Toward the close of the century, procedure was steadily and rapidly gaining greater importance, it being increasingly seen, in the manner of all modern legal systems, as the backbone of the law. The highly formalized and complex procedural protocols represented a large domain in which the Shariʿa was almost totally replaced.

The final series of major acts aimed at consolidating the Ottoman state's legal powers began in 1879. A Ministry of Justice, which was to bring under its authority the Shariʿa and Nizamiyye courts, was established in 1879, thus unifying a hitherto fairly heterogenous system. Several codes pertaining to the competence of tribunals, judicial salaries, public prosecution, and civil and criminal procedure came into existence. In 1888, a new system of examinations and rules for the appointment of judges was established. In the new system, judges were assigned by the Ministry of Justice, abrogating the policy of their election instituted earlier. Another act of 1888 required the Ministry to maintain – in perfect keeping with the modern state – systematic records on every official working in the judicial system. The Shariʿa courts themselves were also instructed to expand their documentary range, recording every case in detail. This keeping of records was, in line with Western court procedure, occasioned by the establishment of appeal courts where a full review of the appealed case depended upon the submission of extensive documentary evidence. By this point, oral testimony and the traditional procedural laws that were predicated on it had become largely obsolete.

It is true that the modernizing elite in Istanbul was intent on building a highly centralized system and an efficient governance that might one day rid the Empire of European hegemony. Yet the pressures to which Istanbul was subjected were not proportionate to its drive or desire for modernization, these pressures having reached all-intrusive levels short of direct conquest and colonization. The gap between direct colonization and hegemony equipped them with an agency that allowed for some resistance. One might say that Istanbul was not categorical in its desire to dismantle the Shariʿa court system since this jurisdiction reflected a legal domain that was unfavorable to the excessive privileges of European powers. Thus, the highly gradual process by which these courts were marginalized may be explained as part of this resistance and as a defense of sovereignty.

Egypt's drive for modernization

The intertwined and complex relationships between the Ottoman Empire and its autonomous Egyptian province perhaps explain the general similarities in their checkered legal careers as indirect colonies of the European powers (Egypt, in any case, for most of the nineteenth century). The most serious challenge for Muhammad ʿAli, Egypt's powerful governor, was to solve the riddle of European military and naval supremacy. Although the Napoleonic "expedition" of 1798 had failed, the threat of European domination was vigorously renewed, especially by Britain. A way out of falling prey to such conquests was to modernize, which meant for Muhammad ʿAli building a strong army and navy for defense, and a merchant marine for exports that were to be produced by local agriculture and industry.

One of the first projects he undertook was the physical elimination of the Mamluk elite in 1811, as well as the systematic dismantling of the old tax-farming tradition. An integral part of his agricultural reform was to confiscate land that was frequently, if not mostly, under the regime of *waqf* (although the policy of land confiscation was to be partly reversed later). Thus, long before Istanbul decided to commandeer the *waqf*s, Muhammad ʿAli had already done so, promising *waqf* dependants an income via the agency of the state. Several other administrative reforms were carried out, but these appear to have had neither a clear direction nor a unified sense of purpose. A Supreme Council, headed by Chief Justices from the four legal schools, was established in order to deal with, among many other matters, mercantile disputes involving foreigners. This Council appears to have been instituted with the dual purpose of: (a) accommodating extrajudicial commercial litigation arising from the extensive economic hegemony that the Europeans exercised in Egypt; and (b) inserting centralizing elements into the judiciary. Very little else changed on the level of the lower courts, however.

Although Muhammad ʿAli acted as the de facto ruler of Egypt, he remained during the 1830s bound by the spirit, if not the letter, of Istanbul's reformist agenda, represented in the latter's policies leading up to the 1839 Decree. Such demands, however, were not difficult to oblige, as interest in modernization was equally intense in Egypt. But local considerations gave it a particular form and process. In 1836 or there-abouts, French experts, at the invitation of Muhammad 'Ali, submitted to him a report with a number of recommendations pertaining to improve-ments in the military and economic spheres. The crux of the recommen-dations was the forging of a centralized administration, which could regulate nearly every aspect of life in Egypt, from the army and guilds, to public traffic and water supply. These regulations, permeating spheres of life that had never before been subjected to such high-level scrutiny, became the hallmark of Muhammad 'Ali's regime as much as it became that of the Ottomans and every other modernizing regime.

Following the French experts' recommendations, Muhammad 'Ali issued in 1837 the so-called *siyasatname*, a reform plan that, much like the new administrative and judicial measures of the day, consciously took Europe and the European practice of government as models to be emu-lated. The *siyasatname* laid down the general foundations for the changes that were to be carried out during the next few decades. By the time the Ottoman Decree of 1839 was sent to him from Istanbul for implementa-tion, he could confirm that he had already done most of what was required.

In 1828, Muhammad 'Ali sent the first group of Egyptian students to Paris, to study, among other things, law. After a three-year course, they returned to Egypt and were immediately engaged in translating French codes and law manuals. During the late 1860s, they produced an Arabic translation of both the French civil and commercial codes. Other codes of criminal and civil procedure were translated soon thereafter.

In the meantime, the Shari'a courts in theory continued to have general jurisdiction, but with the increasing influence and scope of new, Western-style courts their range was steadily being narrowed down. They were already limited to land and real property in general, matters of personal status and criminal cases involving blood money. Then in the early 1880s their power was curtailed even more drastically, due in large measure to the corresponding development of the new courts.

Reflecting the increased interference of France, Britain and other European countries in the affairs of Egypt, the so-called Mixed Courts were created in 1876. The Europeans further extended their influence via these courts not only to the affairs of foreigners but also to the whole gamut of the country's commercial life. They also introduced the notion of jurisdictional hierarchy, where courts of first instance were established in Cairo, Mansura and Alexandria, with a single court of appeal in the latter. One year before the establishment of these courts, a series of laws – based mostly on French law – was passed in anticipation, namely, the Civil Code, the Penal Code, the Commercial Code, the Code of Maritime

Commerce, the Code of Civil and Commercial Procedure and the Code of Criminal Procedure.

Regulated by French codes and presided over by a majority of European judges nominated by their respective countries, the Mixed Courts in effect constituted a legal and economic regime by which Egypt's financial and, indeed, political life was controlled. Producing "some forty thousand written opinions," and rendering the "Egyptian government ... subject to their jurisdiction and their judgments," there was "practically no litigation of any large or general importance which [was] not attracted to their jurisdiction."[7] And as if to increase the alienation of the native Shari'a courts and their users, the Mixed Courts, which quickly appropriated most of the spheres of law, began to require advocacy as a prerequisite for filing suits before them. In 1877, when the Mixed Bar Association held its first meeting, it boasted seventy-nine members, none of whom was an Egyptian. On the other hand, the 1880 Code of Procedure came to confine the Shari'a courts' jurisdiction to matters of personal status, inheritance, *waqf*, gifts and crime. By 1896, the latter jurisdiction had been removed from their competence, further limiting their sphere of action to family law, broadly so defined. Furthermore, the Shari'a courts were ordered to report all their transactions pertaining to real property to the Mixed Courts of first instance, although the latter were not obliged to reciprocate.

Aside from the increasingly limited jurisdiction of the Shari'a courts, the Mixed Courts extended their sway, and managed to unify the legal system like never before. This fierce tendency to centralize was in the interests of both the Khedive and the foreign powers. Ironically, the machinery and tools of the modern nation-state were called upon by both the colonizers and the colonized, for through these modern governing instruments the colonizers aimed to colonize, whereas the colonized wanted, at most, to decolonize and, at least, to escape colonization unscathed. Yet, strengthening the Mixed Courts was distinctly more in the interests of the Powers than in those of the Khedive. Their growing exclusivity as judicial organs, plus the powers conferred upon their magistrates in terms of spectacular salaries and life-appointments, were all designed to render them more conducive to serving European economic interests. With a majority of European judges applying "free-market" oriented codes, the harnessing of Egypt as an open market became less difficult to accomplish.

---

[7] Jasper Brinton, *The Mixed Courts of Egypt* (New Haven: Yale University Press, 1930), xxiii–xxiv.

As with many colonial projects, the Mixed Courts became a bone of contention among the competing European powers. Until 1882, Britain refused to expand its jurisdiction or any aspect of its influence lest its colonialist competitors seize such an opportunity to shift the balance of power. But once Britain occupied Egypt after crushing the 'Urabi revolt of 1882, it felt secure enough to permit the Egyptian government to create the so-called national courts. When the Council of Ministers began deliberating the creation of these courts, it was thought that, by accepting some European presence on the benches of these new courts, it would be possible to bring a quicker end to the nationally abhorred Mixed Courts. And so it was determined that the national courts would include one foreign judge at each court of first instance and two foreign judges in each court of appeal. The new court system began work in March 1884, with only one court of appeal in Cairo (not to be reinforced until 1925, when a sister court was created in Asyut). In order to eliminate diversity – inconsistent with the aims and nature of the modern state system – the Court of Cassation was abolished, thereby limiting the new system to two tiers or levels, a constitution also consistent with the Mixed Courts' structure, on which the national courts was modeled. Yet, the new courts also adopted the substantive laws that were applied in the Mixed Courts (and reissued in 1883), save for the code of preliminary enquiry and the penal code, which were to be drafted in accordance with the demands of local conditions. Other codes, including a new commercial code, were compiled by European lawyers who wrote them first in the French language, whence they were translated into Arabic.

On the other hand, the Shari'a and its courts were progressively marginalized, not through changing Islamic law itself, but rather by means of procedural amendments which deprived it of application. For example, in a series of procedural restrictions starting in the 1870s and culminating in 1911, the courts were expressly precluded from hearing litigation in the absence of written evidence. The systematic ousting of oral testimony, the cornerstone of the Shari'a courts' operation, was followed by a reconstituted law of procedure that reflected a written – in contradistinction to oral – tradition that served the state's purpose of counting, accounting, surveillance and control. The marginalization of the Shari'a was thus itself an act not only of dismantling but also of building a system of courts and law that functioned to serve the state.

Iran attempts reform

Before we discuss the legal reforms in Iran, it is essential to say a few things about Shi'i jurisprudence, which was introduced by the Safavid dynasty

(r. 1501–1732) into Iran at the beginning of the sixteenth century. Twelver-Shiʿi jurisprudence came to differ from its Sunni counterpart on a number of essential points, three of which are important to us here. The first relates to the divine appointment of the IMAMATE, which begins with the fundamental assumption that there exists a qualitative dissimilarity between human and divine qualities. Man's intelligence is ultimately defective, with the implication that his understanding of the law is incomplete. This premise entailed that God is bound by duty to make legal obligations known to the human mind. As a means of communicating His signs that embody His Will and Law, God chose a number of persons possessed of superior qualities and made them Prophets and Imams. The Imam is neither a second-class Prophet nor a deputy, as the early Sunnite caliphs were conceived by the Sunnis. He is a substitute for the Prophet, taking on the tasks and functions of the Prophet in his absence.

The second premise takes the Imam to be a sinless, infallible and perfect being. By virtue of having been chosen as an Imam, he combines qualities that are superior to any other human living in his age. If it were not for the convention of religious texts, the Imam would be no less a prophet than the Prophet Muhammad himself. As one distinguished Shiʿi jurist observed, "it is divine law that forbade our Imams being given the name of prophecy, not reason."[8] The Twelver-Shiʿi Imams are thus not subordinate to the Prophet Muhammad but rather his peers. Indeed, whereas he is deemed to be a fallible human, they are deemed immune from error. On the other hand, the Prophet was an instrument of revelation, whereas none of the Imams was chosen for this task. But since their knowledge is infallible, their ability to convey the divine Law to their followers has the status of certitude. (This divine empowerment of the Imams must be kept in mind when we turn later to the legal and political developments in modern Iran, for the elevated status accorded the Imam appears to run counter to the claim that the master-jurist can replace and fully represent the Imam in the latter's absence. In fact, the Imams did not delegate their powers to anyone, and were reported to have condemned as fraudulent any political governance in their name.)

The third premise was constituted by historical events. Around the year 874, the twelfth Imam disappeared, and since then he has been presumed to be in hiding as a result of the persecution he suffered. Yet, while hiding, he continues to bear the knowledge of law in its best,

[8] Cited in Joseph Eliash, "The Ithna ʿAshari-Shiʿi Juristic Theory of Political and Legal Authority," *Studia Islamica*, 29 (1969): 24.

infallible and most perfect form. In many ways, he in effect takes on a divine status, since – according to a number of Twelver-Shi'i jurists – there can be no access to God's mind without resort to the Imam. The Imam thus represents for Twelver-Shi'ism the locus of the law, if not its source. At the end of time, the Imam will reappear, implementing his just law with full force, but until then several functions that the Imams had fulfilled must somehow be discharged, and the jurist-in-charge was the one to do so.

Now, for various reasons to do with political legitimacy, the Qajars of Iran invested heavily in the religious institution, dedicating much property in the way of *waqf*. This gesture, however, failed to coopt the Twelver-Shi'i ulama into the power structures of the ruling dynasty. As it happened, by the time the Qajars established their rule, Twelver-Shi'ism had come to reassert itself with renewed vigor. Thus, by the time of European encroachment, the religious establishment and its personnel (recipients of major endowments and religious taxes) stood in a more powerful position *vis-à-vis* the political establishment than had their pre-sixteenth-century Sunni predecessors, and most certainly their Ottoman counterparts (whose power was manifestly dependent on the political sovereign).

In part as a result of the resistance mounted by the Shi'i legists, most reform plans initiated by the Qajars never materialized on any large scale. Instead, changes were piecemeal, initially reflected in such acts as sending, around 1828, students to Europe in order to follow courses in a variety of new disciplines. Western education was accompanied by a stress on translating European works into Farsi. But such reform proposals as the one drafted in 1851 – and modeled after the 1839 Ottoman Gülhane Decree – categorically failed. Failure also attended the series of reforms begun in 1858, when the newly established Council of Ministers set up provincial departments of justice that were aimed at centralizing the judiciary.

Another serious plan was drafted in 1871, suggesting, among other things, the creation of a system of Western-style, hierarchical courts with special codes to be applied in them. Yet not only these but all other attempts at reform failed, and there was little, if anything, accomplished by 1906. Even the National Consultative Assembly, established during that same year, could produce no more than a Basic Law that affirmed the supremacy of the Shari'a, and, for the purpose of ensuring this supremacy, a five-*MULLAH* committee was formed. However, the Basic Law did introduce the idea of the separation of powers, and granted judges life tenure in an effort to enhance the concept of the rule of law.

Nonetheless, the Qajar legal reforms – if they can be called that at all – were ineffective. Compared with the Egyptian and Ottoman reforms, they cannot be said to have started in earnest until the reign of Reza Shah (1925–42). The reason for this was the fact that Iran was difficult to centralize. Between the collapse of the Safavids in 1732 and the consolidation of the Qajars in 1794, the country had enough time to fall prey to multiple competing tribal chieftains who aspired to general control. The Qajars arrived in the midst of this scene, and were too weak to bring the chieftains under their control. Their fiscal system also adopted the abhorrent practice of selling tax-farming offices to the highest bidder who, to recuperate the high fees, had to extort taxes at the price of depleting local resources. Peasants and all tax-paying subjects developed a great deal of resentment and distrust of the ruler.

The problem of decentralization and the severe lack of government control were further aggravated by the rise, not only of chieftains, but also of powerful Shi'i legists who stepped in to fill the vacuum. Beginning with Isma'il (r. 1501–1524), the Safavid shahs had proclaimed themselves representatives of the hidden Imams, thus investing themselves with attributes of infallibility and divine authority that embraced both the political and the legal realms. Neither the Qajars nor any of their political competitors made such religious or legal claims, thereby creating a void. Replacing the religious powers of the Safavid shahs, the Shi'i legists stepped in and proclaimed their own divine representation on behalf of the Imams, thus complementing the exclusively temporal competence of the Qajars. After the decline of the Safavids, but certainly by the rise of the Qajars, Twelver-Shi'ism developed a grass-roots constituency, standing apart from the ruler and his government. The *fatwa*s of the great legists (the *mujtahid*s) could therefore pronounce any imperial decree invalid with impunity, and for such acts it was easy for these *mujtahid*s to garner massive support from their followers, namely, the majority of the population that had been overly burdened by excessive taxation and maltreatment.

The ulama thus continued largely unperturbed in their control over the judiciary and education, and the nascent secular schools – unlike the new Ottoman and Egyptian schools – were ineffective in producing a Westernized elite that would form a cadre sufficient to push for reform. Whereas hundreds of thousands of new bureaucratic positions opened in the wake of applying Ottoman and Egyptian centralization policies (thus permitting the formation of new reform-minded generations), the Qajar bureaucracy – which barely reached the outskirts of the capital – was too small to accommodate even the relatively few graduates of the new, secular schools. Real reform had thus to await the end of the first quarter of the twentieth century.

Algeria under the French

In July 1830, a French naval expedition captured Algiers, beginning an extraordinarily brutal occupation that was to last for no less than a century and a quarter. It would not be until a decade after this conquest that the occupation forces were able to extend their power beyond the littoral and into the interior of what is today known as Algeria. But the French were very quick to use the law as a tool of conquest, and the Algerian experience provides a supreme model of the use of raw legal power to accomplish colonialist objectives. What made the Algerian case an especially intense colonial experiment were such crucial facts as: (1) the French perceived themselves as replacing the Ottomans as masters of a colony that had never enjoyed a sovereign status – in effect, what had belonged to the Ottomans now belonged to them; (2) a large, and in time powerful, French population settled in this colony as permanent residents, claiming it as their land; (3) France, in time, began to harbor a design to claim the country, not as a colony, but as an integral part of France; and (4) the French settlers continued for decades to exercise tremendous pressure on their Paris government to facilitate their commercial ambitions by granting them land or by permitting them to purchase real property from the natives on a large scale.

Thus, while the colonial interest in the Ottoman Empire was to penetrate the local consumer markets, in Algeria the French interest was direct appropriation and exploitation of the agricultural and mineral resources of the country. The problem, as the French saw it, was that too many Muslims lived in the country and, what is more, that these natives somehow possessed all the lands coveted for commercial exploitation. As genocide involving a population of over 2 million natives was – at least at the time – not a practical option for the colonial authorities, freeing the land from the grip of the natives by other means dominated all considerations, in the legal field no less than in the political.

The coveted land happened to be under various types of ownership, all regulated by Islamic law. In addition to freehold title and state land, there was the all-important *waqf* land (known in North Africa as "*HABOUS*") which alone constituted no less than one-half of all arable land. The latter, as elsewhere in the Muslim world, also formed a substantial part of non-landed real property, especially religious and educational institutions, as well as residential buildings. By hook or by crook, the French settlers managed to amass a good deal of property deriving from the *waqf* domain, sparking what became a common practice for many natives who were beneficiaries of the endowments, i.e., suing for restoration of the sequestered property to its original *waqf* state.

During the first year of conquest, France had already declared the entire colony, including *habous* or *waqf* lands, as belonging to the public domain. In 1844, the *habous* were confiscated and the administration was charged with the task of funding the religious and educational endowments and their employees. (This centralizing act – simultaneously depleting the income of these endowments – was nearly identical to the *waqf* centralization policy adopted by the Ottomans in 1826 and thereafter.) Furthermore, disputes over illegally seized *waqf* property had just been resolved in 1840 when a decree retroactively declared all property in the hands of the *colons*, whether acquired lawfully or not, to be lawfully owned by its colonial usurpers. Deprived of their *waqf* income and support, the legitimate Muslim beneficiaries were left to fend for themselves.

By 1844, all aspects of property law in the Shari'a were replaced by French law, which by design was made to facilitate the commercial ambitions of the settlers. Further steps toward this goal – and specifically toward forcing the *waqf* properties onto the open market – were taken when, against every principle in Islamic law, all *waqf* property was deemed to be, legally speaking, alienable. Nevertheless, the Muslim natives generally refused to sell or buy *waqf* property, rendering this policy somewhat ineffective.

The legal fray that accompanied the *habous* appropriation, as well as the attendant political and military policies that undergirded that dispute, were not the domain of politicians alone. French lawyers, jurists and academicians who knew anything useful about North Africa (and some who knew very little) began to discourse on matters legal and otherwise. Many of them were *colons* who were mostly both scholars and civil servants, and who often became involved in the colonialist administration of justice. After the middle of the century, they began to produce what became a massive bulk of legal literature about Islamic law in its North African context, especially about the theory and practice of the dominant Maliki school. (This literature, it is worth noting, was to become an integral part of Western scholarship on, and therefore Western knowledge of, Islam.) Certain of these writings acquired an academic guise but some were in the nature of legislation, exemplified in the so-called *Code Morand*. This juridical and legislative body of discourse came to be known as the *droit musulman-algérien*, somewhat cognate to, but larger in scope and academic interest than, the British colonialist notion of Anglo-Muhammadan Law.

Like their British and Dutch counterparts, French Orientalists – co-founders of the field of Islamic legal studies – proved to be quite helpful in the implementation of the government's and settlers' policies. As far as *habous* was concerned, for instance, the French administration attempted to control the religious endowments through a series of legislative enactments, aided along the way by the French Orientalists who "campaigned to discredit the institution among the Algerians themselves."[9]

This campaign, if not struggle, to "conquer minds" was as essential a project for the colonists as any material conquest. And much of this project revolved around the production of cultural and academic discourse. There ensued a flood of argument to the effect that there exists a fundamental distinction between family and public *waqf*s – a notion that had never acquired the same meaning in Muslim cultures. Since French scholars by then understood the importance of the Quran in Islam, they began to argue that family *waqf* was a development that occurred subsequent to the formative and foundational phase of the religion, distinctly implying that it was an inauthentic accretion, a bad innovation, so to speak. They concluded that these family endowments circumvented the Quranic law of inheritance which operates by the principle of shares (and therefore led to the fragmentation of family property). Accordingly, family *habous* and Quranic inheritance were declared – on behalf of Muslims – mutually exclusive; and since the *raison d'être* of the former was the skirting of the dictates of the latter, family endowments were deemed both immoral and illegal. This argument was offered in parallel to another: that family endowments inherently tied up property and prevented it from "efficient" exploitation, a fact that ineluctably led to economic stagnation. From here, it was a short and easy step to link this stagnation with cultural malaise and, indeed, a stunted civilizational progress.

The singling out of family endowments as reprobate appeared in the 1850s as a move concomitant with an unusually liberal call by the *colons* and their government to the effect that Islamic law must be centralized in an effort to build an Algerian religious unity. The condemnation of the family endowments, while underscoring the Quran's integrity – which was part of a call to maintain the "true" form of Islam – constituted a two-in-one strike aimed at opening the gates to the application of Quranic rules of inheritance which would, perforce, break up property held in joint ownership. This material ambition combined with the fear that, if Islamic law were to be completely dismantled and assimilation were to run its full course, the Algerian Muslims would demand full political rights.

The contradictions between the need to absorb and control the law and its native subjects, on the one hand, and keeping these colonized subjects

---

[9] David Powers, "Orientalism, Colonialism and Legal History: The Attack on Muslim Family Endowments in Algeria and India," *Comparative Studies in Society and History*, 31, 3 (July 1989): 536.

at bay and away from the exercise of political power, on the other, under-lined much of the colonial policy of the French. But it still served several ends at one and the same time. The Islamic legal system was asserted but centralized and bureaucratized, thereby imposing on it a form of European rationality that was alien to it. And maintaining it not only served enormous economic interests but provided an example to the Ottomans to afford their subjects at least the *"liberté et égalité"* of the French Revolution.

Having prepared the way to dispense with family endowments, the *colons* and the supporting Orientalists moved to the next stage. Toward the end of the century, enormous areas of cultivable land had already fallen into the hands of the *colon* entrepreneurs, with the result that the need to maintain the argument for the Quran's integrity had by then largely vanished. Thus, having already accepted the premise that the Quranic law of inheritance was fragmentary (which in the first place had caused Muslims themselves to circumvent it), the Orientalists now set out to reform the Islamic law of succession, at least by writing scholarly treatises on it. In this project, they enlisted the efforts of Middle Eastern students who had come from various Arab regions to study with French Orientalists. For example, Professor M. Morand, President of the Faculté de Droit d'Alger, supervised doctoral works by such students who called for reforming the Quranic law of inheritance or setting it aside altogether. (It must be emphasized that the discourse of this campaign – against *waqf* in particular but also against the Shari'a in general – was inseparable from the Ottoman discourse which took its inspiration from French cultural models.)

On another front, French penal law was promulgated in 1859, while in 1873 the so-called *Loi Warnier* decreed that all land in Algeria was to be regulated by French law and, what is more, that the Muslim courts would henceforth be confined to adjudging cases pertaining to personal status, including inheritance. The displacement of the penal system reached a high point in 1881 with the promulgation of the repressive *Code de l'indigénat* which empowered civil administrators to mete out harsh pun-ishments, without due process, against Muslim subjects charged with any of forty-one specified offenses. These penalties included detention with-out trial, collective punishment and discretionary confiscation of prop-erty. The *Code* continued in force until 1927.

The French, however, did not limit their attention to criminal and commercial matters. As promulgators of a "civilizing" mission, they saw themselves as advocates of causes that went beyond efficient exploitation of natural resources and labor. Whereas in most other parts of the Muslim world no government, whether local or foreign, risked the introduction at the time of any changes in civil law, the French repeatedly attempted to implement a civil law that would alter what were seen as unprogressive, if not uncivilized, rules. From the middle of the nineteenth century and for many decades thereafter, they promulgated and retracted many codes and decrees, including the famous *Code Morand* of 1916, which was never applied. Like several other decrees, this *Code* attempted to effect a number of fundamental changes to matters of personal status.

By 1871, the Algerian legal class was in disarray, in part because certain of their numbers lost moral authority by cooperating with the French. This coopting was the inevitable byproduct of the French reordering of local political organization, a reordering reminiscent of the Ottoman reconstructive introduction of the municipal councils. While many of the legists serving on these councils represented the interests of their fellow Muslims, there were others – together with notables and landed aristocracy – who cooperated, or appeared to cooperate, with the French beyond what were seen as appropriate bounds. But the more significant reason for the decline of their status and power had to do with the depletion of the resources that had been at their disposal and that now largely vanished into the hands of the French after the centralization and large-scale confiscation of *waqf*s. These transformations in the *habous* system affected not only their economic status but their command of the field of education, on both the elementary and the law college levels. Like the Ottomans before them, the French acquired an educational monopoly on the production of Muslim legists and *qadi*s. The *madrasa*s of Algiers, Tlemcen and Constantine became the official colleges from which future *qadi*s were to be recruited. But the poor (now centralized) funding of these *madrasa*s, among other factors, contributed to a dramatic lowering of the standards of legal education, and consequently of the quality of *qadi*s and law professors (a phenomenon that persists in the great majority of today's Muslim countries). Simultaneously, the streamlining of education permitted the French to inject a pro-colonialist reading into the legal training of these men, another phase in the project of "conquering the mind." The French judges also began to displace *qadi*s and religious courts, while all litigation pertaining to real property and crime, even when the parties to the litigation were all Muslim, was removed from the purview of Shari'a jurisdiction. The effect of the overall tendency to encroach on the domain of the Shari'a led to a dramatic reduction in the number of Muslim courts in the country, from an already reduced 184 in 1870 to 61 in 1890. By the time Algeria gained its independence in 1962, the Shari'a was reduced to no more than a regime of family law.

Methods of legal reform

By 1900, the Shariʿa in the vast majority of Muslim lands had been reduced in scope of application to the area of personal status, including child custody, inheritance, gifts and, to some extent, *waqf*. In the Malay states and the Indonesian Archipelago, its sphere was even narrower, partly because of the *adat* which had long prevailed in some of these domains, and partly because of massive Westernization of its contents and form. The present chapter therefore focuses on personal status, following the fortunes (indeed misfortunes) of Islamic law roughly from the end of World War I until the dawn of the twenty-first century.

The Islamic law of personal status was saved from the death blows dealt to other Shariʿa laws (except rituals) by virtue of the fact that it was of no use to the colonial powers as a tool of domination. Even this disinterest was turned into an advantage, however, for colonialist Europe and its academics promoted the idea that the personal law was sacred to Muslims and that, out of sensitivity and respect, colonial powers left it alone. However, once the laws of personal status were *culturally* marked as such, they were taken as the point of reference for the modern politics of identity. If family law emerged as "the preferential symbol of Islamic identity,"[1] it did so not only because it was built into Muslim knowledge as an area of a sensitive nature, but also because it represented what was taken to be the last fortress of the Shariʿa to survive the ravages of modernization.

While the popular Muslim imagination, even today, appears to hold these remnants of the Shariʿa to be an authentic and genuine expression of

---

[1] Marie-Aimée Hélie-Lucas, "The Preferential Symbol for Islamic Identity: Women in Muslim Personal Laws," in Valentine M. Moghadam, ed., *Identity Politics and Women: Cultural Reassertions and Feminisms in International Perspective* (Boulder, CO: Westview Press, 1994), 391–407; Annelies Moors, "Debating Islamic Family Law: Legal Texts and Social Practices," in M. L. Meriwether and Judith E. Tucker, eds., *Social History of Women and Gender in the Modern Middle East* (Boulder, CO and Oxford: Westview Press, 1999), 150.

traditional family law, the fact of the matter is that even this sphere of law underwent structural and fundamental changes that ultimately resulted in its being severed from both the substance of classical religious law and the methodology by which this law had operated. For to maintain this methodology would have amounted not only to maintaining the linguistic and legal interpretive system, but also the human and institutional bearers of this complex tradition. This, in other words, would have required the maintenance of the very system that produced the entire sociology of legal knowledge, including the institutions of *waqf* and *madrasa*. But we have seen that these otherwise independent institutions stood in the way of the emerging state and its culture, which is to say that they represented an impediment to centralization, be it fiscal, legal or otherwise. Thus, it was both essential to and an inevitable consequence of the ways of the nation-state that personal status had to be severed from its own, indigenous jural *system*, its own ecological environment, so to speak.

This severance was effected through various devices that included both administrative and interpretive techniques. Attributed to nebulous origins in Islamic tradition and history, these devices were cultivated and augmented to yield results that had never been entertained before. The first of these devices was a concept that has come to be used, often implicitly, to justify any and all change in the law. In traditional Islamic law, one was permitted to avoid harm to oneself even if this entailed a violation of the law, e.g., consuming ritually impure food if one is threatened with starvation. This substantive legal principle, the concept of "necessity" (*DARURA*), was fundamentally transformed by modern legists in two ways: first, it was transposed from the domain of substantive law (where it regulated relatively few cases) to the realm of legal theory that in turn came to regulate the construction and operation of POSITIVE LAW generally. Second – and partly derivative of the first – the scope of the principle was widened beyond recognition, so that instead of delimiting the boundaries of "necessity" within those of the law, the law in its entirety was (re)defined within utilitarian principles of necessity. The legal principle was thus turned on its head, from being subordinate to the larger imperative of the law to being the dominating and all-encompassing principle.

The second device was procedural, which is to say that, without changing certain parts of Islamic substantive law, it was possible through this device to exclude particular claims from judicial enforcement, thus in effect leaving significant provisions of Islamic law mere ink on dusty paper. For instance, for many decades during the reform period, child marriage was not explicitly outlawed, but to cancel the effects of this law, the bureaucratic offices – which now in effect possessed the authority to declare what was legal and what was not – were instructed not to register any contract in which the parties to it had not attained the age of majority. A similar change was effected in the area of oral testimony and oral evidence, where the courts were instructed not to hear claims lacking documentary or written evidence.

The third device, one of the most effective methods by which new positive law was created from the virtual dispersal-cum-restructuring of Shari'a law, consisted of an eclectic approach that operated on two levels: *TAKHAYYUR* and *TALFIQ* (lit. "selection" and "amalgamation," respectively). The former involved the adoption as law not only of "weak" and discredited opinions from the school, but also of opinions held by other schools. The options created by this device seemed boundless, since not only could Twelver-Shi'i opinions be absorbed by the codes of Sunni countries, but so also could those of long defunct schools. *Talfiq* involved an even more daring technique. While *takhayyur* required the harvesting of opinions, for a single code, from various schools, *talfiq* amounted to combining elements of one opinion from various quarters within and without the school. In some countries, notably Egypt and Iraq, this double-tiered device was used to produce radical changes even in inheritance law, e.g., making lawful a bequest in favor of an heir (prohibited in Sunni but not in Shi'i law), with the proviso that the total bulk of the bequeathed property not exceed one-third of the estate. The consent of the other heirs was furthermore no longer required. It may be noted that traditional Islamic law made it forbidden for both the jurists and "state authorities" to resort to such devices.

The fourth device is the so-called neo-*ijtihad*, an interpretive approach that is largely free of traditional legal interpretation. In a sense, the device of *takhayyur*-cum-*talfiq* rests on this general approach, since the act of combining different, if not divergent, elements of one opinion entails a measure of interpretive freedom. But there are other examples of a new kind of interpretation, such as limiting the period of pregnancy to one year, a period which some authoritative classical jurists, attempting to keep conceptions out of wedlock within family bounds, had extended at times to up to four years. Another example is the 1956 Tunisian Code of Personal Status which prohibits polygamy on the grounds that the Quran explicitly predicated the permission to marry up to four wives on the man's ability to treat them with complete fairness and justice, a requirement that was interpreted by modern law-makers as essentially idealistic and impossible to achieve.

The fifth and final device, much like the first, represents a new application of the old but restricted principle that any law that does not contradict the Shari'a may be deemed lawful. Prohibition of child marriage and of unilateral divorce by the husband are seen as belonging to this category of law.

In their entirety, these devices, directly as well as obliquely, did the bidding of the state in absorbing the Islamic legal tradition into its well-defined structures of codification. But the most substantive of these devices were the third and the fourth, with the former literally supplying much of the law, remolding it with a view to producing particular, intended effects. We will discuss the most important of these effects in the next section, but for now we must note the most salient byproduct of this structural difference between the traditional law and the codified law of modern states. As we have seen, one of the hallmarks of the Shari'a is its plurality of opinion (at times reaching a dozen viewpoints on one and the same case or issue). This plurality was in part responsible not only for legal change, but also for flexibility in the application of the law. Women, for example, could resort to any school, and the *qadi* in actual practice could apply any opinion from within that school to accommodate a particular situation. Codification, on the other hand, eliminates almost all such juristic and hermeneutical possibilities, leaving both the litigants and the judge with a single formulation and, in all likelihood, a single mode of judicial application. For it is eminently arguable that unifying and homogenizing the law is one of the primary concerns of the modern state.

Family law and a new patriarchy

The engineering of these devices and their orchestration to produce particular effects was the work of the modern state, the appropriator and possessor of the law. That this institution was the most central and commanding modern project ever to enter the world of Islam is nothing short of a truism. As the primary and leading institution of European modernity, it constantly defined, redefined and influenced nearly every entity with which it came into contact. Whether incorporated into the Muslim world by imposition or by mimesis, its defining, constitutive and fundamental features were nearly identical everywhere. It claimed the exclusive right to wage war outside and, with the same exclusivity, to exercise violence within its own domains; it declared itself sovereign while developing systemic mechanisms of surveillance and discipline; it lived on nationalism as the body lives on circulated blood; it appropriated the exclusive right to make and enforce law; and in all of this it was the "big father" of the citizen. As a man was head of the family, the state was the head of society. The nation-state thus combined among its attributes the power to rule and subdue, and the right and duty to defend, promote, and claim possession of the nation, nationhood, nationality, and their subject – the citizen.

Nationalism has always been a masculine conception subordinating the feminine. It is, at one and the same time, a distinctly racial conception that stems from a certain assumption, if not a "scientific" premise, of purity of blood. The conception would evaporate into absurdity if the French nation were to be seen to have been formed with the assistance of Italian, Arab or Chinese sperm. And yet it was this conception of biological workings that maintained the uniqueness of nations. From this logic followed the idea that it is the man, not the woman, who determined national attributes, which is another way of saying that man defined and literally constituted the nation as the subject of the state. As an archetypal figure, he likewise constituted it as an object of sovereignty. In this design, women became instruments of reproduction, while the modern state appropriated the right to determine "the uses of women's reproductive skills."[2]

The nation-state that the Muslims encountered was – and continues to be – a masculine entity and, in its nineteenth- and early twentieth-century form, a thoroughgoing patriarchal order. And it was the French legal model that dominated the colonialist scene in the Middle Eastern (and African) countries. Even Egypt, an otherwise British protectorate, opted for that model. Nor is it difficult to see why this should have been the case. One of the most salient features of the nation-state is its totalistic appropriation of the domain of law, an appropriation that presupposed centralization and bureaucratization of the legal system. There was no room for judges' law-making, otherwise a defining attribute of the British case law system. Case law is a diffused phenomenon, lacking in concentricity, a clear voice of authority and a textual homogeneity that can pronounce the laws of the state in an authoritatively clear and unmistakable fashion. A strong colonialist regime (and later nationalist governance) thus required the code, the statute and the act as tools of total control. Even the British engaged in this form of legislation in their legal reconstruction of the colonies.

It was no coincidence that the code, the very tool that represented and embodied the agendas of the nation-state, was also the chief method by which the legal systems of the Orient were reengineered. And the French model not only supplied the political form of the nation-state's hegemony; it also – and importantly – furnished the legal content that bolstered this hegemony. If blood and sperm were seen to constitute the nation, so was the state's law. But for it to make the nation, shape it and represent it, the

---

[2] Mervat Hatem, "The Professionalization of Health and the Control of Women's Bodies as Modern Governmentalities in Nineteenth Century Egypt," in M. Zilfi, ed., *Women in the Ottoman Empire* (Leiden: Brill, 1997), 67.

law had to be equally national, the very embodiment of the nation's will, aspirations and worldview. In the final analysis, the law is and must be the quintessential expression of the state's will.

Inasmuch as the law is a manifestation of the state and its will to power, the family, as a prototype of the nation, is the reconstituted invention of the state, whether in Europe or the Muslim world. The ideal family, consisting of a two-parent household, lacks the complex social networks that otherwise engender loyalty among and between the many members of the extended family and clan. The nuclear family, constituted by national ideology and a capitalist mode of production (both inherent to the structures of European and most other states), is thus the object of the social engineering project; it is, in fact, quintessential to the imagining of the state and its ideological and political practices. And having been assigned to fulfill this role, the family is shaped by the state's law through regulation of marriage, divorce and inheritance, as well as an array of practices that define and dictate those relationships producing the family. Yet, the family itself arguably stands with the state in a mutually constitutive relationship where the state's power to authorize and dissolve marriage manifests itself as a set of practices from which it derives its own sovereignty, while the family has thus contributed to shaping the modern state, though on terms that suit the state and its systematic and systemic programs to reengineer (or sanction preexisting parts of) the social order, among others.

During the colonial period, when the nation-state was being imported into the Muslim world from Europe, the agenda of the colonial powers did not extend to the reengineering of the Muslim family, since the construction of states *qua* states in the lands of Islam was not what the colonists originally aimed to accomplish. Material exploitation, the quintessential project of colonialism, did not require this reengineering, a situation that allowed (as we saw earlier) colonial apologists to make a virtue of non-necessity. As we will see in due course, many Islamic countries indirectly embarked on modifying family law as early as the second decade of the twentieth century, but the project of reengineering the family via legal mechanisms did not begin in earnest until the colonies acquired autonomy or independence. Nevertheless, as we saw earlier, the colonial powers did, directly and obliquely, cause the dismantling of the *waqf* institution, which was undoubtedly linked in numerous structural ways with family life and the laws that regulated that life. Furthermore, when France developed the unique colonial idea of absorbing Algeria into the French nation, it repeatedly attempted to alter the personal laws of the Shari'a and replace them with what was seen as more progressive and civilized rules. From the middle of the nineteenth century onward, the French attempted to enforce many codes and decrees, most notably the *Code Morand*, a code that was devised, inter alia, to redesign the Muslim family along lines conceived by the *état suprême* of post-Revolutionary France. In the end it was due to the determined resistance of the Algerians that such attempts resulted in failure, and surely not to the lack of French effort.

As the nationalist elites slowly began to displace the colonists, the project of governance could no longer be limited to the unidimensional aim of material exploitation. The basic structures of the state apparatus were already in place, and the goal would now become total rule, a desideratum that all nineteenth-century European states had already attained at home. This type of rule, together with what the French had attempted to do in Algeria, would become one of the primary objectives of the new nationalist elites. The recently independent states in the Islamic world would continue a project of governance that the colonists had little motive to pursue in the colonies, for the project, in its full manifestation, did not serve colonialist goals. But once political independence was secured, the nationalist leadership pursued state-building in earnest. Tellingly, what this leadership had resisted under colonial rule, it would insist upon after independence. For instance, under the French, the Tunisian and Algerian nationalists vehemently opposed any change in the law of personal status, but as soon as the French were made to leave, and as soon as the former assumed power, they almost immediately embarked on a program of "reform" in this presumably sensitive legal sphere.

The early, half-hearted Ottoman codification of personal status, as well as the later nationalist codification projects, found their inspiration in the only available model of governance: the European nation-state in general, and the French version of it in particular. The French Civil Codes (from 1804 until the middle of the twentieth century), to which the Ottoman Empire, the post-colonial nation-states and so much of Africa owed a debt, did not hesitate to declare the man to be the predominant figure in the home. In the 1804 Civil Code, and thereafter until its 1938 successor, it was unambiguously stated that the "husband owes protection to his wife, the wife obedience to her husband."[3] Even as late as 1970, in French law the husband still stood as "the head of the family." (Similarly, until 1949, the West German Civil Code granted the husband the right to "decide all matters of matrimonial rights" while the so-called Equality Law of 1957 [art. 1356.I] opens with the statement that "The wife's

[3] Mary Ann Glendon, "Power and Authority in the Family: New Legal Patterns as Reflections of Changing Ideologies," *American Journal of Comparative Law*, 23, 1 (1975): 6–9.

responsibility is to run the household.") Therefore it was this legal culture, directly arising from the nation and its state, that defined the parameters of post-colonial nationalism. Partha Chatterjee's apt description of the Indian context equally applies to others: nationalism, Chatterjee observed, "conferred upon women the honor of a new social responsibility and by associating the task of female emancipation with the historical goal of sovereign nationhood, bound them to a narrow, and yet entirely legitimate, subordination."[4]

This subordination finds ample manifestation in the provisions of the Ottoman Law of Family Rights of 1917, a law that represented in the Ottoman domains the first state-sponsored codification of the Islamic law of personal status. The significance of this Law lay not only in the fact that it was the first attempt of this kind, but, more importantly, in its spatio-temporal propagation. For whereas Turkey seceded from the entire edifice of Islamic law in 1926, the Law of 1917 remains in effect as the Muslim denominational law of Lebanon and Israel to this day, and continued to be the official law of Syria until 1949 and Jordan until 1951. What adds to the significance of this Law is not only the fact that it is the major survival of the Shari'a in the post-Ottoman era, but that it purportedly set out to improve the lot of Muslim women. But did it?

The Family Law of 1917 generally did not depart from the provisions of the Shari'a, but it did codify them, and thus subjected them to the rigidity of a single linear language devoid of the plurality and multiple juristic nuances and variations that the traditional law had afforded. The hallmark of this codifying transmutation was, as we have repeatedly noted, the appropriation of the law by the nation-state, a transmutation that announced the clear message that even when the law was both substantively and substantially that of the Shari'a, it was ultimately the state that determined this fact and what part – or what combination thereof – was or was not law. This precisely is the meaning of sovereignty, and sovereignty is no one else's business but the state's.

Yet, in the very process of reenacting Islamic law into a codified body of rules, linguistic presentation, focus, brevity, detail and attention, all played a significant part in recasting and remolding the law, all of which factors entered into the calculation of what effects the law was supposed to produce. Thus, while the traditional law provides a staggering body of discourse respecting the wife's right to various types of support from her husband, the 1917 Law reduces this discourse to two articles whose brevity deprives the modern court of the full view of these rights.

---

[4] Partha Chatterjee, "Colonialism, Nationalism, and Colonized Women: The Contest in India," *American Ethnologist*, 16, 4 (1989): 629–32.

(In pre-modern Hanafi law, by contrast, the wife's rights to support were extensive and her treatment as a juristic topic often occupied dozens of pages.) All that emerges from the multiplicity of pre-modern rights is that she is entitled by law to a "house," language that might be interpreted by modern judges in light of customary practice (thus maintaining a measure of continuity), but a practice that was constantly shifting in favor of new realities that tended, with time, to supersede the earlier ones, if not remove them from judicial memory. Affording a "house," together with the provision (art. 72) stressing the wife's right to refuse living with the family of her husband, seems to be a recognition of the rising importance of privacy and companionate marriage, but it simultaneously takes away, again through silence, the pre-modern set of rights that "constructed the wife as a social being with needs for companionship that must be accommodated by the presence of relatives, neighbors, or even hired companions."[5]

Yet, the legal reduction of the matrimonial relationship (formerly predicated upon complex social relations within an extended family structure) to companionate marriage simultaneously constituted a step toward constructing the wife as a housewife in a family unit headed by the husband, a notion that is entirely absent from the traditional religious law. Indeed, article 73 of the 1917 Law requires the husband to treat his wife kindly, but imposes on her the obligation of obedience. The latter, in Shariʿa narrowly defined in terms of sexual availability, is now dissociated from an intricate system of obligations to which the husband too was bound. "Obedience" has undergone abstraction and expansion, and has furthermore been merged into the highly unrestricted French civil notion of wifely obedience marshaled to produce an effective means of subordination. Little of this changed even much later. A recent study of the 1957 Moroccan family law convincingly argues that the so-called reforms in that country have indeed produced a consolidated patriarchal hold within a reinterpreted field of the Shariʿa, while simultaneously undermining the intricate guarantees and multi-layered safety nets that the Shariʿa had provided in practice before the dawn of modernity and its nation-state.[6]

A further index of women's subordination relates to the post-colonial promotion of the man/husband as head of the family, to be obeyed and even revered. The pre-modern Muslim jurists regarded the inability of the husband to fulfill his marital duties as constituting disobedience, in which

---

[5] Judith Tucker, "Revisiting Reform: Women and the Ottoman Law of Family Rights, 1917," *Arab Studies Journal*, 4, 2 (1996): 11.

[6] Ziba Mir-Hosseini, *Marriage on Trial: A Study of Islamic Family Law* (London: I. B. Tauris, 2000).

case he was required to grant his wife a *khul*ʿ without remuneration to him. Husbands, in other words, were almost as much subject to the charge of disobedience as wives, although their liabilities were assumed to take different forms. In modern national codes, disobedience becomes exclusively a woman's liability, the result of failure to perform a variety of functions assigned to her by the law. Thus, in the Algerian code, the wife can be accused of disobedience simply for failure to accord the husband respect as head of the family; in Libya and Yemen, disobedience arises for failing to attend to the needs and affairs of the matrimonial home; in Morocco, it arises even for failure to show respect to the husband's parents.

These grounds for obedience were clearly not so expansive in pre-modern Islamic law, having been mainly limited to sexual inaccessibility. In traditional law, the family was constructed as a social group based on kinship, a group whose members had rights and duties, but where no one was *legally* designated as head. Materially and economically (a wide scope of social existence), women were legally independent, having the same rights as men. Husbands could not legally control their wives' property. Nor was the woman required to respect her husband's parents any more than he was required to respect hers. Nor, moreover, was she required by law to attend to the affairs and daily needs of the matrimonial home (much less her husband's family), it being explicitly stipulated as the husband's duty. But this is not all. A host of rights that women enjoyed in traditional law were entirely lost in modern legislation, not the least of which was the husband's responsibility to pay for suckling his own children, for the cleaning and cooking expenses of the matrimonial household, and for servants to attend to his wife's personal needs.

These gender-based transformations were made possible by several factors that combined to produce multiple effects in different sites, effects that invariably served to increase the subordination of women. One of the crucial factors was the collapse during the nineteenth century of local markets in most countries of the Muslim world, a far-reaching phenomenon causally linked to the European domination of the newly created open markets in these countries. Integral to this economic transformation, which led to the rise of alternative modes of economic production, was the disappearance of the home economy (involving, inter alia, weaving and spinning), in which women had not only played a crucial role, but also, through their economic performance, benefited from the financial independence that this afforded.

A second factor was the rise of new political, legal, economic and bureaucratic elites that were either essential to building the new state system or subordinated to its structures. Taking as their model late nineteenth-century Europe – which had barely begun to grant its women the right to full personhood (be it in terms of suffrage or owning property in marriage) – the new Muslim elites (almost exclusively male) filled the gaps in the changing structures of power through mimesis.

Third, and arising from the second factor, was the importation by the new national elite of European systems and philosophies of education which assigned to women the role of raising the national citizen of the future. Women, important and sublime as their role was in manufacturing the successful and productive nation, were nonetheless expected to stay at home, with their children.

Yet another factor enhancing this prejudicial transformation was the gradual rise of a new and anomic psycho-social order, one that grew concomitantly with the continual reduction of the extended family and the simultaneous increase in the prominence of the nuclear family. That this socio-familial transformation – to which we shall return later – was due to the changing modes of economic production is clear, but what has not been sufficiently taken into account is the dialectical relationship between these social and economic transformations and the new notion of individualism. While the incomes of extended family members largely belonged to an indistinguishable fiscal pool that was often perceived as group-owned and that consisted of goods and commodities along with cash, in the emerging nuclear family, and because of the rise of a massive bureaucratic elite, the man's salaried income was an individualized act of remuneration, an income earned through a narrowly defined job in which no other family member took part. An increasing sense of individualism, combined with a male-oriented national state, a new male-oriented economy and bureaucracy, and a wholesale collapse of the domestic economies that had been the exclusive domain of women, all combined to produce legal codes and legal cultures that, under the banner of modernity, tended to subordinate women rather than liberate them.

Equally important in the 1917 Law, and analyzable in the same fashion, is its haunting brevity in dealing with the modes of marital dissolution afforded to the wife. The Law quietly affirmed the husband's absolute right to effect unilateral divorce by his own accord while, at the same time, severely abridging the discourse about *khulʿ*, formerly a common recourse available to women who wished to rid themselves of a bad marriage. Article 116 makes mention of it in passing, without describing any of the substantive or procedural legalities associated with it. As one scholar has perceptively noted, "[o]nly the closest reader of the Law would notice that such a divorce had legal standing."[7] By contrast, traditional law

---

[7] Tucker, "Revisiting Reform," 12.

consecrated pages upon pages to discussing this form of marital repudiation. Furthermore, while Islamic law had in practice permitted women to sue for marital annulment only after one year of a husband's failure to provide support (due, inter alia, to insolvency, desertion or disappearance), the 1917 Law expanded this period to four years (art. 127), thus exacerbating the wife's plight. On the whole, the 1917 Law reduced the multiple and multi-layered traditional legal rights of women instead of expanding them.

Yet, while maintaining many of the male legal prerogatives versus the female, the new law restricted male rights in other respects, though all in favor of closer state control and surveillance over family life. The overall result was one that intercalated women into a regimented domestic sphere, and all this on the ruins of what had once been a largely open social public space that allowed extraordinarily free latitude to economic transactions in both the private and public domains.

The rise of proto-feminist movements in Euro-America during the first half of the twentieth century redefined colonial cultural discourse, with the result that promoting the feminist agenda immediately resounded in the Muslim world at large. Whereas the "segregated Muslim woman" had, in the nineteenth century, been the focus of European and American commentary and criticism, in the twentieth century she had become in this critical commentary the victim of a merciless patriarchy, from which she had to be rescued. Yet there was little, if any, recognition that the new forms of patriarchy were directly caused by the displacements/transformations just outlined. As part of the cultural discourse of domination, the critique chimed with the agenda of the ruling elites of the Muslim states, and was reflected in the changes that these states made to the substance of the law. Women had become a priority in fashioning the new nation, and redesigning the law was yet one more means of achieving this end.

Reengineering family law

Integral to the project of social engineering was a specific effort to increase the contractual options of the wife. Through the methods of *takhayyur* and *talfiq*, most states reconstituted the marriage contract along the lines of Hanbali doctrine, which permitted the inclusion of as many terms as the parties might wish to stipulate, as long as no term was contrary to the aims of the contract. By implication, this reconstitution also meant that the terms and conditions could not violate the established principles of the law or the parties' interests as ensured by the contract itself. This widely adopted contractual doctrine permitted women to include stipulations that served to protect their own interests within marriage, such as the right to work outside the marital home; to divorce her husband; to forbid him from taking a second wife; or, on penalty of divorce, to prohibit him from moving the marital home to another locale without her consent.

These terms, apart from the first, had for centuries been included in marriage contracts, but this was not a systematic practice. Only some people had recourse to it. What the twentieth-century state accomplished in this respect was to systematize (through state, centralized action) the right to these inclusions, thereby raising the minimal scale of women's rights. Yet, Muslim women did not leap to take advantage of the newly available contractual options. In an effort to increase this proportion, the state began actively to encourage the use of such options by women. In 1995, for instance, the Egyptian Ministry of Justice prepared a draft marriage contract that could be used by couples as a model and be modified in accordance with their wishes and needs – this contract's purpose was to make the entire range of legal possibilities known to the average citizen.

Furthermore, by setting the terms and conditions in a ubiquitously available and standard document, the conditions would acquire a routine-like character, thereby making them in effect an integral part of the law rather than an addendum that women would have to negotiate or for which they would have to bargain. A similar, standard contract had been drafted in Iran in 1975, and reformulated under the Islamic Republic in 1982. The new model contract, reflecting changes in positive law, contained several standard conditions, including the wife's right to take half of her husband's assets that he had accumulated during marriage, provided that he divorced her for no fault of hers. (The 1982 Law also gave the woman the right to the value of all her labor during the marriage, if she were determined by the court not to be at fault in the breakdown of the marriage.) By the terms of the model contract, she would also be entitled to divorce him should he abandon or mistreat her, marry another, or default on maintenance. This standard(ized) contract had something of a Shari'a-law appearance, since the husband, by accepting these conditions – which he now had to – could be said to have delegated to his wife the power to divorce herself from him should he default on any of the stipulated conditions. (Incidentally, these powers of "delegated divorce" were fully recognized and intricately elaborated in the Shari'a, but never integrated into any standard contract, an unknown practice in the first place.)

As we said earlier, the insertion of such conditions was nothing new, and the traditional Shari'a courts of virtually all schools have in practice accepted the inclusion of such conditions. But this inclusion had been the exclusive prerogative of the wife, a piece of ammunition with which she was supplied as a matter of protection. Nevertheless, in many modern "reforms," partly out of a preoccupation to equalize the rights of men and women, this prerogative of inserting conditions has now been bestowed on men in several Muslim countries, thereby enhancing the subordination of women in the name of equality.

Financially, marriage in the nation-state was to be reengineered supposedly in order to strengthen the position of women. Integrated into the legal institution of marriage were guarantees as to the maintenance to which wives are entitled by operation of the law, i.e., even if the guarantees were not stipulated as part of any agreement. This is classical doctrine reenacted. As the Shariʿa had done for centuries, the modern reforms made maintenance (which consists of provisions of clothing, shelter and food) an inextinguishable obligation on the part of the husband toward his wife – which means that failure to provide maintenance would render his estate liable for seizure by the court in order to defray these costs.

Likewise, a wife was contractually entitled to a dower. This remained both a legal requirement and a social and customary practice. Although in India and Pakistan the extravagant stipulations of dower caused legislation to counter abuses in this domain (forcing the parties to stipulate reasonable amounts of dower), most states, especially in the Arab world, continued to enhance this feature of the marriage contract. In Egypt, for instance, not only did dower continue to be an essential feature in the validity of the marriage contract, arising by operation of the law, but the wife also retained priority of claim over all other claims of debt against the husband's estate. Her right to dower is inextinguishable, and the husband's failure to pay it could land him in prison. And in order to enhance the husband's ability to surrender the amount of the dower to his wife, he is required to provide a guarantor, who will be equally culpable upon failure to pay. (It is remarkable that these rights continue to be stated according to a logic and language that is highly gendered. In a world where an increasing number of Muslim women nowadays hold more lucrative jobs than their husbands, who may occasionally be unemployed, the law has not yet managed to neutralize its language to reflect the rights of the husband in cases where women are the breadwinners.)

In the great majority of Muslim states, especially those traditionally of Maliki affiliation, several restrictions were placed on the powers of the marriage guardian who was normatively defined as a male relative who had significant powers in determining who his ward should or would marry. Some of these male prerogatives were maintained until about the middle of the twentieth century, but they have increasingly come under attack since. Under pressure from feminist groups, the Moroccan government, for instance, came to change some of the assumptions about guardianship by proclaiming it "the woman's right," a change that actually reflects a reversal of rights. In the Shariʿa, the guardianship of the senior male agnate amounted to a representational right whereby the interests of the family and the group would be considered together with the marital interests of the ward. The Moroccan legislature sought to guarantee this right by stipulating that marriage could not be concluded "without her consent," but it also found it impossible to ignore the fact that Moroccan society, like nearly every other Muslim society, places a premium on the family as well as on inter-familial relations. Article 12 of the Code of Personal Status thus offers a guarantee for the family, as represented by the guardian, to the effect that the social network within which the marriage is embedded must play a role in the contractual process. While her consent is indispensable, the guardian, this article stipulates, "concludes the marriage on her behalf."

Guarantees were also installed in favor of a woman whose guardian might refuse to conclude a marriage that she desired. Several states thus permit women of marrying age to petition the courts to obtain permission to marry against the objections of relatives, including male guardians. On the other hand, according to the laws of Pakistan and India, a minor girl married by her father or grandfather must wait until the age of eighteen before she can seek judicial dissolution of her marriage.

The Moroccan case exemplifies what may be called the transitional problematics of modernizing societies, where traditional communal norms coexist alongside, yet simultaneously oppose, modern notions of individualism. Expanding the freedom of the individual within the interests of the enveloping group – however modified these interests may be – appears to represent a new stage in the transition toward more individualism and less communalism. It may be a matter of time before the law moves on to the sphere of exclusive individualism, where the extended family and community can be declared, for legal purposes at least, defunct. It is always worth remembering that while the institution of guardianship represented – even in practice – a certain power of patriarchy, it was not only about that power, as modern scholarship often makes it out to be. The guardian, we recall, also represented the voice of the nuclear and extended family, and even the immediate community. For marriage in Muslim societies, past and present, has never been an affair relevant only to the couple.

Together with changing notions of community and individualism came another transformation in the social values that define adulthood, a transformation that has largely been due to major shifts in economic structures and modes of production. Early in the twentieth century, most Muslim states raised the age of marriage (generally prescribed in classical texts to start with puberty), and some have criminalized the marriage of minors. The 1929 Indian Child Marriage Restraint Act prescribed penalties for any marriage where the bridegroom had not reached eighteen or the bride fifteen. The latter was raised to sixteen in Pakistan's 1961 Muslim Family Laws Ordinance. In other countries, such as Egypt, no code (yet) explicitly prohibits marriage of minors, but by instituting strict registration requirements (see p. 116 above) severe restrictions were placed on such practices. All countries in the Middle East now prescribe the age of eighteen for bridegrooms, but the age has varied in the case of brides: Iraq requires eighteen, Jordan and Syria seventeen, Algeria sixteen, and Tunisia and Morocco fifteen.

None of these areas of the law was so politically charged as that of polygamy, however. The first step taken in further limiting the scope of this practice was the Ottoman Law of 1917 which provided that, in her marriage contract, a wife might stipulate that, should her husband take a co-wife, she had the right to claim a judicial divorce. This device, centuries old, became commonplace in subsequent legislation throughout the Muslim world, but was often combined with other measures – also centuries old – empowering wives to sue for dissolution should certain unfavorable conditions arise in their marriage. These means consisted of (a) predicating the husband's unilateral divorce upon the occurrence of certain conditions (i.e., if X happens, then divorce shall take effect), and (b) delegating the husband's power to divorce to the wife herself (as well as to a third party). This delegated power was to be exercised by her upon the occurrence of particular conditions that she construed as disadvantageous to her, including her husband taking a co-wife.

Yet another approach to curbing polygamy was taken in a number of Egyptian legislative proposals during the 1920s, but these were not to become actual law until the 1950s and 1960s, and in such countries as Syria and Tunisia before Egypt itself. The device was administrative in nature, requiring any man desiring to take a co-wife to petition the court for permission. The 1961 Muslim Family Law Ordinance of Pakistan made the consent of the wife a further requirement alongside the court's permission. The court, however, could still refuse his request independently of the wishes of the wife, and this on either of two grounds: his financial inability to support two wives, or his inability to treat them in an equally just manner. These considerations, especially the latter, were based on the Quranic verse 4:3, which enjoins a husband to treat his wives justly and equitably. Some countries, such as Syria, opted for financial considerations as the chief grounds for a decision, while other countries deemed the notion of justice (which does not, in its widest interpretation, preclude financial considerations) as paramount. The most drastic position taken on the issue of justice was that of Tunisia. In the 1956 Law of Personal Status, polygamy was declared a criminal infraction, categorically prohibited on the grounds that it is impossible for any man to be just, as the Quran requires, in the same manner to two wives.

Equally fundamental changes to the law were effected in the sphere of paternity. In the interest of preserving social harmony and the integrity of the family, the Shari'a stretched the limits of conception and pregnancy with a view to ascribing children, as much as possible, to the "marriage bed." The basic and primary legal assumption was that "children belong to the marriage bed." The Islamic legal schools differed with regard to the minimal period in which, after the marriage begins, the child may be deemed legitimate, as well as in regard to the maximum period after the marriage is dissolved or the mother widowed. The former period, in minimalistic doctrine, was fixed at six months, while the latter extended to between two and five years, depending on the particular school. The Twelver-Shi'is constituted an exception in fixing it at ten months, although they were a numerical and doctrinal minority. In general, there-fore, the Shari'a promoted the integration of children into family units, discouraging any tendency to single out children as illegitimate. To prove a child illegitimate, evidence had to be beyond any doubt, "reasonable doubt" being insufficient. In other words, there could not exist even a semblance of doubt. Furthermore, mere acknowledgment by the father that the child was his was deemed conclusive, even if the physical union of the parents may have been impossible for any period prior to six months before the birth.

Much of this has been changed in favor of, first, limiting the scope of legitimacy, and, second, the de-privatizing of paternity claims and decla-rations. In India and Pakistan, following English law, the father's acknowledgment is inadmissible if physical union between him and the mother was impossible before the marriage took place, and if the child is not born within 280 days of that marriage. The Arab states have preserved some elements of Shari'a doctrine, while at the same time rejecting the highly tolerant limits that it stipulated and that must have significantly conduced to resolving disputes that might otherwise have arisen. Thus, the Egyptian Law of 1929 places a one-year limit on the determination of legitimacy after divorce or after the death of the husband, declaring the period of gestation to be no longer than one year.

Although prior to the nineteenth century unilateral divorce by the husband was not the most common form of dissolving marriage, the culture of modernity has made it a morally repugnant instrument, asso-ciated with male domination, capriciousness and downright oppression.

Associated and combined with the exclusive male right to polygamy (a relatively infrequent practice), this type of divorce came to symbolize, on the one hand, the tyranny of the Eastern male and, on the other, the wretched existence of the Muslim female. The male's absolute right to divorce was therefore to be curbed, in whole, and, if this proved impossible, at least in part. The foremost of these reforms was the declaration as invalid of any pronouncement of divorce made as an oath, under duress, in a fit of anger, while intoxicated, or – in some countries – during the menstruation period of the wife. Only statements made with the intent to dissolve a problematic marriage were now deemed valid, although they might not necessarily lead to dissolution. Also abolished in most Muslim countries was the so-called "triple divorce," a formula that abridges into a single statement the three pronouncements by the husband of his will to divorce, each of which should be made during a period when the wife is free from menstruation.

In most Muslim countries, the mere declaration of unilateral divorce by the husband (valid and effective in traditional jurisprudence) has been held ineffective without its being registered in court. In Morocco, for instance, a husband need not petition the court for such a divorce, nor, therefore, does he need to vindicate it on any grounds, but he must register it. On the other hand, a woman who seeks a judicial divorce must (consistent with traditional law) explain to the court the reasons for her petition. In some countries, the husband may apply for divorce without having to state any grounds, while in other countries both parties are equally obliged to state the grounds for their request. In Iranian law under the Shah (1967), while both parties faced the same procedural obligation, women's scope for these grounds was expanded beyond that available for husbands. Under the Islamic Republic of Iran, the 1967 Law was struck down, but several elements of it survived in the Special Civil Courts Act. A wife's consent to the husband's divorce continues to be a requirement, although the husband no longer needs to provide grounds for his wish to divorce when petitioning the court.

In the great majority of Muslim countries, wives are now said to be able to file for marital dissolution on two additional grounds, namely, the husband's failure to provide spousal or family support, or his taking another wife. This does not mean, however, that such rights were not available to women before the twentieth century, for, as we saw earlier, it was in fact the common practice of both the courts and society in the case of the first grounds (i.e., failure to maintain) and a contractual option available to women in the case of the second (i.e., taking on another wife) that guaranteed such rights. The difference now is that the law is declared, made explicit and sanctioned by the state, the procedure having been bureaucratized and formalized. Most importantly, perhaps, it allows state officials to wrap themselves in the robes of reform, though the substance has surely not changed to any notable extent.

In the same vein, much of the Shariʿa law of marital dissolution was integrated into the civil codes of Muslim states in the name of reform, but a reform deprived of the complex system of checks and balances that Islamic law had extensively supplied. In addition to the two grounds for judicial divorce listed in the previous paragraph, the legislators included the following: defect in body or in mind that makes married life intolerable or dangerous; impotence that renders normal sexual relations impossible; cruelty and maltreatment, which included – depending on the definition of the particular state – anything from physical abuse to taking on another wife; absence for a prolonged period of time; and, finally, marital discord. As we saw, a woman in the Shariʿa could petition the *qadi* for dissolution of her marriage for almost any reason, including all of the above, as well as for such reasons as "disliking her husband due to his ugly appearance or as a result of discord between the two."[8] The Egyptian Law of 1929 stipulates that "if a wife claims that her husband is causing her harm in such a way as to make it impossible for people of her social class to continue the marital relationship, she may petition the judge to dissolve the marriage, whereupon he shall grant her a single, irrevocable divorce, provided that the abuse is proven and he has failed in reconciling them. If, however, the judge denies her petition and she subsequently reiterates the allegation but cannot prove the abuse, the judge shall appoint two arbitrators."[9] Thus, in the modern system, the procedural requirement of proving maltreatment must obtain before a wife is liberated from a bad marriage. Moreover, in some Muslim countries, while a woman can sue for, and obtain, divorce on any of these grounds, she is obligated to pay the husband a consideration decided upon by the court. Islamic law, by contrast, acknowledged the woman's inability to cohabit as intrinsic grounds for dissolution, although arbitration and reconciliation before a final verdict remained, in effect, a mandatory requirement.

Modern Muslim codes continue to affirm the importance of the traditional Islamic concept of mediation between husband and wife, a necessary step before the dissolution of a marriage is effected. In

---

[8] Abu Ishaq al-Shirazi, *al-Muhadhdhab fi Fiqh al-Imam al Shafiʿi*, ed. Zakariyya ʿUmayrat, 6 vols. (Beirut: Dar al-Kutub al-ʿIlmiyya, 1995), IV, 253–54. Similarly, see Abu Muhammad Mahmud al-ʿAyniʿ, *al-Binaya fi Sharh al-Hidaya*, ed. Muhammad ʿUmar, 12 vols. (Beirut: Dar al-Fikr, 1990), V, 506.

[9] See Article 6, Law of 1929, cited in Immanuel Naveh, "The Tort of Injury and Dissolution of Marriage at the Wife's Initiative in Egyptian *Mahkamat al-Naqd* Rulings," *Islamic Law and Society*, 91 (2002): 22, note 16.

twentieth-century codes, it has become formalized and homogenized in almost every country, and it has become an official requirement to be fulfilled before effecting any type of divorce, including – perhaps especially – unilateral divorce by the husband. Needless to say, the necessity for mediation in pre-modern law was normative, both in the sphere of the *qadi* and in the social site in which the marital conflict occurred. We simply do not know whether mediation was involved in the social context of a husband's unilateral divorce, although in all probability this form of divorce did not reach the *qadi* in his official capacity as judge, and thus it would be difficult to see how the latter's official mediation (directly or by proxy) was involved. In today's civil codes, on the other hand, mediation appears as a ubiquitous stipulation, formalized in specific procedural requirements.

The method of *takhayyur* was also deployed to effect changes in the law pertaining to the mother's right to child custody, which extended, according to the Hanafi school, to seven years for boys and nine for girls. Traditionally Hanafi countries have raised this bar to some extent. For example, the 1929 Egyptian Law stipulated ten years for boys and twelve years for girls, and the 2005 Law (No. 4) has further raised the age to fifteen years for both. But these countries could have adopted a more significant change, as the Maliki school already granted the mother the right to custody of boys until puberty and girls until marriage. While most of North Africa and the Sudan have adopted this Maliki doctrine, Tunisia, a traditionally Maliki country, has opted for a policy more in line with the Hanafi doctrine. In the Iranian Civil Code of 1382 H (2003), the age was raised to seven for both boys and girls, this being based on a minority view in Twelver-Shi'i law. At the same time, many other Muslim countries left to the *qadi*'s discretion decisions on custody according to the best interests of the child. Yet, irrespective of where the children live, the father remains responsible for their maintenance, and, in several countries, for their education. In this respect, there was little to no change from the rules of Islamic law.

The sphere of inheritance, on the other hand, was subjected to significant changes. The Sunni system of succession in effect arose from a modified tribal system that served the interests of the extended, agnatic relations, i.e., those who guaranteed the survival of the group and whose entitlement to the estate of the deceased was repayment for the security they extended to the propositus and to his/her immediate relatives while he or she was alive. The Quran incorporated into this system much to serve the interests of mothers, daughters, wives, sisters and sons' daughters. But the system remained, in a particular way, largely patriarchal, and the emphasis continued to be focused on agnatic relations that guaranteed the group's security. The concatenation formed by these relations translated into an extended family that permeated the Bedouin as well as the urban environment. The extended family, in other words, was the relevant unit of social and economic support within both the clan and the neighborhood.

The introduction of modern forms of capitalism and the attendant fundamental changes in modes of production have led, inter alia, not only to the collapse of the earlier modes of production but also to a transformation in the social map: a society whose typical family structure was of the extended type has become characterized by the widespread and growing phenomenon of the nuclear family. Loyalties are no longer to fathers, uncles and the other "patriarchs" of the family who once formed a veritable safety net for the needy of the family: the ill and the infirm, and orphans, and divorcees and their children. Each family unit was henceforth "on its own," the unit having become the parents, their children and grandchildren, and their fathers and mothers, whenever all these coexisted. It is this unit that reflects the "model family" promoted by the modern state, not only because this is the predominant European model – the exporter of this state – but also because the new "Islamic" nation-state could more easily secure the loyalty of such a nuclear family on the defined and articulated site of the good citizen. The loyalties within clans and tribes, being quasi-political, can hardly be divided. Thus, the modern nation-state, which also was fundamentally engaged in, and intertwined with, the new forms of capitalism and new economic modes of production, had a profound interest in refashioning the modern family into a family that is distinctly nuclear.

In reengineering the law of inheritance, the legislators of the modern state leaned heavily on the method of *takhayyur*, combining elements from various schools to produce effects that were inconceivable under the traditional legal system. An important material source on which the legislators drew was Twelver-Shiʿi law, regarded for centuries as unorthodox and even antithetical to Sunni doctrine and practice. The Twelver-Shiʿi system of succession drastically departs from agnatic arrangements as conceived by Sunni law. It just so happens that the Shiʿi system of succession – which represents the site of the greatest difference between Sunni and Twelver-Shiʿi legal conceptions – has become more suitable to the realities and demands of the modern nuclear family than any configuration that its Sunni counterpart can produce. Accordingly, many of its elements were introduced in several Sunni countries, and in Iraq it was made the law of the entire population, including Sunnis and Kurds. Twelver-Shiʿi law favors a nuclear conception of the family and pays special attention to the females in it. Thus, in the case of a daughter who survives her father together with an uncle, the father's estate in Sunni law will be divided into two equal shares between the two heirs. In Twelver-Shi'i law, on the other hand, the daughter inherits the entire estate, certainly a modern way of devolving family property.

Some legislators, such as those of Tunisia, opted to modify and augment the Maliki system of succession while drawing on complex principles of other Sunni legal schools, avoided in countries that traditionally followed these schools. But the results were virtually identical to the effects produced in the Twelver-Shi'i system, in that daughters were given precedence over agnates. Also of Twelver-Shi'i inspiration was the unrestricted principle – adopted in Egypt, Iraq and Sudan – that while the bequest cannot exceed one-third of the testator's total inheritable wealth, the latter can choose an heir whose normal share will then be augmented with the additional one-third.

The modern permissibility of "bequeathing to an heir" has also afforded a solution to the problem of the son of a predeceased son who, according to Islamic law, was entirely excluded from his grandfather's inheritance. The nature of the support dynamics within the extended family was such that an orphaned grandson was usually taken care of by his grandparents, uncles and aunts, which explains why Islamic law did not see good reason to allot the deceased father's share to his surviving son by representation. Orphans were routinely and as a matter of course absorbed by the family unit in which their parents had lived, which also explains why the relatives continued, over the centuries, to be the recipients of the deceased's share. With the emergence in modernity of the nuclear family as an archetype, and with the exponential rise in mobility, such orphans needed protection, as the extended family which used to take care of them has suffered a major decline (in many areas disappearing entirely). No solution from within Islamic law was forthcoming, since inserting the orphaned grandson into the equation of Islamic inheritance would wreak havoc with the entire system. The solution was instead pioneered by Egyptian legislators and consisted in the statutory decree that any grandfather who has orphaned grandsons must make a will that allots them what their father would have inherited had he been alive, with the proviso that such an allotment not exceed one-third of the grandfather's total estate. In the event that the latter did not make such a bequest, or if his bequest did not observe the decreed rule, the court had to rectify the will accordingly.

By the year 2000 no fewer than eight countries in the Middle East had made the estate of the grandparent liable for an obligatory bequest in favor of the orphaned grandchild. This solution was not welcomed in all Muslim states, however, with Pakistan voicing strong opposition on the grounds that such legislation makes compulsory what the Quran intended to be a freely chosen act. We shall discuss the case of Pakistan in the next chapter.

The laws of succession and bequests were closely tied in with reengineering the law of *waqf*, especially in the Middle East and North Africa. In the previous chapter, we saw that *waqf* was a prime target of attack in the modernizing project initiated by both the colonialist powers and the native nationalist elites. The discourse generated by the French Orientalists during the 1840s filtered through to the Ottoman territories and, later, to the successor states. This discourse – aided by both the nationalist elite and native scholars who had studied at the feet of the European Orientalists – manufactured a distinction between family and public *waqf*s, a distinction that Muslim cultures had not made. It further injected into the nationalist ideology the notion that family *waqf* was a development in Islamic history from after the FORMATIVE PERIOD, and therefore without legitimacy, since it was based neither on Prophetic tradition nor even on that of the Companions; the implication here being that later developments, modern ones included, were as good as any other, especially if the "modern" developments excelled earlier ones in "civilizational sophistication."

Even more remarkable was the creation in this discourse of a causal link between the "invention" of family endowments and an attempt by Muslim societies over the centuries to circumvent the stipulations of the Quranic law of inheritance, which operates by the principle of shares and which, therefore, leads to the fragmentation of property. What is noteworthy about this discourse in the context of mid-twentieth-century nation-states is that the *waqf*'s "betrayal" of the Quranic spirit was one that – ironically – contradicted an invented spirit designed to promote the nuclear family and, unwittingly, to conform to Shi'i law.

As if this did not furnish them with enough ammunition for the attack on *waqf*s, the French colonists, the Ottoman ruling elite and the counterparts of the latter in the successor nation-states furthermore blamed economic malaise on the *waqf* since, it was argued, family endowments inherently tie up property in perpetuity and prevent it from efficient development in a free market economy. And since the economy is indispensable to modern development, then impeding material progress amounts to halting the march toward civilization. Thus *waqf*, the main prop of civil society in Islamic civilization for over a millennium, and a chief instrument of its social welfare and safety-net, became synonymous with civilizational retardation and regress. In Kemalist Turkey, the entire institution of family *waqf* was abolished in 1926, while charitable non-family *waqf*s were nationalized as public welfare institutions.

The process of eradicating *waqf* was nowhere as sudden as it was in Turkey, however. Before the elimination of family *waqf*s altogether in a number of other Muslim countries, the nationalist governments attempted to restrict the scope of the Shari'a laws of *waqf* by aligning them with their policies of refashioning the "model (nuclear) family." But in order to accomplish this, the *waqf* administration was not allowed to continue in accordance with its former independent practices, where private administrators acted independently of the "state" although they were generally supervised and occasionally inspected, or audited, by the *qadis*.

With their centralization within the framework of government ministries, the *waqf*s were subjected to unprecedented rules, foremost among which was the requirement of registration for any act pertaining to the creation, revocation, renovation or alteration in the income distribution of any *waqf*. Egypt led the way in the Middle East region. It declared in 1946 that religious *waqf*s, especially mosques, would be henceforth designated as perpetual, as had been the case under the Shari'a; but not so private or family *waqf*s, which were now limited to sixty years (as in Lebanon) or to the lifetimes of two series of beneficiaries. Upon the dissolution of the *waqf*, the property would have to revert either to the beneficiaries or to the founders' heirs, depending on the particular conditions the law set for each circumstance.

There was, in both Egypt and Lebanon, yet another major limitation on the freedom of *waqf* founders to establish a foundation whose value was larger than one-third of their inheritable estate. In the event that the *waqf* did exceed the one-third limitation, then the excess on the one-third had to be divided among the heirs according to their shares in the inheritance of that property. This limitation soon became common legislation, having been passed as recently as 1992 in the Yemen.

In 1949, Syria went even further, centralizing the administration of all public *waqf*s in a government ministry, and abolishing all *waqf*s whose beneficiaries were in whole or in part members of a family. The same drastic measure was enacted in Egypt in 1954, and in 1957 all agricultural lands that had been established as *waqf* were confiscated as part of Nasser's nationalization program. A similar program of nationalizing land was undertaken in Algeria in 1971. A number of other countries also followed suit in abolishing family *waqf*s, some of the last being Libya, in 1973, and the United Arab Emirates, in 1980.

Yet another method devised to reduce the family *waqf*s was the lifting of several restrictions that ensured perpetuity under traditional Islamic law. The 1991 Algerian Law stipulated (in addition to abolishing family *waqf*s) that a founder may revoke his own *waqf* deed or change any of its terms. The 1992 Yemeni Law went so far as to bestow on the beneficiaries of a family *waqf* the right to revoke the deed and to distribute the property according to their shares in the inheritance.

In South-East Asia, there were fewer changes in the *waqf* law, since by the dawn of the twentieth century the fundamentals of that law had already changed in the region, as they had in the Indian subcontinent. In the Malay States and the Straits Settlements, much of the *waqf* had been transformed into what were in effect English trusts, a fact that significantly reduced the interest of donors, which in turn drastically diminished the size of family and even public endowments. In Indonesia, the basic law that regulated *waqf* was promulgated in 1937 under Dutch colonial rule, but its effects on the *waqf* and its administration have been purely procedural, regulating the modalities of founding and registering *waqf*s. Generally speaking, the economic role of *waqf* in South-East Asia does not seem to have been as central as it was throughout Central Asia, the Middle East and North Africa; which explains why colonialist pressures to abolish so much of the *waqf* did not arise in South East Asia as they did in other parts of the Muslim world.

Definitions: state, ulama, secularists and Islamists

In the previous chapter, we discussed the processes by which the law was modernized, as well as the cultural and other forces that underlay these transformations. Notable Westernizing trends began in India at the end of the eighteenth century, and in the Middle East at the beginning of the nineteenth, culminating in the 1940s and 1950s. The changes, as we saw, were massive, involving the structural dismantling of the Shariʿa legal system, and leaving behind a distorted and gradually diminishing veneer of Islamic law of personal status.

At one point, it seemed that Islam as a religion of legal norms was out of favor, having once and for all lost to the modernists and their new states. But the 1970s and early 1980s saw powerful events that appeared to halt the collapse of this religious force. The questions that confront us then are as follows. What were the sources of the re-Islamization trends that appeared during and after the 1970s? How far back do the origins of these sources extend? Are they a reenactment of pre-modern Islamic tendencies or are they, strictly speaking, the results of the modern project? What have they managed to accomplish in terms of converting the secularist legal changes, the engineered law of the state, into an Islamicized narrative? What methods and means have they pursued in order to accomplish this end, and where and when have they been successful?

To produce a manageable account of legal developments since the 1970s, a number of assumptions have been made about the "actors" involved. I take it as a reasonably valid proposition that there are four major actors on the legal scene who are not always neatly distinguished from one another, namely, the state, the "secular" modernists, the ulama and the Islamists.

Throughout the two previous chapters, we have pointed out several features that have necessarily made the nation-state in the Islamic world a *modern* entity. This is to say that governance in Islamic lands had to acquire modernist structures by force of necessity in order for the

nationalist elite not only to challenge direct and indirect Western colonialism but also, while attempting to accomplish this task, to rule their
own populations efficiently. But this project involved an absurdity: to
resist Western political and military hegemony, the state had to adopt
modern technology, modern culture and modern institutions – in short,
modernity in as mature and complete a form as could be imported or
assimilated, according to need.

Yet, the modernization process, forced to depend for all its major
features on a capitalist economy and/or technology, led to economic and
other forms of dependency on one Western country or another (and in the
1950s and 1960s on the Soviet Union as well). Thus, to free themselves of
the clutches of colonialism (a quintessential phenomenon in, and inherent
to, modernity), Muslim states adopted modern institutions and cultures
that led them to don new colonialist trappings. The state – the most
overpowering project of modernity – has therefore come to the Muslim
world to stay, in effect creating this most fundamental dilemma for
Muslims around the world: if Islamic law governed society and state for
over twelve centuries, and if the rule of law had a significance beyond and
above the modern state's concept of such rule, then how is that sacred law
accommodated by the irretrievable fact of the state, in effect the maker of
all laws? This is the question that permeates the fabric of all the discourse
and practice of politics and law in today's Muslim world.

The second actor is the camp commonly described as secularist-
modernist, a significant camp during the 1940s and 1950s, though it
slowly declined over the next three decades, becoming something of a
minority after the early 1990s. Whatever strength it could garner since the
1990s appears to have stemmed from its association with the state, whose
tendencies, generally speaking, have all along been on secular lines (with
the obvious exception of such countries as Saudi Arabia and, later, Iran).

Marginally stronger than the secularists (at least until recently) are the
ulama who, as a rule, survive as pockets in various Muslim countries, but
not by any means in all of them. South East Asia, Pakistan, Iran and Egypt
represent more prominent sites of ulama strength, Iran especially, where
they have been commanding the state since 1979. In Saudi Arabia they
constitute a powerful actor in domestic politics and especially in the legal
system. Yet, thus far, in no Sunni country has the Iranian experiment of
almost exclusive ulama rule been replicated. In Egypt and Pakistan, as we
shall see presently, the ulama play a not inconsiderable role versus the
state, at times standing in tension with it, at others in accommodation.

The latest but by far the most significant actor is the Islamist camp,
distinguishing itself from the ulama in two critical ways, among others of
lesser significance: the first is that the ulama, strictly speaking, continue to

uphold their "traditional" methods of interpretation or a semblance thereof, which is to say that they generally espouse the authority of their legal sources, treatises, legal schools, leading jurists and ways of instruction (although none of these spheres is an exact replica of its historical antecedents). A second important difference is the ulama's professional loyalty to their area of specialization: they have continued to dedicate themselves to religious knowledge, either by acquiring it as students or by imparting it as teachers, professors, *mufti*s or preachers. Although their functions are now nearly exclusively educational (i.e., not legal in the sense that obtained before the nineteenth century), they remain largely dissociated from other technical professions. (But this is not to say that such religious universities as Azhar do not offer extensive programs of study in the sciences.)

By contrast, the Islamists since the 1980s have come to represent an influential and pervasive camp, stretching across the entire Muslim world, and spanning the whole gamut of the social and economic orders. Generally speaking, they are not trained in traditional disciplines, nor (in part as a consequence) do they read the classical sources with the same perspective as the ulama. They are trained in a wide variety of modern technical disciplines, ranging from engineering and medicine to accounting, business and teaching in "secular" schools. Those of the Islamists who discourse on matters religious and legal seem willing to employ any modern interpretive amalgam. The interpretive methods they employ – what they say, how they say it and why – are of complex hybridity. They are not bound by an established or a given reading of the Quran and the Prophetic Sunna, as the ulama generally are. Their interpretive techniques with respect to these sources can invoke a wide range of principles ranging from the social to the natural sciences. In other words, having shed the mantle of traditional juristic and hermeneutical authority, the Islamists do not feel bound by the cultural and epistemic systems developed throughout Islamic intellectual and legal history. The recent proliferation of *fatwa*s on the Internet, in print media and in video-recordings attests to a multifarious production of "religious knowledge" that has consistently lacked any axis of authority. Aside from Pakistan's Mawdudi and Egypt's Sayyid Qutb, whose writings have attracted significant numbers of Muslim readers around the world, and apart from a few other secondary writers, the Islamists, in terms of religious–legal authority, have thus far not unified their ranks under any clearly identified banner or ideology, which is to say that their camp – if the term is at all apt – is highly diverse.

But this diffusion of authority is also endemic, though to a lesser extent, among the ulama as well as the so-called secular modernists. The latter cannot be classified in any uniform terms, for they may range from atheists and Gnostics (who are relatively few) to believers in God who do not wish to see religion play any role in the state, its politics or the public sphere. On the other hand, some ulama have effectively, though not formally, joined the Islamist camp, as is the case with certain members of the lower echelons of Egypt's famous Azhar. Their Islamist affiliation is attested not only by the political positions they adopt, but also by their hybridized interpretive mechanisms which are no longer loyal to the Azharite juristic methods of interpretation. Arguably, the reverse is also true, namely, that the Islamists have penetrated Azhar's lower ranks, and continue to do so. The boundaries are never neat, not even on the level of state involvement.

In the following pages, we will discuss the main contours of juridico-political developments in five key Muslim countries, where trends have been set and where tensions and accommodations between and among these camps have had noticeable but varied effects.

Egypt

We begin with Egypt, as it offers, after British India (whose relevance for us is now limited to Pakistan), the longest experiment in legal modernization and, simultaneously, perhaps one of the fiercest tendencies to contest secularization of the law in the name of one Islamic ideology or another. Since Muhammad 'Ali, Egypt has enjoyed a relatively strong state, and from the middle of the nineteenth century it began to develop upper social classes imbued with vehemently secularist tendencies. But at no point was Egypt devoid of influential Islamic groups. The Azhar and its ulama were still forces to be reckoned with even after the exhausting effects of the nineteenth-century reforms. In fact, despite the chipping effects of Nasser's institutional and administrative engineering around the middle of the twentieth century, Azhar grew phenomenally in size, increasing the number of its institutes from 212 in 1963 to 3,161 in 1993. Its student population increased from about 65,000 to almost a million during the same period. But even more phenomenal growth occurred in another religious movement that was to become far more popular and pervasive. In 1928, Egypt witnessed the birth of the Muslim Brothers, an association created by the Arabic language teacher Hasan al-Banna (1906–49). Spreading in the 1950s to Jordan, Syria, Sudan, Iran, Pakistan, Malaysia and Indonesia, the movement has continued to gain momentous strength, in Egypt as well as outside it, partly by virtue of an influential ideologue in the figure of Sayyid Qutb, later considered a martyr after being executed by Nasser's regime in 1966.

These two Islamic camps, represented by Azhar and the Brotherhood, have advocated different visions of the Shariʿa, but view its implementation in the social order as a matter of principle, a desideratum. Regarding themselves as custodians of the traditional religious law and its methods, the Azharis, generally speaking, advocate a conventional version of the Shariʿa, largely derived from the legal doctrine expounded by the legal schools.

The Muslim Brothers, on the other hand, have a wider view of juridical possibilities, allowing for an Islamic law that can be modified to reflect the changing realities of the world, in ways comparatively far more open to interpretive possibilities. But the change is not to be of the sort dictated by the Western colonizer, for that form of change is precisely what has to be resisted and overcome. The colonizer's change has been as detrimental to Muslim spiritual and social life as the conservatism of the Azhar ulama, whom the Muslim Brothers vehemently oppose. Modernity, which in the Brothers' discourse appears distinct from Westernization, does not however pose any particular problem, that is, if we can assume that modernity *qua* modernity consciously posed itself as an intellectual subject in the thought of – at least – Banna and Qutb. But this perhaps is too much to assume, for it seems that the effects of science, technology and industry are not, according to the thought of these two men, appreciated in the social and moral realms. Although the Muslim Brothers, including Banna and Qutb, have never explained exactly what form of Shariʿa might be adopted in the new, avant-guarde Muslim society, it is clear that religious morality is expected to lie at the center of the social order.

Morality represents the fundamental basis of any project of rebuilding a new Muslim society, and as such the Shariʿa, to be implemented, would have to rest on a moral social order. Living a moral life appears even as a predicate to the introduction of any Shariʿa order and explains at least in part the formation, in the 1980s, of local grass-roots Islamist communities throughout Egypt. Somewhat similar to the pre-modern neighborhoods, these mostly urban, lower-middle-class communities fashioned themselves into cohesive neighborhoods with their own systems that encompassed schools, hospitals, mosques, preachers, "banking" operations for mutual financial support, and other social-communal services. (Similar phenomena have also emerged in Gaza and Southern Lebanon, Hamas's and Hizbullah's networks being, respectively, prime examples.) Most of these Egyptian neighborhoods are populated by Islamists (who are by no means political activists in the majority of cases), although lower-ranking, techno-Azharites have also come to share these habitats. Indeed, the growth of this religious movement would ultimately bring unprecedented pressure upon the government to take seriously the popular request to implement the Shari'a. But how did the state finally deal with these pressures?

The fundamentals of the politics of law that we have discussed in chapter 6 continued to be, in their bare essentials, largely operative on the Egyptian scene during the twentieth century. The regime needed Azhar to legitimize its nationalist and socialist projects, which were intended, as elsewhere, to reengineer the social order in the image of the ideal nation which is materially and culturally productive, just, successful and, most importantly, independent and free. On the other hand, Azhar, having become subordinated more than ever to the state and its apparatus, could not but oblige. Nasser's regime brought Azhar to heel, first by nationalizing much of the *waqf* property in 1952, then by excluding its personnel from the national courts in 1955. But it was the 1961 reform that had the most drastic effect on Azhar, in both more and less predictable ways. The first major change was the introduction of scientific subjects into the curriculum, such as engineering and medicine, which, on the one hand, predictably liberalized Azhar but, on the other, created a class of techno-Azharites who – unpredictably – came in the 1970s to share and indeed strengthen the ranks of the Islamists. Nasser also subjected Azhar's entire administration to the state, and made the appointment and dismissal of its head (Shaykh al-Azhar) a direct responsibility of the President's office. Having mercilessly suppressed the Muslim Brothers and outlawed their political formations, and having systemically and systematically subordinated the Azhar to the state, Nasser and his regime could easily afford to ignore all religious sentiments that voiced a concern about the implementation of the Shari'a.

These concerns might have continued to fall on deaf ears had the Arab regimes been more successful in their projects, including their conflicts with Israel. The crushing defeat of 1967 ultimately brought Nasser himself to his knees, and the Muslim Brothers sprang back – from imprisonment, torture and deprivation – with a great deal of resentment. Azhar dramatically transformed its discourse, now invoking notions of repentance, and casting the so-called Setback (of 1967) as a lesson from God and exhorting Muslims to reconsider their erroneous ways, not least of these being Nasser's socialism. Even Nasser himself spoke of the Setback as a divine intimation, a call for purification.

It was Sadat's liberalizing policies that ushered in a new stage in the rise of the Islamist movement. Alleviating the oppression against the Muslim Brothers and releasing the groups' members from prisons, Sadat began his rule with a policy of appeasement – promising, furthermore, to consider ways to implement the Shari'a. Article 2 of the 1971 Constitution stipulated that Islamic law is "a principal source" of legislation. (In 1969, a Supreme Court had been created and in 1971 it was renamed as the Supreme Constitutional Court [SCC], whose function was to curb infringements by the legislative and executive branches.) Although a legislative parliamentary committee was to prepare laws in line with Article 2, and although Azhar was supposed to, and did, provide direction and assistance in drafting these laws, nothing came of what was, with the benefit of hindsight, little more than an act of lip service on the part of the regime. With a judiciary and a Parliament staffed by a liberal and secularized majority, Article 2 appeared to be no more than a rhetorical ploy.

In the meantime, the Islamist movement gained strength, and the ruling elite needed Azhar more than ever to combat the increasing pressure coming from the Islamists. The more Azhar was needed and the more it offered its support to the regime, the more assertive it became, and the more it called for the implementation of the Shari'a. And to avert the political sting of the Islamists, the regime was willing to make concessions on the less innocuous legal front, concessions that happened to favor its ally, Azhar. And so in 1980 the Constitution was amended, and Article 2 changed to stipulate that the Shari'a "is the principal source of legislation."

But not much happened. No Islamic laws were passed, and no new cases were to constitute any step in that direction. Frustrated by the government's lack of legislative action, the Islamists mounted challenges to the SCC, bringing cases regarding laws they alleged (often rightly so) to be in contradiction to the Shari'a, and requesting that the SCC declare them, by virtue of Article 2, unconstitutional. This challenge also included Law No. 44 of 1979, the so-called Jihan's Law (which extended the duration of child custody for divorced mothers, and, even more importantly here, made a husband's marriage to a second wife an element automatically constituting harm to the first wife and therefore giving rise to divorce by operation of the law). But this Law and the other cases reviewed were dismissed without reference to their (in)compatibility with Article 2, which was one way for the SCC to avoid defining, once and for all (it was thought), what is exactly meant by the term "Shari'a" mentioned in Article 2. Jihan's Law was struck down on the grounds that it was passed through unconstitutional means, and the cases were dismissed on grounds of non-retroactivity. The Shari'a of Article 2 was left undefined.

It was not until 1993 that the SCC delivered a definition of what the Shari'a, in its opinion, meant. Under overwhelming pressure from the Islamists, it pronounced that the Shari'a in effect amounts to the broad legal principles laid down in the Quran, as defined by the consensus of jurists over the centuries. These were defined as fundamental principles, not specific rules, and as general and universal principles they are applicable to any society in any age. A case in point is the principle that law should not be harmful to Muslims. Accordingly, any law that does not violate any of these principles is one that does not stand in contradiction to the Shariʿa. But who is to make a determination of these general principles, and how? How is the actual power, or mere potential, of laws to harm or to benefit to be determined?

In answer to these questions, the SCC took the bold position that any judge presiding in the national courts can be a valid interpreter of these general Shariʿa principles; which, in effect, amounted to the proposition that these principles are so general that any person having basic knowledge of "Islamic law" – but who is sufficiently trained in modern law – can derive such principles from the Quran and the consensual practices of the jurists over the preceding twelve or thirteen centuries.

The SCC's answer became the new bone of contention between the state and the Islamists. The challenge put forth by the latter was as much legal as political. The Islamists insisted – as their ideologue Qutb had done half a century earlier – that such exercises in interpretation are nothing short of human legislation producing a system where men rule over each other. The secular training of the national-court judges equipped them, even with the best of intentions, to extract nothing more than the most general of principles. Their well-nigh ignorance of Shariʿa's rules, of Quranic exegesis, of *hadith* (which the SCC largely ignored), and even of basic skills in classical legal Arabic, largely barred them from any genuine understanding of what Shariʿa's rules signified or even technically meant.

It is common knowledge – for anyone familiar with the modern Arab legal profession – that this profession as a rule considers the Shariʿa's discourse as culturally remote, juristically complex and a judicially obscure system of rules. For those members who have little sympathy for the Islamists, Shariʿa's system of rules is downright primeval, ultra-conservative and anti-modern. Nevertheless, the Islamists pushing the SCC to adopt a more sensitive position toward a "genuine" Shariʿa have insisted – and rightly so – that deriving such inordinately broad principles not only leads the court to indulge in utilitarian reasoning about law and society, but also lodges it in an arbitrary world where judges who know next to nothing about the religious and legal texts will be able to pronounce on God's law. Indeed, a close analysis of some of the cases that the SCC has decided shows this much. Thus far, in the Egyptian experiment at least, a definition of Shariʿa that can garner popular and majoritarian legitimacy continues to be elusive.

Pakistan

Another country witnessing a significant push toward Islamization of laws, Pakistan emerged from the ruins of British India with a distinct Islamic identity, articulated by the anti-colonial nationalists as justification for their independence. It was emphasized that its reason for coming into existence was neither geographical nor ethnic, but rather religious. God was declared in the March 1949 Objectives Resolution as the sole sovereign of the Universe, a sovereign whose authority was "delegated to the State of Pakistan." This assertion, from the very dawn of independence, betrayed the tension between the sovereignty of God and that of the state, for the legal history of Pakistan has been characterized by a potent tension implicit in the claims of "delegated" sovereignty. The political ruling elite, including Muhammad Ali Jinnah, was modernist and Westernizing, promoting the political, administrative and bureaucratic interests of what, in every way, was a nation-state. Yet, the Objectives Resolution, while insisting on purely Western concepts of governance, promised that "Muslims shall be enabled to order their lives ... according to the teachings and requirements of Islam as set out in the Holy Quran and the sunna."[1]

The 1949 Objectives Resolution was regarded as a Preamble to the Constitution, which was not to be promulgated until 1956. In the interim, the ulama maintained an organized and sustained pressure on the government toward implementing the promises made in the Resolution. One of the specific proposals on which they insisted was that the government should review Pakistani legislation with a view to expunging any law that stood in contravention of the Shari'a. The prevalent idea appears to have been that the Shari'a is constituted of the traditional set of rules adopted by the historical schools, not the sort of general principles later advocated by the Egyptian SCC. When the Constitution was finally promulgated in 1956, Article 198 stipulated that "no law shall be enacted that is repugnant to the Injunctions of Islam as laid down in the Holy Quran and the Sunna."[2] However, the potential effects of this Article were restricted by clauses 2 and 3. In their aggregate, these two clauses required that a temporary advisory committee submit a proposal to the National Assembly seeking to rectify any law contrary to the Shari'a, but they effectively precluded the courts from hearing any cases that bore on Article 198.

---

[1] Cited in Daniel Collins, "Islamization of Pakistani Law: A Historical Perspective," *Stanford Journal of International Law*, 24 (1987–88): 550.

[2] Cited in A. An-Na'im, *Islamic Family Law in a Changing World* (London: Zed Books, 2002), 230.

The 1958 crisis that led to the abolition of the Constitution prevented the appointment of any committee and thus the National Assembly never carried out the provisions of Article 198. By the end of that year, Ayyub Khan had seized power and embarked on implementing a policy of modernization. One such far-reaching legislation was the Muslim Family Laws Ordinance of 1961, a law that was at the time typical in the Middle East but that ran against the wishes of a relatively strong Pakistani ulama constituency. One indicator of the legal tensions in Pakistan was the inheritance problem, which we have already discussed in regard to the children of a predeceased son. The 1961 Ordinance, acknowledging the principle of representation, decreed that the child of a predeceased child had the right to inherit what his or her parent would have inherited had he or she been alive. The next year saw the enactment of a new Constitution that was modernist in tenor, omitting not only any mention of Pakistan as an "Islamic Republic" (as in the 1956 Constitution) but also the entirety of the repugnancy clause. However, public discontent and pressure forced Ayyub Khan to restore both provisions, although these alterations remained superficial and were no more than a form of appeasement.

The repugnancy provision was in effect left dormant, and the law of Pakistan continued to preserve, until the late 1970s, its Anglo-Muhammadan form, whereby the courts continued to apply the law according to the common law case method. The civil war of 1971, the political changes occurring as a result and the new 1973 Constitution brought no change, although the repugnancy clause was included, again to no effect, in this Constitution.

But the Middle East and the Islamic world had changed by the 1970s. As mentioned earlier, the 1967 Arab defeat had caused a major self-reassessment, accompanied by a rediscovery of Islam as a political force. A gradual yet potent increase in Islamic consciousness spilled over beyond the Arab world, augmenting the local and nation-specific problems of each country. The 1979 Iranian Revolution was not the spark that ignited this consciousness, but was rather a powerful symptom of the currents sweeping the region, as well as the Islamic world at large, since 1967. The 1970s may well be called the decade of Islamic incubation. In 1979, Zia al-Haqq seized power and it was clear that his growing religious constituency could no longer be ignored or silenced through legislative lip service. As in Sadat's Egypt, the political legitimacy of the regime rested squarely on satisfying this constituency. Zia al-Haqq immediately made it clear that his regime would pursue a program of Islamization, and he followed up on his promise by enacting a number of Islamic laws which closely followed traditional Shari'a rules.

Receiving by this point no concrete constitutional status, the Objectives Resolution of 1949 was formally incorporated as the Preamble to the Constitution, and the statutory language pertaining to repugnancy issues was strengthened. Furthermore, each High Court was supposed to have a Shariat Bench, but this was streamlined into a single Federal Shariat Court (FSC) in 1980. The latter was to decide on which laws contravened the Shari'a, and once a law was found by it to be repugnant, it would cease to have any effect. Yet, the FSC's power was constrained by structural and other limitations. First, appeals to the Supreme Court could reverse the FSC's decisions. Second, the FSC could not adjudicate the full range of the law: the Constitution, fiscal law, procedural law and law of personal status were entirely excluded from its jurisdictional purview. Third, in its early period, the five judges who staffed the FSC all came from the national courts, which is to say that none of them was a member of the ulama class. It was not surprising then that the FSC's decisions were not always consistent with the Shariat ordinances promulgated by General Zia, nor were they in conformity with the traditional Shari'a rules.

In due course, however, the FSC's bench began to be populated by members of the ulama class, and General Zia renewed his commitment to Islam as part of his bargain for political legitimacy. The price of the bargain was the 1988 Enforcement of Shariat Ordinance which decreed that the Shari'a was the "supreme source of the law in Pakistan and the Grundnorm for guidance of policy-making by the state." But the earlier substantive exclusions from the purview of this court as well as appeals of its decisions to the Supreme Court remained in place, showing, at the end of the day, where true legal power lay.

The aforementioned exclusions were challenged in 1981 by the Peshawar Shariat Bench, which interpreted the exclusions as bearing on the Shari'a itself, not the state's legislative pronouncements on personal status. Accordingly, it ruled that the inheritance rights prescribed by section 4 of the 1961 Muslim Family Law Ordinance were repugnant to Shari'a and that the orphaned grandchild was not entitled to his or her parent's share had the parent been alive. The decision was appealed by the Government, and the higher court overturned it on jurisdictional grounds, stating that the Peshawar Bench was not empowered to make such a determination, and that this matter fell to the competence of the legislature alone (including its advisory Council of Islamic Ideology).

The persistence of the 1961 Ordinance is a marker of the modest extent to which substantive Islamization took place in Pakistan. No less is it a marker of the political uses the founding fathers and subsequent politicians made of the Shari'a. But the few changes that have occurred in this sphere during the last several years are indicative of a larger trend, as we shall see shortly. The FSC declared that as of March 2000, section 4 allowing orphaned grandchildren to be represented in inheritance would no longer have effect, and delegated to the legislature the task of finding a solution for those grandchildren who, with this decision, were left to fend for themselves.

The Court agreed with the proposal of the Council of Islamic Ideology that a requirement be placed upon the aunts and uncles of orphaned children to provide and care for them as members of their own families. But the social and moral conditions, the Court agreed, were not yet ready for such an obligation to be imposed. Although a moral community does not require external interference (one form of which is a legislative enactment), there must exist at least an elementary form of this community for such an enactment, first, to be accepted, and second, to have a constructive effect on the emergence and full formation of the moral community. In its decision, the Court wrote: "If the piety which is a prerequisite of an Islamic Social Order had been prevalent, it [viz., imposition of obligation upon uncles and aunts] could well have been a good solution but in the situation in which we are placed, we are of the view that the better solution would be the making of a Mandatory will in favor of the orphaned grandchildren."[3]

The Court's imposition of a mandatory will, and not a duty of care upon relatives, appears to be grounded in the conviction that with the modernizing changes in society and the virtual non-existence of a moral community, a duty of care will end in failure, and will meet with stiff popular resistance. This view, echoing Sayyid Qutb's ideas, rests on the assumption that the social order must first develop its moral character before it is ready for the implementation of Shari'a. Whether or not the Court articulated the moral–legal ramifications of the case in these terms, its decision certainly demonstrated that at least it arrived at an intuitive understanding of the functional and organic interdependence between and among the moral, communal and legal spheres *within* the Shari'a. But the tenacity of the 1961 Ordinance and the entanglement of Pakistan's ruling elite in "modernizing" policies – in good part dictated by international hegemonic powers – have carried the day, effectively leaving the Court, the Islamists and the ulama, however differently they articulate Islam, in a minority position.

---

[3] Lucy Carroll, "The Pakistan Federal Shariat Court, Section 4 of the Muslim Family Laws Ordinance, and the Orphaned Grandchild," *Islamic Law and Society*, 9, 1 (2002): 75 f. In the mandatory scheme, the bequest must apportion to orphaned grandchildren what their deceased parent would have inherited had he or she been alive, with the proviso that such apportioning not exceed one-third of the grandfather's total estate. Should the parent not make such a bequest, the court must assume that the grandparent did do so.

Iran

As noted in chapter 7, significant changes to the Shariʿa did not take place until Reza Shah Pahlavi assumed power in 1925. With the assistance of the British, and in a bid to centralize his rule, the Shah subdued the tribal chiefs (who nearly incapacitated the Qajars), and embarked on a project of weakening the ulama and their institutions. He confiscated their *waqf*s and placed their administration in the hands of the Ministry of Education. Any ulama retained as administrative or educational personnel were now paid by the government, depriving them of their traditional independence. This was a victory for the state that lagged behind its Ottoman counterpart by about three-quarters of a century.

Very much in line with changes the Ottomans had long since effected, the Pahlavi regime immediately introduced two new and important enactments: the Code of Judicial Organization and the Principles of Civil Procedure (both in 1927). A new state system of courts was thus established, with judges and prosecutors as civil servants. In 1931, the Act of Marriage was promulgated, implementing changes that reflected – as we saw in the previous chapter – the increased interest of the state in the reengineering of family life. This Act was the result of preparatory work conducted by a commission composed of ulama and European-trained lawyers. The rest of the legislation on family law, including inheritance and gifts, was enacted in 1935. The years 1967 and 1975 witnessed two further waves of changes to family law, the latter year having introduced the Family Protection Act, the hallmark of which was the abolishing of the husband's right to unilateral divorce. Needless to say, the sphere of family law was the only reserve of the Shariʿa, however thin it had become. To all intents and purposes, the rest of the law and legal system were of entirely Western inspiration, the French influence manifestly dominating.

The monumental Iranian revolution of 1979 produced colossal political and conceptual ruptures, within Iran and outside it no less. Yet, interestingly, the sphere of law, the supposed hallmark of the Islamic Republic, experienced a relatively small, indeed nominal, measure of Islamization for years after the Revolution took place.

In chapter 7, we had occasion to speak of the distinctive Shiʿi theory which holds the Imam to be the lawgiver and the inspector of its application. But since the Imam is in hiding, and since law must continue in operation, several functions that the Imams would have fulfilled must now be dispensed – by proxy – by the Jurist-in-Charge. This delegation of duty has become known as Vilayat-i Faqih, the theoretical foundation of governance in the new Islamic Republic.

Building on three centuries' worth of Twelver-Shi'i doctrine, but simultaneously charged with intense anti-colonialist sentiments, Ayatullah Khomeini (the charismatic leader and theorist of the Revolution) expanded on this theory and argued that, as long as the Imam remains in hiding, the Jurist-in-Charge, the MARJA'-TAQLID, must fulfill the role of political and religious ruler, representing the Imam's functions in all worldly and spiritual affairs. This doctrine became formally enshrined in the 1979 Constitution of the new Republic, where Article 5 states that the Jurist – or a group of such Jurists – who has fulfilled the qualifications of *ijtihad* (mastery of the law) is entitled to exercise leadership, provided the Imam continues to be absent. The extension of the Jurist's powers to the political, military and other secular realms was justified, in Khomeini's discourse, by reasoning to the effect that, for an Islamic state to be run in genuine compliance with the Shari'a, it must be supervised and administered by the ultimate expert in the law, the Marja'-Taqlid.

Khomeini's position, it must be noted, represented an expansion on the doctrine he elaborated during the decade or so before the Revolution. In that earlier version, the Marja'-Taqlid assumed a supervisory role – very much like that prescribed by the 1906 Constitution – whereby the Jurist or Jurists evaluate(s) all legislation in order to ensure that laws stand in conformity with the rules of the Shari'a. As we just saw, this position was revised shortly before 1979 so that governance, including the supreme exercise of political power, might rest exclusively in the hands of the Marja'-Taqlid. In both versions of the doctrine, the Marja' is responsible for exercising *ijtihad* in those unprecedented cases that may befall the community and its state, but otherwise the Marja' is to regard and treat the established law of the Shari'a, at least in its broad outlines and foundational principles, as unchangeable. This permanency of the law as structure and principles constituted the essence of the Islamic rule of law, a feature that continues to be advocated and cherished by the majority of Islamists today.

Toward the end of his life, however, Khomeini modified his doctrine for the second time. Now he maintained that the Marja' is not bound by the Shari'a and its laws, and can make his own determination of what the law is. The Marja' can abrogate even the essential pillars of Islam – such as pilgrimage – and demolish mosques, among other things, if "the interests of the Islamic country" are threatened. Very much in the spirit of the modern state which sees itself – and acts – as a system whose function is to create and impose discipline with a view to correcting any deviation from the self-established norm, Khomeini fully absorbed this modernist perception of the law's function. He adopted the view, unknown – in its modernist *political connotations* – to pre-modern Islamic jurists of any strand, that: "Islam regards law as a tool, not as an end in itself. Law is a tool and an instrument for the establishment of justice in society, a means for man's intellectual and moral reform and his purification."[4]

As one historian has argued, this doctrine grants the Marjaʿ absolute authority over and above the law, and it is precisely for this reason that the Sunni ulama shied away from it. For "in the guise of upholding Islam the state might make it subservient to its own goals and ultimately absorb it within itself."[5] It is this "guise," representing no more than a thin veneer, that marks the superficial difference between a self-declared secular state and a self-declared Islamic state. The ulama as well as the Islamists – Sunni and Shiʿi – have yet to discover that, in the final analysis, a state is a state, no matter what name one gives to it.

Be that as it may, very little in Khomeini's doctrine was implemented immediately, for even the Marjaʿ himself, the Supreme Leader, could not overhaul the Pahlavi state with the speed he hoped for, and in fact he died before much of his legal ideology was implemented. Part of the reason may lie in the paradox of his conception that Islamic governance grounded in the Shariʿa's rule of law was gradually fading away in favor of a modernist perception of governance (a change that can be explained by the weight of his experience as a political leader of a modern state which, under the Shah, had cultivated a sophisticated system of surveillance and bureaucracy). Yet Khomeini's paradox was that of the Islamic Republic as well, for the tension between the Islamic ideal, even in its modernized form, and the reality of the modern state was and remains dominating.

This tension is exemplified in several features of the Republic. Consider, for instance, the limitations in the 1979 Islamic Constitution. Article 4 requires that "All civil, penal, financial, economic, administrative, cultural, military, political laws and other laws or regulations must be based on Islamic principles ... absolutely and generally."[6] Yet, the mechanism created to implement Islamization of laws was not programmed in absolute Islamic terms. The Constitution provides for a supervisory council (COUNCIL OF GUARDIANS) consisting of six Shariʿa jurists and another six Western-trained lawyer-jurists whose task it is to ensure that all bills presented to the Parliament stand in conformity with Islamic law.

---

[4] Ruhollah Khomeini, *Islam and Revolution: Writings and Declarations*, trans. Hamid Algar (Berkeley, CA: Mizan Press, 1981), 80.

[5] M. Qasim Zaman, *The Ulama in Contemporary Islam: Custodians of Change* (Princeton: Princeton University Press, 2002), 107.

[6] Hassan Rezaei, "The Iranian Criminal Justice under the Islamization Project," *European Journal of Crime*, 10, 1 (January, 2002): 57; Asghar Schirazi, *The Constitution of Iran: Politics and the State in the Islamic Republic*, trans. John O'Kane (London and New York: I. B. Tauris, 1997), 10.

The juristic qualifications of the latter six members might well be questioned, at least on grounds of lack of scholarly expertise in Shariʿa's traditional law and its interpretive system.

Furthermore, according to Article 167, the court judges are supposed to adjudicate each case on the basis of codified law, and in the absence of such a law their decisions must conform to a *fatwa* issued by a learned Shariʿa jurist. This article effectively preserves much of the Pahlavi legal system, since it was understood by all parties concerned that the transformation aspired to in the various Articles that require comprehensive Islamization cannot obtain except through a piecemeal process. And this is in fact what happened. As late as 2000, the Procedure of General and Revolutionary Courts replicated most of these stipulations, stating that if any law is inadequate or unclear or does not exist in regard to a case at issue, the court must make recourse to a *fatwa* based in Islamic legal principles or the judge himself must perform *ijtihad*. However, should the law be found by the judge to contradict the state's enacted law, the case must be sent to another court for adjudication. The state, as we shall see further below, must reign supreme, a situation that hardly squares with Khomeini's own assertion that "[Islamic] law alone ... rules over society. Even the limited powers given to the Most Noble Messenger and those exercising rule after him have been conferred upon them by God ... in obedience to divine law."[7]

In the first months of the Revolution, the symbols that touched on the sensitive images of the Shariʿa received the first attention, for this was the testing ground. How can an Islamic state, an Islamic revolution, continue to uphold the idolatrous laws of the sacrilegious Shah? So night clubs, alcohol shops, music (including videos and cassettes), dancing and the sale of pork were immediately outlawed. The Constitution shortly thereafter came to prohibit usury, mentioning it by name (Art. 43). And within four months of the new Republic's birth, the Islamic penal laws were instated in lieu of the Shah's criminal code, which was based on the 1816 French Penal Code. However, even this instatement of penal law was tenuous, requiring additional enactments in 1982, 1988, 1989, 1992 and 1996 to give it a concrete and more complete form.

Furthermore, in installing the so-called discretionary punishments (*taʿzir*), the Republic faced a dilemma. In the Shariʿa, offenses ranged from the moral to the monetary and homicidal. Some of these (i.e., adultery/fornication, wrongful accusation of adultery/fornication, drinking alcohol, theft and highway robbery) were known as *HUDUD*, and

---

[7] Khomeini, *Islam and Revolution*, 56–57.

happened to be regulated by the Quran and the Sunna. But there were other offenses whose punishments were to be determined by the judge in light of the particular facts and circumstances of each case. In no case can the punishments for these offenses exceed the *hudud* penalties, nor can these punishments be predetermined. Acting in the manner of a modern state, the Islamic Republic, however, fixed the penalties for such offenses, in effect taking away the most characteristic property of what makes *ta'zir* what it is, namely, the judge's social, moral and legal evaluation of a particular and unique situation which every case represented. It was the ad hoc balance that the *qadi* struck among these three and other considerations which gave *ta'zir* its features and distinguished it from *hudud*. Failure to recognize that the conceptual foundations of *ta'zir* have always assumed that each case presents unique moral conditions was a reflection not only of the moral community's undoing but also of the modern state's inherent role in metamorphosing the otherwise independent Shari'a into a form of state law. The reasoning behind creating this uniformity – i.e., that different penalties were imposed by judges for the same crimes – bespeaks the inevitable discomfort that the modern state displays in the face of heterogeneity: the Subject must always be uniform.

The supremacy of the state was not merely a conceptual residue of modernist influences on Islamic modes of governance, but rather a conscious choice of how the Islamic Iranian experience, or at least the influential Khomeini and other Ayatullahs surrounding him, articulated its own concept of political modernity. In effect, Khomeini viewed Islamic law not merely as a tool by means of which certain social and moral goals can be accomplished, but one that is derivative of the state, the cardinal ordinance of God. "The state is the most important of God's ordinances and has precedence over all other derived ordinances of God." The state does not operate within the framework of the law; rather, it is the law that operates within the state. "If the powers of the state were [only] operational within the framework of God's ordinances, the extent of God's sovereignty and the absolute trusteeship given to the Prophet would be a meaningless phenomenon devoid of content."[8]

This vision of the state entirely comports with Khomeini's other pronouncements that, in the name of the state, the Marja' could suspend with impunity Shari'a rules, major and minor, if the "country's" interest required doing so. In this vision, institutionalized checks and balances, both Western and Islamic, are absent. In theory and in practice, the Marja' and the Council of Guardians have arrogated to themselves the "stately"

---

[8] Khomeini's speech (1988), cited in Schirazi, *Constitution of Iran*, 230.

power to pronounce on what is and what is not Islamic. But this power of determining the law in the name of the state in no way reflects the tradition of the Shari'a, wherein the conjoined effects of the stability of the law and its supremacy guarantee, as they in fact did, that the "state" always operates under the rule of law.

In the meantime, little in the way of Islamization was accomplished. This was clear from the frustrations Khomeini himself expressed in a 1982 speech. After that speech, the Parliament began to push toward Islamic legislation in earnest, declaring that all laws in the Republic deemed by the government institution applying them to be un-Islamic must be submitted to the Council of Guardians for review. But the Council immediately countered by affirming that, as long as a law was not officially declared un-Islamic, it should be applied provisionally until further notice, which would be presumably after the Council of Guardians had reviewed its substance. As it turned out, this position of 1982 expressed the Republic's gradual approach to Islamization over the next two and a half decades. It was an approach that adopted a pragmatic policy, where the accommodation of legal practice on the ground took precedence over any consideration of Islamization that might cause paralyzing or harmful ruptures to the political system.

The first manifestation of this pragmatic policy was the re-legalization of music on radio and television, trade in videos, chess and other forms of entertainment. The reasoning, embodied in a *fatwa* that Khomeini issued, resorted to the juristic distinction between harmful and beneficial forms of entertainment, and what was restored, it was said, was entertainment of the latter form. But the reality behind re-legalization of "permissible" entertainment was the ineffectiveness of the 1979 prohibition, which brought to the fore the inability of the government to ban popular practices. Although this was presented to the public not as a retreat but as a policy operating in favor of public interest, to the religious leadership it was, as their *fatwa*s suggest, a mitigated concession in favor of modernity's pernicious effects, for such legislation would at least allow Islamic television programs and classical Iranian music to compete with their Western counterparts. It was an act of opting for the lesser evil. Prohibition on all forms of music would have meant that only black market, and thus Western, music was being consumed.

This retreat had a parallel in the law of *ta'zir* whose penalties, as we noted, were fixed by the state. Faced with criticism by some of the Ayatullahs themselves (on the ground that the discretionary nature of *ta'zir* is of the essence), the government could neither abrogate them nor restore their discretionary features. So the law had perforce to stay, but – in order to vitiate the criticism of the *mullah*s – it was given the designation "state regulations," a nomenclature that amounts to a declaration of withdrawing these penalties from the sphere of Shariʿa. Like all Shariʿa elements that have come to symbolize and capture the *modern* essence of "Islamic law," penal law was pursued with particular vigor, but, like much else, several modernizing adjustments to the traditional system had to be made. Other modern institutions within the judiciary had to be accommodated and given a Shariʿa-like veneer. For instance, the jury, required in trials of "political and press offenses," was claimed to have a Shariʿa pedigree, represented – as we have seen – in the habitual attendance of jurists in pre-modern courts of law, an attendance whose intent and purpose was to ensure "due process" and fair trials, but not to pass judgments. (Apparently, the immeasurable gap between the legal knowledge of these sit-in jurists and that of the jury does not appear to have been taken as a relevant factor in the analogy.)

Similar adaptations were made to rationalize and justify the legal profession, lawyerly practices and related matters – all of which had been introduced to Iran from the West. In the final analysis, the great majority of laws adopted before and *after* the Revolution were Western in inspiration and content, and they remain so. International laws, international conventions and treaties continue to be ratified every year, the traditional law of *jihad* notwithstanding.

Indonesia

The vigorous Dutch push on behalf of *adat* since the end of the nineteenth century – which aimed to privilege these *adat* over the Shariʿa – generated massive resentment, not least because the Dutch were seen to be tampering with legitimate authority in both legal spheres. What exacerbated the matter further was the Dutch decision to eliminate the Islamic courts during the last few years before their final departure in 1950. All in all, it can be safely said that these policies did nothing but strengthen the Indonesian popular resolve to persist in their commitment to their religion and its juridical institutions. (In fact, this phenomenon is attested in several other colonized regions, where Shariʿa's importance grew significantly as a response to colonialism and – for the first time in history – as a rigid marker of political identity.)

On the other hand, the structures of political and legal power bequeathed by the Dutch to the largely secular native elite were maintained after the country's independence (gained practically in 1950). All commercial laws and laws of industrial property and patents were maintained, as were all *adat* laws applicable to Indonesians. The Shariʿa in its restricted family spheres was initially kept as before, and Indonesian

Christians continued to be governed by their own Marriage Law. The laws that the Dutch had applied to the Europeans were now applied to the Chinese, though certain parts of these laws were generalized to all Indonesian nationals. The near absence of legal change in the Republic was given official sanction in Article 2 of the 1945 Constitution which stipulated that "All existing institutions and regulations of the state shall continue to function so long as new ones have not been set up in conformity with the Constitution."

One result of the political compromise the Dutch had to make before their departure was the establishment in 1946, after the defeat of the Japanese occupation, of a Ministry of Religion. In part, this was also a competitive measure, calculated to match the efforts expended by the Japanese to promote Islam as a means of controlling the population. Many Islamic institutions were subsumed under the administration of this Ministry. The Directorate of Religious Justice became the Ministry's division responsible for the administration of Muslim courts. In the long run, this Ministry came to play a significant role in the promotion of Islamic law, both in terms of spreading its courts and judicial practices, and in creating an educational system that was conducive to the development of an Indonesian religio-legal identity. This Ministry tended, then as now, to be staffed by persons who did not hail from the upper Westernized elite that the Dutch had bequeathed to the country, an important fact in light of the power dynamics that were to determine the extent to which the Shari'a was to be accommodated.

Together with support from Islamist parties, the Ministry of Religion (later Ministry of Religious Affairs) pressed for the creation of Islamic courts on various Indonesian islands – this in defiance of the influential Ministry of Interior that was backed by the largely anti-Islamic, secularist nationalist elite. By 1957, Shari'a courts (Mahkamah Syariah) were convened in Sumatra and Java, and appellate religious courts for the other islands were established in Java. But in all of these developments, the Dutch colonial legacy was considerable, for these courts amounted to very little not only in terms of their jurisdiction; the scope of this jurisdiction was at times very different from one place to the next. The Dutch judicial policies established for Java and Madura (and later Kalimantan) between 1882 and 1937 reduced the Shari'a courts in these islands to the adjudication of cases pertaining to marriage, and more specifically to divorce; on the other hand, the newer courts of Sumatra and elsewhere adjudicated spheres as varied as *waqf*, public funds (including religious alms-tax), gifts, bequests and inheritance. The unification of the judicial system thus posed a great challenge to the independent state, as the Javanese courts wished to acquire wider jurisdiction, especially over inheritance, while the other courts, especially in Sumatra, resisted giving up what they had already gained at high cost.

During the first years after formal independence, the Shari'a courts were affected by a number of factors. Internal administrative and procedural inconsistencies, coupled with inadequate funding for both administration of the courts and training their officers and magistrates, remained something of a debilitating problem for years. More importantly, however, these courts were only part of a wider ethnic, religious, legal and cultural diversity which the state was assiduously trying to homogenize. The elite's knowledge that law is a powerful mechanism of social engineering led to the promulgation of the 1947 Law No. 7, which positioned the Supreme Court and Chief Public Prosecutor at the pinnacle of authority in the legal system. Law No. 23 of the same year abolished the customary courts of Java and Sumatra, areas that had locally governed themselves under the Dutch. It is significant that this law asserted, in defensive terms, the sovereignty of the new Republic, stating that the Republic was not "merely the successor of the Netherlands-Indies Administration."[9] The process of unification continued unabated. A year later, in 1948, Law No. 19 introduced a three-tiered court system (first instance, appeal and supreme court) but did not account in these provisions for the *adat* and Shari'a courts.

An attempt at organizing the Shari'a courts came in 1957, when the central government defined the functions of these courts and the procedures for appointing their officers. No principles or laws of the Shari'a were stated, and the courts, modeled after their civil counterparts, were collegiate – another Dutch legacy. The laws of evidence were those used in civil courts, not those of the Shari'a, and so were the description and reporting of court cases. Following the Dutch policy, the new nation-state adopted the principle that the Shari'a courts should not deal with property and financial matters, which were, as noted earlier, deputed to the civil courts. Needless to say, such a dichotomization of divorce and property jurisdiction is artificial, and proved to be problematic, since in landowning rural communities the two spheres were inseparable.

The national debate during the 1950s was redolent of the discourse over the places of *adat* and Shari'a in the country's legal system. The pluralism of *adat* ran against the wishes of the secular nationalists whose strategy was to depict the *adat* as backward and anti-modern. Likewise, the weaker voices in this secularist-nationalist camp made similar arguments against the Shari'a. The proponents of *adat*, though, were powerful

---

[9] Daniel Lev, "Judicial Unification in Post-Colonial Indonesia," *Indonesia*, 16 (October, 1973): 20.

enough to gain some concessions in the 1960s, when the Basic Law of Agrarian Affairs declared that the *adat* law provides a source of law in the Republic, taking the place of colonial law. But this concession was sharply limited by the introduction of conditions to the effect that any use of such customary laws should not impede the construction of a just and prosperous society. In substance, therefore, colonial law persisted quietly under a nationalistic guise.

On the other hand, the Shari'a courts survived this debate more successfully, partly owing to the aura of legitimacy that Islam generated, and partly because the legal "code" by which they were regulated (mainly of Shafi'i pedigree) was, unlike the pluralist *adat*, consistent with the aims of the national unification project. It is also very likely that the government realized the relevance of these courts to the daily lives of the rural population. Whereas no secular courts could play the role of a mediator, the Shari'a courts fulfilled a major role in arbitrating and mediating disputes *before* reaching the level of formal adjudication. Thus, Law No. 14 of 1970 affirmed the judicial powers of Shari'a courts, thereby appeasing a majority of citizens to whom the legislation was not just a legal act, but also a symbolic and political one. On the one hand, the law in effect was curbed through the concomitant affirmation of the "silent" colonial principle that Shari'a court decisions, to be effective, required the ratification of the secular courts. The religious Marriage Law of 1974 was, in application, subject to these very limitations.

In time, however, these limitations were removed. Under the increasing pressures of Islamization and of the Islamists of Indonesia, as well as the emergence of strong civil Islamic movements, and despite the stiff opposition of the "secularist" and non-Muslim groups, Law No. 7 (1989) was passed, unifying the Shari'a courts throughout the islands and, significantly, reversing the principle of ratification, known as *executoire verklaring*. Henceforth, the Shari'a courts' decisions were self-validating, needing no sanction from the secular courts. As of 1991, these courts began to base their decisions on the new Compilation of Islamic Law in Indonesia, which reflected a modernized version of Islamic law that was also intended to create more consistency and uniformity within the country. In this Compilation polygamy remained legal under certain conditions and inter-faith marriage continued to be banned.

After the collapse of the Suharto regime in 1998, the process of decentralization (known as Otonomi Daerah) took on a new dynamic that resulted in a number of developments, often contradictory, on both the federal and district levels. Laws No. 10 and 32 of 2004 recognized the relative autonomy of Indonesia's districts, giving the federal government exclusive powers over national and international policies, but leaving the domestic affairs of the districts to be decided largely by the districts themselves. Sixteen districts have since signed on to the Sharia District Regulation (Peraturan Daerah Sharia; abr. Perda Sharia), including Aceh, Padang, Banten, Cianjur, Tangerang, Jombang, Bulukumba and Sumbawa. The main content of the Regulation is the application of Shari'a teachings, understood and expressed variably by different districts. Some have passed laws requiring the donning of Muslim dress, whereas others limited it to civil servants; other districts also criminalized prostitution and the sale and consumption of alcohol, and regulated the collection of religious tax. On the other hand, in 2004, and under pressure from international and local human rights groups, the Ministry of Religious Affairs proposed a draft law to replace the 1991 Compilation. The proposed law – in which polygamy was to be strictly outlawed, and inter-faith marriage unconditionally legalized – led to a protracted national debate that continues until this day.

10   Shariʿa then and now: concluding notes

For over a millennium, and until the nineteenth century, the Shariʿa represented a complex set of social, economic, moral, educational, intellectual and cultural practices. It was not just about law. It pervaded social structures so deeply that no ruler could conceive of the possibility of efficiently ruling the population without succumbing to a great extent to the dictates of the Shariʿa order. Involving institutions, groups and processes that resisted, enhanced and affected each other, Shariʿa as practice manifested itself as much in the judicial process as in writing, studying, teaching and documenting. It manifested itself in political representation, and in strategies of resistance against political and other abuses, as well as in cultural categories that meshed into ethical codes and a moral view of the world. It lived and operated in a deeply moral community which it took as granted, for it is a truism that the Shariʿa itself was constructed on the assumption that its audiences and consumers were, all along, moral communities and morally grounded individuals.

The Shariʿa also involved a complex and sophisticated intellectual system in which the jurists and the members of the legal profession were educators and thinkers who, on the one hand, were historians, mystics, theologians, logicians, men of letters and poets, and, on the other, contributed to the forging of a multi-layered set of relations that at times created political truth and ideology while at other times confronting power with its own truth. It involved the regulation of agricultural and mercantile economies that constituted the vehicle for the maintenance of material and cultural lives that spanned the entire gamut of "classes" and social strata. It rested on a theological bedrock that colored and directed much of the worldview of the population whose inner spiritual lives and relationships were in daily touch with the law. Indeed, this theological base encompassed the mundanely mystical, the esoterically pantheistic and the rationally philosophical, thereby creating complex relations between the Shariʿa and the larger spiritual and intellectual orders in which, and alongside which, it lived and functioned. The Shariʿa then was not only a judicial system and a legal doctrine whose function was to regulate social relations and resolve and mediate disputes, but also a pervasive and systemic practice that structurally and organically tied itself to the world around it in ways that were vertical and horizontal, structural and linear, economic and social, moral and ethical, intellectual and spiritual, epistemic and cultural, and textual and poetic, among much else. The Shari'a was as much a way of living and of seeing the world as it was a body of belief and intellectual play.

While in its textual and technical exposition the Shari'a was, by necessity, of an elitist tenor, very little else in it was elitist. As we saw in the early chapters of this book, the Shari'a cultivated itself within, and derived its ethical and moral foundations from, the very social order which it came to serve in the first place. Its personnel hailed from across all social strata (especially the middle and the lower classes), and operated and functioned within communal and popular spaces. The *qadi*'s court, the professor's classroom and the *mufti*'s assembly were typically held in the mosque's yard, and when this was not the case, in the marketplace or a private residence. That these sites served, as they did, a multiplicity of other social and religious-communal functions strongly suggests that the intersection of the legal with the communal was a marker of the law's populism and communitarianism. The same can be said of legal knowledge, which, as we saw, could scarcely have been more widespread across the entire range of society, free of charge. The Shari'a defined, in good part (and together with Sufism), cultural knowledge. Enmeshed with local customs, ethics, and economic and cultural practices, it was an encompassing system of social values.

Substantive Shari'a law gave direction and method to, but generally did not coercively superimpose itself upon, social morality. Because the *qadi* was an immediate product of his own social and moral universe, he was constituted – by the very nature of his function – as the agency through which the so-called law was mediated and made to serve the imperatives of social harmony. Procedurally, too, the work of the court appealed to pre-capitalist and non-bureaucratic social constructions of moral integrity that sprang directly from the local site of social practice. The institution of witnessing would have been meaningless without local knowledge of moral values, custom and social ties. Without such knowledge, the credibility of testimony itself – the lynchpin of the legal process – would have been neither testable nor demonstrable. Rectitude and trustworthiness, themselves the foundations of testimony, constituted the personal moral investment in social ties. To fail their test was to lose social standing and the privileges associated with it. Thus, the communal values of honor, shame, integrity and socio-religious virtue entered and intermeshed with legal practice and the prescriptive provisions of the law.

Furthermore, legal pluralism – a pervasive and fundamental feature of the Shari'a – not only was a marker of a strong sense of judicial relativism but also stood in stark contrast with the spirit of codification, another modern means of homogenizing the law and, consequently, the subject population. Nor was Shari'a's substantive law limited to being merely a mechanical and interpretive manifestation of divine will. It was also a socially embedded system, a mechanism, and a process, all of which were created for the social order by the order itself.

From this perspective, then, religious law operated in a dual capacity: first, it provided an intellectual superstructure that culturally positioned the law within the larger tradition that conceptually defined Islam, thereby constituting it as a theoretical link between metaphysics and theology on the one hand, and the social and physical/material world on the other; and second, it aimed discretely at the infusion of legal norms within a given social and moral order, an infusion whose method of realization was largely mediation rather than imposition. The Muslim adjudicatory process was therefore never remote from the social world of the disputants, advocating a moral logic of distributive justice rather than a logic of winner-takes-all. Restoring parties to the social roles they enjoyed prior to the legal process called for moral compromise, where each party was permitted to retain a partial gain. Preserving social order presupposed both a court and a malleable law that is acutely attuned to the system of social and economic cleavages. For despite the fact that cleavages – including class and other prerogatives – constantly asserted themselves, morality was the lot and indeed the right of everyone.

Moreover, in the world of practice, religious law did not constitute a totalizing statement of what *must* be done, nor was it engaged in transforming reality or managing or controlling society. Attributing to this law roles of control and management would be a distinctly modern misconception, a back-projection of our notions of law as an etatist instrument of social engineering and coercion. This misconceived attribution perhaps explains why modern scholarship has for long insisted on the "divorce" between "Islamic law" and social and political realities since the early ninth century, saving only for the areas of family law and, obviously, ritual. What this scholarship took to be a divorce was really a state of affairs in which the legal system allowed for the mediation of the agency of custom and social morality. In this picture, flexibility and accommodation were not taken for their constructive values, but were construed as signs of inefficiency, weakness and decline. It would be a mistake then to equate the Shari'a and its so-called law with *law* as we conceive and practice it in our world of modernity.

Shariʿa law was a process of explicating doctrine, an intellectual engagement to understand all the possible ways of reasoning and interpretation pertaining to a particular case. It was not the case that was of primary importance, but rather the principle that governed a group of cognate cases. On balance, the particular cases were more illustrative than prescriptive. Individual opinions, therefore, did not constitute law in the same sense in which we now understand the modern code, regulation or "case law," nor was it the "legal effect" of stating the will of a sovereign that the Muslim jurists intended to accomplish in any way. Their law was an interpretive and heuristic project, not "a body of rules of action or conduct prescribed by [a] controlling authority."[1] It was not a "solemn expression of the will of the supreme power of the state,"[2] for there was – as we repeatedly said – no *state* in the first place. The religious law was the intellectual work of private individuals, jurists whose claim to authority was primarily based on their erudition, legal knowledge, and religious and moral distinction. It was not political in the modern sense of the word, and it did not involve coercive or state power. The jurists were civilians and as such commanded neither armies nor troops. Nor was the Shariʿa subject to the fluctuations of legislation, reflecting the interests of a dominant class – as the modern state is. In its stability, but without rigidity, the Shariʿa represented an unassailable fortress within which the rule of law compared very favorably to its much-vaunted modern counterpart.

Furthermore, Shariʿa's law was not an abstraction, nor did it apply equally to "all," for individuals were not seen as indistinguishable members of a generic species, standing in perfect parity before a blind lady of justice. Each individual and circumstance was deemed unique, requiring *ijtihad* that was context-specific. This explains why Islam never accepted the notion of blind justice, for it allowed the rich and the powerful to stand on a par with the poor and the weak. In the Shariʿa, the latter had to be protected, and their disadvantage was turned into an advantage in the Shariʿa courts of law. This in part explains why there was no point in *stating* the law in the way that it is recorded in today's legal codes. Rather, the law was an *ijtihadic* process, a continuously renewed exercise in interpretation. It was an effort at mustering principles as located in specific life-situations, requiring the legists to do what was right at a particular moment of human existence. Even in its most detailed and comprehensive accounts, the law was mostly a juristic guide that directed the judge and all legal personnel on the ground to resolve a situation in due

---

[1] A standard definition of (Western) law. See *Black's Law Dictionary*, 5th edn (St. Paul, MN: West Publishing Co., 1979), 795.
[2] *Ibid.*

consideration of the unique facts involved therein. As a fully realizable and realized worldly experience, Islamic law was not fully revealed unto society until the principles meshed with social reality and until the interaction of countless social, moral, material and other types of human relations involved in a particular case was made to come full circle. In other words, Islamic law is not that found in the books of the jurists, but rather the outcome of a malleable and sensitive application of rules in a complex social setting. To know what Islamic law was, therefore, is to know how actual Muslim societies of the past *lived* it; but most certainly it is not merely the law as abstracted in the books of jurists.

The foregoing characterization of Islamic law, partial as it may be, bespeaks a complex reality that has largely disappeared. Over the past two centuries or so, the Shari'a has been transformed from a worldly institution and culture to a textuality, namely, a body of texts that is entirely stripped of its social and sociological context – its ecological environment, so to speak. Furthermore, this textuality has been engaged in a kind of politics that its pre-modern counterpart did not know. Which is to say that the surviving residue of the Shari'a, its entexted form, functions in such uniquely modern ways that this very residue is rendered foreign, in substance and function, to any of its historical antecedents.

This profound transformation was the outcome of the confrontation between the Shari'a and the most significant and weighty institution that emerged out of, and at once defined, modernity, i.e., the state. Conceptually, institutionally and historically, the state came into sustained conflict with the Shari'a, initially coexisting with it in a condition of contradiction, but soon succeeding in displacing it once and for all. Among the specific effects of this contest for mastery over the law was the desiccation and final dismantling of the Shari'a's institutional structures, including its financially independent colleges and universities, and the legal environment and culture that afforded Muslim legists the opportunity to operate and flourish as a "professional" group. This dismantling (with the benefit of hindsight, inevitable and expected) finally led to the extinction of this group as a species, to the emergence of a new conception of law, and, in short, to the rise of new legal and cultural systems. Shari'a's subject matter became no more than positive law, emanating from the state's will to power. The transformation was embodied in, and represented by, a complex process that operated at nearly every level in the uneven relationship between colonialist modern Europe – the creator and exporter of the modern state – and Muslim (and other) societies around the world. The forces behind the transformation were, among many others, centralization, codification (in the widest sense of the word), bureaucratization, homogenization and – to ensure totalistic compliance – ubiquitous militarization, all of which are in fact the props of the modern state project.

As we saw, it was in British India that the "entexting" of Islamic law first occurred – where, that is, it was *fixed* into texts as a conceptual act of codification. British India, subjected to direct forms of colonialism, displayed the processes and effects of crude and naked power more clearly than, say, the Ottoman Empire, although the latter was no less affected by the domination of modernity, in all its aspects, than any other directly colonized subject. The Indian experiment (and no less the Ottoman) served an immediate function in the colonialist articulation of Islam, in *knowing* and managing it. What amounted to a large-scale operation by which complex Islamic legal and social practices were reduced to fixed texts created a new way of understanding India and the rest of the Muslim world. Integral to this understanding was the pervasive idea that to study Islam and its history was to study texts, and not its societies, social practices or social orders. Entexting the Shari'a therefore had the effect of severing nearly all its ties with the anthropological and sociological legal past, much like the consignment of events to the "dark ages" or medieval period in the European historical imagination.

Once the anthropological past was trampled under by an entexted Shari'a, the very meaning of Islamic law was severely curtailed, if not transformed, having been emptied of the content and expertise necessary for a genuine evaluation of Shari'a-on-the-ground, and of its operation within an "ecological" system of checks and balances. It was also, as a consequence, stripped of much of its previous relevance. The new nationalist elites, endowed with the legacy of colonial state structures, aggressively pursued this severance of Shari'a from its anthropological past. Entexting served the nation-state's project of social engineering very well.[3]

I have already noted that the entexted Shari'a was also engaged in a new world of politics, a world that its pre-modern counterpart did not know. The act of severance, in other words, was almost perfectly correlated with the process by which the surviving residue, the entexted body of Shari'a, was transplanted into a new environment. The transformation was then two-pronged, engendering juristic rigidity through entexting,

---

[3] With the obvious exception of such countries as Saudi Arabia, whose continuing application of the Shari'a renders this severance largely unnecessary. Yet, this is not to say that the modern Saudi state structures did not transform the Shari'a in other, fundamental ways. On the place of Shari'a in the Kingdom of Saudi Arabia, see Frank E. Vogel, *Islamic Law and Legal System* (Brill: Martinus Nijhoff, 2000).

and politicization through transplantation. Whereas pre-modern Islamic law operated largely outside dynastic rule, the entexted and transplanted Shari'a had now come to be lodged *within* the structures of the state. To say that this transformation subjected the Shari'a to a profound process of politicization is merely to state the obvious. The Shari'a, however conceived by its modern followers, stands today as the centerpiece of political contention.

The road to politicization began at the moment when the so-called reforms allowed the state to appropriate the law as a legislative tool, changing dramatically a thousand-year-old situation in which the typical Islamic proto-state administered a law neither of its own making nor subject to the ruler's will to power. "In the modern state," as Talal Asad poignantly observes, "law is an element in political strategies – especially strategies for destroying old options and creating new ones."[4] Values centering on the family as a discrete social unit, on property, crime, punishment, a particular sexuality, a particular conception of gender, of rights, of morality and of much else, have all been created and recreated through the law. Yet, the intractable presence of the state – the virtually all-powerful agent exercising the option of reengineering the social order – has preempted any vision of governance outside its parameters. To practice law in the modern era is to be an agent of the state. There is no law proper without the state, and there is no state without its own, exclusive law. "Legal pluralism" can no doubt exist, but only with the approval of the state and its law. State sovereignty without a state-manufactured law is no sovereignty at all.

If the way to the law is through the state, then Islamic law can never be restored, reenacted or refashioned (by Islamists or ulama of any type or brand) without the agency of the state. More importantly, none of these restorative options can be realized without the contaminating influence of the state, rendering extinct the distinctiveness of pre-modern Shari'a as a non-state, community-based, bottom-up jural system. This distinctiveness would be impossible to replicate. In the modern state, politics and state policy mesh with law, creating a powerful ideological and cultural technology as well as producing other potent instruments that are wielded in the service of the state in fashioning and refashioning the social order, whose habitus is precisely that machinery which produces the citizen.

And so when the Shari'a (however imagined) is reasserted in any Muslim country, as happened, for instance, in Iran in 1979 and thereafter,

---

[4] Talal Asad, "Conscripts of Western Civilization," in Christine W. Gailey, ed., *Civilization in Crisis: Anthropological Perspectives* (Gainsville: University Press of Florida, 1992), 335.

the entexted conception combines with another conception of state-appropriated law to produce an aberrancy, one whose domestic advocates (seeking legitimacy) and external foes (seeking condemnation of Islamic revolutionary regimes) are equally happy, though for entirely different reasons, to call what ensues "Shari'a." Given the absence – in political and popular circles – of knowledge about Shari'a's anthropological past, both its advocates and its foes are left wandering in the dark. Inasmuch as the Shah's state, like all states in the West and the East, virtually destroyed and then refashioned its social order and reconstituted (without much success) its moral fabric, the new Islamic Republic, inheriting an utterly inescapable state apparatus, attempted to reinstate the Shari'a and fill the perceived moral void through the now familiar tools of state engineering. The Shari'a became the state's tool, for only to the state could it have been subordinated. Theft, homosexuality, extra-marital sex, music, American cultural icons and much else became the focus, if not the rhetoric, of the new reengineering in the name of the Shari'a. Yet, this reengineering was the work of a moralizing state, and was by no means dictated by the mechanisms associated with Shari'a's traditional ways of functioning.

At the end of the day, the Shari'a has ceased to be even an approximate reincarnation of its historical self. That it would be impossible to recreate it along with the kind of social order it presupposed and by which it was sustained is self-evident. To claim, however, that its modern expression can be altogether dispensed with is unrealistic. The Shari'a has indeed become a marker of modern identity, engulfed by notions of culture and politics but, ironically, much less by law.

Glossary of key terms

Terms defined here reflect a particular understanding of the Islamic legal tradition. To be understood properly, the book should therefore be read with these definitions in mind, since some terms here are given a specificity of meaning that they do not possess in the works of other writers (who may give them their own nuances). For instance, as I use it here, the word "jurist" has a particular meaning that should not be confused with such concepts as "judge" or "legist." The same is true of the terms "school," "substantive law" and so on.

abrogation: making a revealed text supersede another. The grounds on which abrogation can be made are many, one of which is the chrono-logically later provenance of the repealing text (reflecting a change of mind or position adopted in the earlier text); another reason for abrogation is when one text itself commands the abandonment of a matter specified in another text.

adat: usually unwritten customary laws prevailing in Malaysia and Indonesia.

amicable settlement: *see* peacemakers.

author-jurist: a highly learned legist (q.v.) who is capable of exercising certain faculties of *ijtihad* (q.v.) in writing legal manuals and/or long treatises on law.

Azhar: a religious university in Egypt (based mainly in Cairo) that origi-nated as a *madrasa* (q.v.) and that has incorporated into its twentieth-century curriculum many fields in the sciences.

caliph: the political and religious head of Islamic government; a deputy of the Prophet, also known as the Commander of the Faithful and Imam (q.v.). After the ninth century, and with the ascendancy of tribal dynas-ties hailing mainly from Central Asia, the caliph lost his political and military powers, and was progressively reduced to a religious symbol. The effective ruler became the sultan. In 1924, the caliphate was abolished by Kemal Atatürk.

certifying-witness: functionary of the court whose task it was to examine and certify the integrity of witnesses produced, inter alia, by the litigating parties.

charitable endowment: *see waqf.*

chief justice (*Qadi al-Qudat*): in the early period, the judge sitting in the capital, who appointed *qadi*s to the provinces and cities of the empire; later, especially under the Ottomans, each province or city could have a chief justice, since the authority that appointed them was the Shaykh al-Islam (q.v.), the chief mufti of the Empire. A chief justice, however, could not quash or reverse decisions of other *qadi*s, not even those whom he appointed; thus the hierarchy was administrative – one of appointment to office and dismissal – and not of legal authority.

circle: *see* study circle.

consensus: generally, the agreement of the community on a particular matter; the third source of Islamic law, technically defined as the agreement of *mujtahid*s (q.v.) in a given age on a particular point of law. Consensus was determined in a back-projected manner, namely, when jurists looked back at earlier generations and observed that there was no disagreement amongst them on a particular point of law. Juristic disagreement, however, was the norm, whereas rules subject to consensus were relatively few. While a *mujtahid* (q.v.) was required merely to know the cases subject to consensus, the hallmark of his *ijtihad* (q.v.) was intimate knowledge of the reasons for juristic disagreement (an intellectually demanding field of enquiry).

Council of Guardians: having the powers of a constitutional court in the Islamic Republic of Iran, it consists of twelve members, six of whom are Shari'a jurists while the rest are experts in other areas of the law; it has the power to veto any bill introduced by the Majlis (Parliament) on the grounds that it is repugnant to Shari'a norms.

Court of Cassation: a high court that holds the power to review and overturn the decisions of lower courts; in some countries, it is the highest of all courts while in others it stands below the constitutional court.

***darura*:** a legal principle, mainly in the law of rituals, allowing a person to set aside the law in a particular circumstance if fulfilling the legal obligation is believed to lead to undue hardship or harm. For example, stopping, while on travel, to pray is an obligation that may be waived if the life or security of the worshiper is in danger (for example, the threat of highway bandits).

divorce: marital dissolution in the Shari'a takes one of at least three forms: (1) unilateral divorce by the husband (*talaq*) whereby he owes his wife financial compensation; (2) contractual dissolution (*khul'*) whereby the wife usually surrenders her entitlement to dowry plus maintenance she would have received for three months had the husband divorced her unilaterally; and (3) judicial divorce by the court.

faqih: a legist (q.v.); an expert in the law; an *'alim* (pl. *ulama*, q.v.).

fatwa: legal opinion issued by a *mufti* (q.v.); although they were formally non-binding, judges adhered to *fatwa*s routinely, as they were deemed authoritative statements on particular points of law.

formative period: the first three and a half centuries of Islam (roughly 620–960 AD) when Islamic law took its full form. Thereafter, the law continued to change in a piecemeal fashion and on a case-by-case basis, but its major principles and chief characteristics maintained remarkable continuity.

four sources: the main sources of the law, i.e., the Quran, the Prophetic Sunna (q.v.), consensus (q.v.) and *qiyas* (q.v.).

habous: see *waqf*.

hadith: Prophetic traditions or reports of what the Prophet had said, done or tacitly approved with regard to a particular matter. The term is both singular and plural. *See* recurrence and Sunna.

Hanafi: a legal school (q.v.); a legist (q.v.) loyal to the principles and substantive law of Hanafism. *See* legal schools.

Hanbali: a legal school (q.v.); a legist (q.v.) loyal to the principles and substantive law of Hanbalism. *See* legal schools.

hudud: severe punishments for certain offenses specified in the Quran, rarely applied in pre-modern Islam because of the strict requirements of procedural law. For example, to prove adultery/fornication, four male witnesses must independently testify to the fact that they have, among other things, seen the man's sexual organ penetrate the woman. Should any of the four testimonies contradict the other three in any fashion (e.g., with regard to the position of the two while having sex or where they were having it), the four witnesses will be charged with slander and whipped eighty lashes each.

ijtihad: legal methods of interpretation and reasoning by which a *mujtahid* (q.v.) derives or rationalizes law on the basis of the Quran, the Sunna and/or consensus; also, a judge's evaluation of customary practices as they bear on a case brought before him. *See also* consensus, *mujtahid* and *qiyas*.

imam: leader of Friday prayer; a preacher in a mosque; a caliph (q.v.) in Sunni Islam.

Imam: The infallible head of the Shi'i Muslim community who is a descendant of Imam 'Ali and who is in hiding (occultation).

Imamate: the institution embodying the Imam in Shi'ism.

istihsan: literally, preference; technically, a method of inference *preferred* over *qiyas* (q.v.) and taking as its basis alternative textual evidence on the grounds that this preferred evidence leads to a more reasonable result that does not involve an undue hardship.

istislah: literally, to find something good or serving a certain lawful interest; technically, a method of inference that does not resort directly to a revealed text as the foundation of reasoning, but rather draws on rational arguments grounded in the five universals of the law, i.e., protection of life, mind, religion, private property and family.

jihad: literally, striving to do, or be, good; acting morally in deed and in thought; technically in law, rules regulating conduct of war and peace treaties.

judge: *see* jurist and *qadi*.

jurist: a legist (q.v.) who achieved a remarkably high level of legal knowledge, usually as a *mufti* (q.v.) and/or an author-jurist (q.v.); every jurist was a legist, but not every legist or even judge was a jurist.

khulʿ: *see* divorce.

legal norm: one of five legal values that a *mujtahid* (q.v.) applies to a case or a particular set of facts; the five norms/values are: forbidden, permissible, obligatory, disapproved and recommended.

legal school: a non-formal association of jurists who share loyalty to a particular set of legal precepts, a particular methodology of interpretation and of deriving law; in Sunni Islam, the legal schools that have survived after the eleventh century are four, the Hanafi (q.v.), Maliki (q.v.), Shafiʿi (q.v.) and Hanbali (q.v.), each named after a master-jurist (q.v.) to whom a particular methodology of doing law is attributed.

legist: someone learned in the law, be it a *mufti* (q.v.), an author-jurist (q.v.), a judge or a law student.

madhhab: a legal opinion or juristic principle adopted by a legist; a legal school (q.v.).

madrasa: college of law that is usually part of an endowment (q.v. *waqf*); *madrasas* regularly taught language, *hadith* (q.v.) and Quranic studies, and often offered study circles (q.v.) in mathematics, astronomy, logic and medicine.

majlis (al-hukm): the Islamic court of law in session.

Maliki: a legal school (q.v.); a legist (q.v.) loyal to the principles and substantive law of Malikism. *See* legal school.

Marjaʿ-Taqlid: a relatively recent Twelver-Shiʿi concept to the effect that a *mujtahid* (q.v.) acts as the legal and political leader of the community whilst the Imam (q.v.) is in hiding.

maslaha: *see istislah*.

master-jurist: a *mujtahid* (q.v.) of the highest caliber who is capable of performing the entire range of *ijtihad* (q.v.), and usually one who is credited with having established a legal school (q.v.). The four doctrinal

schools that survived in Sunni Islam are said to have been founded
by Abu Hanifa (d. 767), Malik b. Anas (d. 795), Ibn Idris al-Shafi'i
(d. 820) and Ahmad b. Hanbal (d. 855).

mazalim: the ruler's courts of grievances that prosecute public officials,
including *qadi*s (q.v.), usually on charges of abuse of power. *See also*
siyasa shar'iyya.

mediation: *see* peacemakers.

mufti: jurisconsult; usually a learned jurist who issues *fatwa*s (q.v.);
a jurist capable of one degree of *ijtihad* (q.v.) or another.

muhtasib: market inspector whose functions ranged from auditing
weights and measures in the marketplace to bringing government
officials to the Shari'a court for abuse of their powers.

mujtahid: a highly learned jurist who is capable of *ijtihad*, i.e., reasoning
about the law through applying complex methods and principles of
interpretation. *Mujtahid*s are of various ranks, the highest of which is
reserved for the one who is said to have fashioned the very methods and
principles that he and others in his school apply, while those who are
loyal to, and capable of applying, these principles belong to lower ranks.
See also consensus, *ijtihad* and master-jurist.

mullah: a Twelver-Shi'i religious intellectual, jurist and/or theologian.

munasaba: *see istislah* and suitability.

necessity: *see darura.*

opinion: statement of law or normative rule espoused by a jurist with
regard to a particular case. A *fatwa* (q.v.) is such an opinion. Islamic
substantive law largely consists of opinions.

Ottoman: referring to the Ottoman Empire that existed between 1389
and 1922, first in Anatolia, but later extending its domains to South-
East Europe, North Africa, Egypt, Greater Syria and the Hejaz.

peacemakers (muslihun): persons who mediate between parties in
dispute with a view to reaching an amicable settlement; such persons
as appointed by a judge, especially in the case of marital discord.

positive law: the body of rules legislated or sanctioned by the modern
state, including those that originally belonged to the Shari'a. The
decrees issued by pre-modern Muslim governments do not qualify as
positive law. *See also* substantive law.

post-formative period: occurring roughly between the second half
of the tenth century and the end of the eighteenth. *See also* formative
period.

qadi: the magistrate or judge of the Shari'a court who also exercised
extra-judicial functions, such as mediation, guardianship over orphans
and minors, and supervision and auditing of public works. When faced
with difficult cases, a *qadi* petitioned the *mufti* (q.v.) who provided a

fatwa (q.v.) or legal opinion (q.v.) on the basis of which he rendered a decision. *See also* jurist.

qadi-'askar: Ottoman chief justice, usually appointed in pairs, one to the European side of the Empire, the other to the Asian side.

qanun: edicts and decrees legislated by the Ottoman sultans, often asserting provisions of Islamic legal doctrine and at times supplementing it on matters related to taxes, land, public order, and court procedure and evidence (e.g., allowing torture to extract evidence). *Qanun*s contradicting Shari'a provisions (which abhorred torture) were at times resisted and ignored by *qadi*s and jurists.

qiyas: the fourth source of Islamic law; a general term referring to various methods of legal reasoning, analogy being the most common; other methods subsumed under *qiyas* are the syllogistic, relational, *a fortiori, e contrario* and *reductio ad absurdum* arguments.

ratio legis ('illa): cause; occasional factor; the attribute or set of attributes common between two cases and which justify the transference, through inference, of a norm from one case (that has the norm) to another (that does not have it). *See also qiyas.*

recurrence: a mode of transmitting Prophetic *hadith* (q.v.). Recurrence obtains when a *hadith* is narrated through so many channels and by so many people that collusion upon forgery is deemed inconceivable (because of the assumption that such a large number of transmitters cannot find ways to conspire amongst themselves); knowledge engendered by this type of *hadith* is considered certain.

Shafi'i: a legal school (q.v.); a legist (q.v.) loyal to the principles and substantive law of Shafi'ism. *See* legal school.

Shaykh al-Islam: before the Ottomans (q.v.), a leading *mufti* (q.v.) who, inter alia, supervised legal education in a city; under the Ottomans, the head of the judicial hierarchy, appointing and dismissing judges, opining on points of law, and wielding significant political powers which he at times exercised to depose sultans.

siyasa shar'iyya: the ruler's governance according to juristic political theory; discretionary legal powers of the ruler to enforce Shari'a court judgments and to supplement the religious law with administrative regulations (*see qanun*); the ruler's extra-judicial powers to prosecute government officials on charges of misconduct (*see mazalim*).

softa: an Ottoman term meaning a law student. *See also* legist.

solitary: a Prophetic *hadith* (q.v.) transmitted through fewer channels than recurrent reports (*see* recurrence). Knowledge engendered by this report is considered probable.

stare decisis: a doctrine of British, American and other Western courts to the effect that judges should stand by precedents and established principles and apply them to all future cases where facts are substantially the same.

study circle: literally referring to the form in which a group *sat down* to study with a professor; a study session with a particular specialization (mostly in law), usually held in mosques (but also in private homes). The circle was the medium of Islamic education.

substantive law: the body of rules and general principles of which the law manuals of Shari'a consist. As there is no technical distinction in the Shari'a between procedural and other laws, the expression "substantive law" may be used to cover procedural law as well. *See* pp. 29–30 above, for a list of topics making up substantive law.

suitability: a rational method of inferring the *ratio legis* (q.v.) in *qiyas* (q.v.). *See also istislah.*

Sunna: the second, but most substantial, source of Islamic law; the exemplary biography of the Prophet. The *hadith*s (q.v.) are the literary expressions and context-specific accounts of the Sunna.

takhayyur: literally, picking, selecting or choosing; a reforming method – prohibited by traditional Shari'a – of selecting opinions from various schools in order to create a modernized body of law. It is mostly applied in regard to the law of personal status.

talaq: *see* divorce.

talfiq: literally, patching, fabricating, amalgamating or concocting; a reforming method of bringing together different parts of a doctrine/opinion from various schools so as to create, on a specific point of law, a modernized doctrine.

tawatur: *see* recurrence.

ta'zir: discretionary punishments; determined and meted out by a *qadi* (q.v.), these punishments cannot reach or exceed *hudud* penalties (q.v.).

traditionist: one who studies and transmits *hadith* (q.v.).

Twelver-Shi'i: follower of the infallible Imam (q.v.), also known as Ja'fari; a theological and political group that believes Imam 'Ali and his descendants to be the legitimate successors to the Prophet; a layperson belonging to the Twlever-Shi'i community, or a jurist who is a member of the Twelver-Shi'i legal school. This community and its jurists are now predominant in Iran, southern Iraq and Southern Lebanon. There are substantial populations of Shi'is in Bahrain and Azerbaijan as well.

ulama: referring to the learned class, especially the legists (q.v.); in this technical sense, the word is of later provenance, probably dating to the twelfth century or thereabouts.

usul al-fiqh: a discipline or a field of study specializing in methods of interpretation and reasoning (q.v. *ijtihad*), with the aim of arriving at new legal norms for unprecedented cases or rationalizing existing ones. This discipline produced many important treatises dealing with the subject, and referred to as *usul al-fiqh* works.

usury (interest; Ar. *riba*): categorically prohibited in Islamic law; literally meaning "excess," *riba* refers to receiving or giving a lawful thing having monetary value in excess of that for which the thing was exchanged; interest charged on a debt is a prime example.

Vilayat–i Faqih: *see* Marja'-Taqlid.

waqf **(also *habous* in North Africa):** a charitable endowment; usually, immovable property alienated and endowed to serve the interest of certain beneficiaries, such as members of the family, the poor, wayfarers, scholars, mystics, the general public, etc. Constituting more than half of real property in many parts of the Muslim world, endowments sustained the legal system and its institutions, and supported public life and a flourishing civil society. Examples of endowments are: mosques, schools and graduate colleges, hospitals, soup-kitchens, public drinking fountains, bridges, street lights and real estate.

Chronology

This chronology is intended to aid beginners in identifying landmarks and important dates in the history of the Shari'a. In the case of movements and historical processes, the dates should be taken as rough estimates of their beginnings and/or ends.

610	Prophet Muhammad receives the first revelation.
622	Muhammad migrates to Medina.
632	Death of Muhammad.
632–80s	Rise of the Prophetic Sunna.
661–749	The Umayyad Dynasty.
680s–	Scholars and early judges begin to study and specialize in Prophetic Sunna.
690s–730s	Rise of the class of private legal specialists (*muftis*) and study circles.
740–	Rise of personal legal schools.
750–	The beginning of systematic exposition of substantive legal doctrine.
767	Death of Abu Hanifa, the eponym and main leader of the Hanafi school.
795	Death of Malik b. Anas, a leading Medinan jurist and the eponym of the Maliki school.
800	Substantive legal doctrine acquires its full-fledged form.
820	Death of Ibn Idris al-Shafi'i, the eponym and doctrinal leader of the Shafi'i school.
820–900	Compilation of Prophetic *hadith*.
855	Death of Ahmad Ibn Hanbal, a distinguished traditionist and eponym of the doctrinal Hanbali school.
860–900	Compilation of Prophetic *hadith* in canonical collections.
860–950	The formation of legal schools as doctrinal entities.
920–70	The first major expounders of a full-fledged theory of law (*usul al-fiqh*).
934–1055	The Buyids rule Iraq, Rayy and Fars.

939	The beginning of the Greater Occultation in Twelver-Shiʿism.
1037	The rise of the Saljuq Empire.
1055–1157	The Saljuqs rule Iraq.
1063–92	Tenure of the Saljuq vizier Nizam al-Mulk.
1077–1307	Saljuq state of Rum.
1250–1517	The Mamluks rule Egypt.
1347–61	Reign of the Mamluk sultan al-Nasir Hasan, interrupted between 1351 and 1354.
1389–1401	Reign of the Ottoman sultan Bayazid I.
1389–1922	The Ottoman Empire.
1453	The Ottomans capture Constantinople.
1501–1732	The Safavids rule Iran.
1520–66	The reign of the Ottoman sultan Sulayman the Lawgiver.
1526–	Beginning of the Mogul Empire in India.
1600	The British East India Company is chartered.
1602	The Dutch East India Company is chartered.
1757	The Battle of Plassey and acquisition of Bengal by the East India Company.
1772	Warren Hastings becomes Governor-General of India.
1779–1924	The Qajar Dynasty in Iran, consolidating its rule in 1794.
1786	Charles Cornwallis becomes Governor-General of India.
1804	The promulgation in France of the *Code civil* (*Code Napoléon*), later influential in several Muslim countries.
1805–11	Muhammad ʿAli consolidates his grip over Egypt, eliminating the Mamluks and preparing for significant reforms.
1826	The abolition of the Janissary corps by Mahmud II.
1826	W*aqf*s are placed under the control of the Imperial Ministry of Endowments, Istanbul.
1826	The Straits Settlements come under the rule of the East India Company.
1828	Muhammad ʿAli sends the first group of Egyptian (law) students to Paris. At, or around, this time the Ottomans and the Qajars do the same.
1830	The French conquer Algiers.
1830–80	Drastic weakening of the ulama class in the Ottoman Empire, Egypt and French Algeria.
1837	The proclamation of the *siyasatname* by Muhammad ʿAli in Egypt.
1839	The proclamation of the Ottoman Gülhane Decree.

1839–76	The age of Ottoman Tanzimat.
1847–69	First major wave of educational reforms in the Ottoman Empire.
1850	A commercial, French-based code promulgated in the Ottoman Empire.
1853–56	The Crimean Wars and Ottoman defeat.
1856	The proclamation of the Humayun Decree.
1857	The Indian Rebellion.
1858	Promulgation in the Ottoman Empire of the Penal Code and Land Law.
1859	French penal code enacted in Algeria.
1860s	Egyptian legal experts begin translating French civil, commercial, penal and procedural codes into Arabic.
1860–80	Gradual restriction of Shari'a's application to personal status in the Ottoman Empire and Egypt.
1864	Promulgation in the Ottoman Empire of the Law of Provincial Administration.
1870–77	The publication of the Ottoman *Majallat al-Ahkam al-'Adliyya*.
1873	*Loi Warnier* pertaining to land promulgated in French Algeria.
1874	The promulgation, in the Ottoman Empire, of the Law of the Shari'a Judiciary.
1874–75	The promulgation in Egypt of the Civil Code, the Penal Code, the Commercial Code, the Code of Maritime Commerce, the Code of Civil and Commercial Procedure, and the Code of Criminal Procedure (all of which greatly influenced by French law).
1875	The promulgation of the Indian Law Reports Act.
1875	The establishment of the Mixed Courts in Egypt.
1876	The establishment in Istanbul of the first modern law school.
1880	Code of Civil Procedure enacted in the Ottoman Empire.
1880–1937	Shari'a in Indonesia is restricted by the Dutch to family law, with the exception of *waqf* in Sumatra.
1881	*Code de l'indigénat* enacted in French Algeria, and applied until 1927.
1906	Iran adopts a new constitution.
1916	*Code Morand* promulgated in French Algeria.
1917	Ottoman Law of Family Rights enacted.
1923	Turkey declares itself a republic.

1924	Atatürk abolishes the caliphate.
1925–42	Rule of Reza Shah Pahlavi in Iran and the beginning of a major wave of legal reforms.
1926	Last purge of the Shari'a in Kemalist Turkey.
1927	The Code of Civil Procedure and the Code of Judicial Organization promulgated in Iran.
1928	The birth of the Muslim Brothers' movement in Egypt.
1929	Indian Child Marriage Restraint Act promulgated.
1931	The Act of Marriage promulgated in Iran.
1935	A new civil code in Iran.
1937	The Dutch enact new laws to regulate *waqf*s in Indonesia.
1945	Adoption of a constitution in Indonesia.
1947	Pakistan declares its independence.
1949	Mixed Courts abolished in Egypt.
1949	Adoption of the Objectives Resolution in Pakistan.
1949	A new civil code in Syria.
1949	Death of Hasan al-Banna, the founder of the Muslim Brothers in Egypt.
1950–	The Muslim Brothers spread their influence to Jordan, Syria, Sudan, Iran, Malaysia and elsewhere in the Muslim world.
1951	A new civil code in Iraq.
1951	Law of Family Rights enacted in Jordan.
1952	Law No. 180 (abolishing family *waqf*s) enacted in Egypt.
1955	Law No. 462 enacted, abolishing Shari'a courts in Egypt.
1956	The Code of Personal Status promulgated in Tunisia.
1956	The promulgation of the Constitution in Pakistan.
1958–69	The presidency of Muhammad Ayyub Khan in Pakistan.
1959	The Code of Personal Status promulgated in Iraq.
1961	Muslim Family Laws Ordinance promulgated in Pakistan.
1963–93	Azhar University expands dramatically.
1964	Adoption of a new constitution in Algeria.
1966	Sayyid Qutb, ideologue of the Muslim Brothers, executed by the Nasser regime.
1967	Family Protection Act promulgated in Iran.
1969	The Supreme Court in Egypt renamed the Supreme Constitutional Court.
1973	The adoption of a new Constitution in Pakistan.
1973	A Constitution adopted in Syria.
1974	A marriage law enacted in Indonesia.
1975	The Family Protection Act amended in Iran.

1975	The Syrian Law of Personal Status amended.
1977–88	The presidency of Zia al-Haqq in Pakistan.
1979	The Islamic Revolution in Iran; the adoption of a new Constitution.
1979	Law No. 44 (Jihan's Law) promulgated in Egypt.
1980–96	A number of changes introduced to the criminal code in Iran.
1985	Law No. 100, replacing Jihan's Law of 1979.
1989	Law No. 7 enacted in Indonesia (for the unification of Shariʿa courts).
1989	The Iranian Constitution amended, expanding presidential powers.
1991	Enactment of the Compilation of Islamic Law in Indonesia (Kompilasi Hukum Islam di Indonesia).
1992	Law of Personal Status (No. 20) promulgated in Yemen.
1996	A new constitution adopted in Algeria, repealing its 1976 predecessor.
2000	The Procedure of General and Revolutionary Courts promulgated.
2003	Iranian Civil Code promulgated.
2003–07	A major wave of legislative enactments in occupied Iraq.

Suggested further reading

Those who wish to pursue the study of Islamic law may follow a certain order in reading works listed here. Numbers found between square, bold brackets at the end of each entry indicate the sequence in which the reference may be read. It is highly recommended that these works be read along the sequence of this book's chapters, covering first the group of works numbered 1, then, again from the beginning, group 2, and so forth until group 5.

In grading the readings on a scale of five, the factors of accessibility and scope of subject matter were taken into account. Those references that are more technical in nature or do not deal with core areas in the field of Islamic law have been assigned higher numbers. Items with hyphenated numbers (e.g., **[3–4]**) are mostly collective works or works of wide coverage that may be relevant to more than one level of reading. Finally, the first five books, with the partial exception of Hodgson's *Venture*, deal relatively little with the Shariʿa, but offer excellent background information for the levels indicated.

GENERAL SOCIAL AND POLITICAL HISTORIES

Hodgson, Marshall G. S., *Rethinking World History: Essays on Europe, Islam, and World History* (Cambridge and New York: Cambridge University Press, 1993). Almost indispensable for understanding modern developments. **[4]**

The Venture of Islam, 3 vols. (Chicago: University of Chicago Press, 1974). **[3]**

Hourani, Albert, *A History of the Arab Peoples* (Cambridge, MA: The Belknap Press, 1991). **[1]**

Lapidus, Ira M., *A History of Islamic Societies* (Cambridge and New York: Cambridge University Press, 1988). **[1]**

Marcus, Abraham, *The Middle East on the Eve of Modernity: Aleppo in the Eighteenth Century* (New York: Columbia University Press, 1989). **[2]**

GENERAL WORKS ON ISLAMIC LAW AND ITS EARLY HISTORY

Calder, Norman, "Law," in Seyyed Hossein Nasr and O. Leaman, eds., *History of Islamic Philosophy*, vol. 1 (London and New York: Routledge, 1996), 979–98. **[2]**

Cohen, H. J., "The Economic Background and Secular Occupations of Muslim Jurisprudents and Traditionists in the Classical Period of Islam (until the

Middle of the Eleventh Century)," *Journal of the Economic and Social History of the Orient* (January 1970): 16–61. **[1]**

Glenn, Patrick H., *Legal Traditions of the World: Sustainable Diversity in Law* (Oxford and New York: Oxford University Press, 2000). At times inaccurate in its single-chapter treatment of Islamic law, but gives an excellent comparative perspective. **[1]**

Hallaq, Wael B., "The Authenticity of Prophetic Hadith: A Pseudo-Problem," *Studia Islamica*, 89 (1999): 75–90. **[2]**

   The Origins and Evolution of Islamic Law, in W. Hallaq, series ed., Themes in Islamic Law 1 (Cambridge: Cambridge University Press, 2005). **[1]**

   Shariʿa: Theory, Practice, Transformations (Cambridge: Cambridge University Press, 2009). **[2–3]**

Khadduri, M. and H. J. Liebesny, eds., *Law in the Middle East* (Washington, DC: Middle East Institute, 1955), chapters 1–5. **[1]**

Weiss, Bernard G., *The Spirit of Islamic Law* (Athens and London: University of Georgia Press, 1998). **[2]**

Yearbook of Islamic and Middle Eastern Law, ed. E. Cotran *et al.*, vols. 1–8 (The Hague: Kluwer Law International, 1995–2003); vols. 9–12 (Leiden: Brill, 2004–8). A good source to follow important legal developments in North African and Middle Eastern countries. **[5]**

Zubaida, Sami, *Islam, the People and the State: Essays on Political Ideas and Movements in the Middle East* (London and New York: Routlege, 1989). **[3]**

   Law and Power in the Islamic World (London and New York: I. B. Tauris, 2003). **[2]**

CHAPTER 1

Hallaq, Wael, *Authority, Continuity and Change in Islamic Law* (Cambridge: Cambridge University Press, 2001), 1–23, 166–235. **[4–5]**

Masud, Muhammad Khalid, Brinkley Messick and David S. Powers, eds., *Islamic Legal Interpretation: Muftis and Their Fatwas* (Cambridge, MA: Harvard University Press, 1996). Introduction **[1]**; rest of the book **[2–3]**

Masud, Muhammad *et al.*, eds., *Dispensing Justice in Islam: Qadis and Their Judgments* (Leiden: Brill, 2006). **[2–3]**

Messick, Brinkley, *The Calligraphic State: Textual Domination and History in a Muslim Society* (Berkeley: University of California Press, 1993). **[5]**

Müller, Christian, "Judging with God's Law on Earth: Judicial Powers of the Qadi al-Jamaʿa of Cordoba in the Fifth/Eleventh Century," *Islamic Law and Society*, 7, 2 (2000): 159–86. **[4]**

Powers, David S., "On Judicial Review in Islamic Law," *Law and Society Review*, 26 (1992): 315–41. **[4]**

   "Legal Consultation (futya) in Medieval Spain and North Africa," in Chibli Mallat, ed., *Islam and Public Law: Classical and Contemporary Studies* (London and Boston: Graham and Trotman, 1993), 85–106. **[3]**

Tyan, E., "Judicial Organization," in M. Khadduri and H. J. Liebesny, eds., *Law in the Middle East* (Washington, DC: Middle East Institute, 1955), 236–78. **[1]**

CHAPTER 2

Hallaq, Wael, *A History of Islamic Legal Theories* (Cambridge: Cambridge University Press, 1997). **[2]**
   "Non-Analogical Arguments in Sunni Juridical *Qiyas*," *Arabica*, 36, 3 (1989): 286–306. **[3]**
   "On the Authoritativeness of Sunni Consensus," *International Journal of Middle East Studies*, 18 (1986): 427–54. **[3]**
   "Was the Gate of Ijtihad Closed?" *International Journal of Middle East Studies*, 16 (1984): 3–41. **[1]**
Kamali, Hashim, *Principles of Islamic Jurisprudence* (Selangor: Pelanduk Publications, 1989). **[2]**
Lowry, Joseph, "Does Shafi'i Have a Theory of Four Sources of Law?" in Bernard G. Weiss, ed., *Studies in Islamic Legal Theory* (Leiden: Brill, 2002), 23–50. **[4]**
Wakin, Jeanette, "Interpretation of the Divine Command in the Jurisprudence of Muwaffaq al-Din Ibn Qudamah," in N. Heer, ed., *Islamic Law and Jurisprudence: Studies in Honor of Farhat J. Ziadeh* (Seattle: University of Washington Press, 1990), 33–53. **[4]**
Weiss, Bernard G., "Interpretation in Islamic Law: The Theory of *Ijtihad*," *American Journal of Comparative Law*, 26 (1978): 199–212. **[1]**
   "Knowledge of the Past: The Theory of *Tawatur* According to Ghazali," *Studia Islamica*, 61 (1985): 81–105. **[3]**
   The Search for God's Law: Islamic Jurisprudence in the Writings of Sayf al-Din al-Amidi (Salt Lake City: University of Utah Press, 1992). **[5]**
   ed., *Studies in Islamic Legal Theory* (Leiden: Brill, 2002). **[3–4]**

CHAPTER 3

Bearman, P. *et al.*, eds., *The Islamic School of Law* (Cambridge, MA: Islamic Legal Studies Program, 2005). **[3–4]**
Hallaq, Wael, *Authority, Continuity and Change in Islamic Law* (Cambridge: Cambridge University Press, 2001), 57–120. **[5]**
   "From Geographical to Personal Schools? A Reevaluation," *Islamic Law and Society*, 8, 1 (2001): 1–26. **[4]**
   The Origins and Evolution of Islamic Law, in W. Hallaq, series ed., Themes in Islamic Law 1 (Cambridge: Cambridge University Press, 2005): 150–77. **[1]**
Melchert, Christopher, *The Formation of the Sunni Schools of Law* (Leiden: E. J. Brill, 1997). **[2]**
   "The Formation of the Sunni Schools of Law," in W. B. Hallaq, ed., *The Formation of Islamic Law*, in L. Conrad, series ed., The Formation of the Classical Islamic World 27 (Aldershot: Ashgate, 2003), XIII. **[2]**
Tsafrir, Nurit, *The History of an Islamic School of Law: The Early Spread of Hanafism* (Cambridge, MA: Islamic Legal Studies Program, 2004). **[4]**

CHAPTER 4

Berkey, Jonathan Porter, *The Transmission of Knowledge in Medieval Cairo: A Social History of Islamic Education* (Princeton: Princeton University Press, 1992). **[1]**

Chamberlain, Michael, *Knowledge and Social Practice in Medieval Damascus, 1190–1350* (Cambridge: Cambridge University Press, 1994). **[4]**

Ephrat, Daphna, *Learned Society in a Period of Transition: The Sunni Ulama of Eleventh-Century Baghdad* (Albany: State University of New York Press, 2000). **[2]**

Makdisi, George, *The Rise of the Colleges: Institutions of Learning in Islam and the West* (Edinburgh: Edinburgh University Press, 1981). **[3]**

Tibawi, A. L., "Origin and Character of al-Madrasah,'" *Bulletin of the School of Oriental and African Studies*, 25 (1962): 225–38. **[4]**

Zaman, Muhammad Qasim, *Religion and Politics under the Early 'Abbasids* (Leiden: Brill, 1997). **[4]**

CHAPTER 5

Antoun, Richard T., "The Islamic Court, the Islamic Judge, and the Accommodation of Traditions: A Jordanian Case Study," *International Journal of Middle East Studies*, 12 (1980): 455–67. **[4]**

Deguilhem, Randi, "Consciousness of Self: The Muslim Woman as Creator and Manager of *Waqf* Foundations in Late Ottoman Damascus," in Amira Sonbol, ed., *Beyond the Exotic: Women's Histories in Islamic Societies* (Syracuse: Syracuse University Press, 2005), 102–15. **[4]**

El-Nahal, Galal H., *The Judicial Administration of Ottoman Egypt in the Seventeenth Century* (Chicago and Minneapolis: Bibliotheca Islamica, 1979). **[3]**

Fay, Mary Ann, "Women and Waqf: Toward a Reconsideration of Women's Place in the Mamluk Household," *International Journal of Middle East Studies*, 29, 1 (1997): 33–51. **[1]**

Gerber, Haim, "Social and Economic Position of Women in an Ottoman City, Bursa, 1600–1700," *International Journal of Middle East Studies*, 12 (1980): 231–44. **[1]**

Jennings, Ronald C., "Divorce in the Ottoman *Sharia* Court of Cyprus, 1580–1640," *Studia Islamica*, 78 (1993): 155–67. **[2]**

"Women in Early 17th Century Ottoman Judicial Records: The *Sharia* Court of Anatolian Kayseri," *Journal of the Economic and Social History of the Orient*, 18 (1975): 53–114. **[2]**

Johansen, Baber, "Legal Literature and the Problem of Change: The Case of the Land Rent," in Chibli Mallat, ed., *Islam and Public Law: Classical and Contemporary Studies* (London and Boston: Graham and Trotman, 1993), 29–47. **[4]**

Marcus, Abraham, "Men, Women and Property: Dealers in Real Estate in Eighteenth-Century Aleppo," *Journal of the Economic and Social History of the Orient*, 26 (1983): 137–63. **[2]**

Meriwether, Margaret L., "The Rights of Children and the Responsibilities of Women: Women as *Wasi*s in Ottoman Aleppo, 1770–1840," in A. Sonbol, ed., *Women, the Family and Divorce Laws in Islamic History* (Syracuse: Syracuse University Press, 1996), 219–35. **[2]**

"Women and Waqf Revisited: The Case of Aleppo, 1770–1840," in Madeline C. Zilfi, ed., *Women in the Ottoman Empire: Middle Eastern Women* (Leiden and New York: Brill, 1997), 128–52. **[2]**

Peirce, Leslie, *Morality Tales: Law and Gender in the Ottoman Court of Aintab* (Berkeley: University of California Press, 2003). **[3]**

Powers, David S., "Four Cases Relating to Women and Divorce in al-Andalus and the Maghrib, 1100–1500," in M. Masud *et al.*, eds., *Dispensing Justice in Islam: Qadis and Their Judgments* (Leiden: Brill, 2006), 383–409. **[4]**

Law, Society, and Culture in the Maghrib, 1300–1500 (Cambridge and New York: Cambridge University Press, 2002). **[3–4]**

Rapoport, Yossef, *Marriage, Money and Divorce in Medieval Islamic Society* (Cambridge: Cambridge University Press, 2005). **[2]**

Rosen, Lawrence, *The Anthropology of Justice: Law as Culture in Islamic Society* (Cambridge and New York: Cambridge University Press, 1989). **[3]**

The Justice of Islam: Comparative Perspectives on Islamic Law and Society (Oxford: Oxford University Press, 2000). **[3]**

Seng, Yvonne J., "Standing at the Gates of Justice: Women in the Law Courts of Early Sixteenth-Century Isküdar, Istanbul," in Susan Hirsch and M. Lazarus-Black, eds., *Contested States: Law, Hegemony and Resistance* (New York: Routledge, 1994), 184–206. **[2]**

Sonbol, Amira, ed., *Women, the Family, and Divorce Laws in Islamic History* (Syracuse: Syracuse University Press, 1996). **[3–4]**

Tucker, Judith E., *In the House of the Law: Gender and Islamic Law in Ottoman Syria and Palestine* (Berkeley: University of California Press, 1998). **[3]**

Zarinebaf-Shahr, Fariba, "Women, Law, and Imperial Justice in Ottoman Istanbul in the Late Seventeenth Century," in Amira Sonbol, ed., *Women, the Family, and Divorce Laws in Islamic History* (Syracuse: Syracuse University Press, 1996), 81–96. **[2]**

CHAPTER 6

Gerber, Haim, *State, Society, and Law in Islam: Ottoman Law in Comparative Perspective* (Albany: State University of New York Press, 1994). **[3]**

Hanna, N., ed., *The State and Its Servants: Administration of Egypt from Ottoman Times to the Present* (Cairo: American University in Cairo Press, 1995). **[3–4]**

İnalcık, Halil, "Suleiman the Lawgiver and Ottoman Law," *Archivum Ottomanicum*, 1 (1969): 105–38. **[4]**

Mardin, Serif, "The Just and the Unjust," *Daedalus*, 120, 3 (1991): 113–29. **[2]**

Zilfi, Madeline C., *The Politics of Piety: The Ottoman Ulema in the Postclassical Age (1600–1800)* (Minneapolis: Bibliotheca Islamica, 1988). **[3]**

CHAPTER 7

Anderson, Michael R., "Legal Scholarship and the Politics of Islam in British India," in R. S. Khare, ed., *Perspectives on Islamic Law, Justice, and Society* (Lanham, MD: Rowman and Littlefield, 1999), 65–91. **[2]**

Christelow, Allan, *Muslim Law Courts and the French Colonial State in Algeria* (Princeton: Princeton University Press, 1985). **[3]**

Çizakça, Murat, *History of Philanthropic Foundations: The Islamic World from the Seventh Century to the Present* (Istanbul: Bogaziçi University Press, 2000). **[2]**

Cohn, Bernard, *Colonialism and Its Forms of Knowledge: The British in India* (Princeton: Princeton University Press, 1996). Although this important work deals mainly with the non-Muslims of British India, its analysis is equally valid as to the Muslim population there. **[5]**

Hooker, M. B., *Legal Pluralism: An Introduction to Colonial and Neo-Colonial Laws* (Oxford: Clarendon Press, 1975). **[4]**

Hoyle, Mark S. W., *The Mixed Courts of Egypt* (London: Graham and Trotman, 1991). **[3]**

İnalcık, Halil, "Application of the Tanzimat and Its Social Effects," *Archivum Ottomanicum*, 5 (1973): 97–127. **[4]**

Kugle, Scott A., "Framed, Blamed and Renamed: The Recasting of Islamic Jurisprudence in Colonial South Asia," *Modern Asian Studies*, 35, 2 (2001): 257–313. **[3]**

Lev, Daniel S., "Colonial Law and the Genesis of the Indonesian State," *Indonesia*, 40 (October 1985): 57–74. **[3]**

Powers, David S., "Orientalism, Colonialism and Legal History: The Attack on Muslim Family Endowments in Algeria and India," *Comparative Studies in Society and History*, 31, 3 (July 1989): 535–71. **[1]**

Singha, Radhika, *A Despotism of Law: Crime and Justice in Early Colonial India* (Delhi and New York: Oxford University Press, 1998). **[5]**

Strawson, John, "Islamic Law and English Texts," *Law and Critique*, 6, 1 (1995): 21–38. **[2]**

CHAPTER 8

An-Na'im, Abdullahi, *Islamic Family Law in a Changing World* (London: Zed Books, 2002). **[1–3]**

Anderson, J. N. D., *Law Reform in the Muslim World* (London: Athlone Press, 1976). **[2]**

Asad, Talal, "Conscripts of Western Civilization," in Christine W. Gailey, ed., *Civilization in Crisis: Anthropological Perspectives* (Gainsville: University Press of Florida, 1992), 333–51. **[3]**

    Formations of the Secular: Christianity, Islam, Modernity (Stanford: Stanford University Press, 2003). **[5]**

Barnes, J. R., *An Introduction to the Religious Foundations in the Ottoman Empire* (Leiden: E. J. Brill, 1986). **[2]**

Buskens, L., "Islamic Commentaries and French Codes: The Confrontation and Accommodation of Two Forms of Textualization of Family Law in Morocco," in H. Driessen, ed., *The Politics of Ethnographic Reading and Writing: Confrontations of Western and Indigenous Views* (Saarbrücken: Breitenbach, 1993), 65–100. **[3]**

Carroll, Lucy, "Orphaned Grandchildren in Islamic Law of Succession: Reform and Islamization in Pakistan," *Islamic Law and Society*, 5, 3 (1998): 409–47. **[3]**

    "The Pakistan Federal Shariat Court, Section 4 of the Muslim Family Laws Ordinance, and the Orphaned Grandchild," *Islamic Law and Society*, 9, 1 (2002): 70–82. **[3]**

Hélie-Lucas, Marie-Aimée, "The Preferential Symbol for Islamic Identity: Women in Muslim Personal Laws," in Valentine M. Moghadam, ed.,

Identity Politics and Women: Cultural Reassertions and Feminisms in International Perspective (Boulder, CO: Westview Press, 1994), 188–96. **[4]**

Lev, Daniel S., *Islamic Courts in Indonesia: A Study in the Political Bases of Legal Institutions* (Berkeley: University of California Press, 1972). **[3]**

"Judicial Unification in Post-Colonial Indonesia," *Indonesia*, 16 (October, 1973): 1–37. **[4]**

Lombardi, Clark B., *State Law as Islamic Law: The Incorporation of the Sharīʿa into Egyptian Constitutional Law* (Leiden: Brill, 2006). **[3]**

Moors, Annelies, "Debating Islamic Family Law: Legal Texts and Social Practices," in M. L. Meriwether and Judith E. Tucker, eds., *Social History of Women and Gender in the Modern Middle East* (Boulder, CO and Oxford: Westview Press, 1999), 141–75. **[2]**

Peletz, Michael G., *Islamic Modern: Religious Courts and Cultural Politics in Malaysia* (Princeton: Princeton University Press, 2002). **[3]**

Tucker, Judith E., "Revisiting Reform: Women and the Ottoman Law of Family Rights, 1917," *Arab Studies Journal*, 4, 2 (1996): 4–17. **[2]**

CHAPTER 9

Cole, Juan Ricardo, *Sacred Space and Holy War: The Politics, Culture, and History of Shiʾite Islam* (London: I. B. Tauris, 2002). **[3]**

Collins, Daniel P., "Islamization of Pakistani Law: A Historical Perspective," *Stanford Journal of International Law*, 24 (1987–88): 511–84. **[2]**

Dahlén, Ashk P., *Islamic Law, Epistemology and Modernity* (New York and London: Routledge, 2003). **[4]**

Eickelman, Dale F., "Islamic Liberalism Strikes Back," *Middle East Studies Association Bulletin*, 27 (1993): 163–68. **[3]**

Euben, Roxanne L., *Enemy in the Mirror: Islamic Fundamentalism and the Limits of Modern Rationality* (Princeton: Princeton University Press, 1999). **[5]**

Feener, Michael, *Muslim Legal Thought in Modern Indonesia* (Cambridge: Cambridge University Press, 2007). **[3]**

Feldman, Noah, *The Fall and Rise of the Islamic State* (Princeton: Princeton University Press, 2008). **[2]**

Haj, Samira, *Reconfiguring Islamic Tradition: Reform, Rationality, and Modernity* (Stanford: Stanford University Press, 2009). **[2]**

Hallaq, *A History of Islamic Legal Theories*, 207–54. **[2]**

Salim, A. and A. Azra, eds., *Sharīʿa and Politics in Modern Indonesia* (Singapore: Institute of Southeast Asian Studies, 2003). **[3]**

Schirazi, Asghar, *The Constitution of Iran: Politics and the State in the Islamic Republic*, trans. John O'Kane (London and New York: I. B. Tauris, 1997). **[4]**

Zaman, Muhammad Qasim, *The Ulama in Contemporary Islam: Custodians of Change* (Princeton: Princeton University Press, 2002). **[2]**

Zeghal, Malika, "Religion and Politics in Egypt: The Ulema of al-Azhar, Radical Islam, and the State (1952–94)," *International Journal of Middle East Studies*, 31, 3 (1999): 371–99. **[2]**

CHAPTER 10

Hallaq, Wael, "What is Shari'a?" *Yearbook of Islamic and Middle Eastern Law, 2005–2006*, 12 (Leiden: Brill, 2007): 151–80. **[2]**

SELECT TOPICS IN SUBSTANTIVE LAW

Bassiouni, Cherif, "Evolving Approaches to Jihad: From Self-Defense to Revolutionary and Regime-Change Political Violence," *Chicago Journal of International Law*, 8, 1 (2007): 119–46. **[3]**

Coulson, Noel James, *Succession in the Muslim Family* (Cambridge: Cambridge University Press, 1971). **[5]**

Encyclopedia of Islamic Law: A Compendium of the Major Schools, adapted by Laleh Bakhtiar (Chicago: KAZI Publications, 1995). **[2–5]**

Hallaq, Wael, *Shari'a: Theory, Practice, Transformations* (Cambridge: Cambridge University Press, 2009), chapters 6–12 (covering rituals, contracts, family law, property, penal law, *jihad*, and evidence and procedure). **[2]**

Ibn Rushd, Muhammad b. Ahmad, *The Distinguished Jurist's Primer*, trans. I. Khan Nyazee, 2 vols. (Reading: Garnet Publishing, 1994–96). A twelfth-century legal text of the Maliki school, covering the entire range of legal topics. **[3–5]**

Kelsay, John, *Arguing the Just War in Islam* (Cambridge, MA: Harvard University Press, 2007). **[2]**

Khadduri, M., and Liebesny, H. J., eds., *Law in the Middle East* (Washington, DC: Middle East Institute, 1955), chapters 0–10. **[1]**

Khalilieh, Hassan, *Islamic Maritime Law: An Introduction* (Leiden: Brill, 1998). **[5]**

Marghinani, Burhan al-Din, *Al-Hidaya: The Guidance*, trans. I. Khan Nyazee, 2 vols. (Bristol: Amal Press, 2006). A twelfth-century text of the Hanafi school, covering almost the entire range of legal topics. **[3–5]**

Misri, Ibn Naqib, *The Reliance of the Traveller*, trans. N. H. M. Keller (Evanston, IL: Sunna Books, 1991). A fourteenth-century text (with a later commentary) of the Shafi'i school, covering a wide range of legal topics. **[2–5]**

Peters, Rudolph, *Crime and Punishment in Islamic Law: Theory and Practice from the Sixteenth to the Twenty-First Century*, in Wael Hallaq, series ed., Themes in Islamic Law 2 (Cambridge: Cambridge University Press, 2005). **[2]**

Schacht, Joseph, *An Introduction to Islamic Law* (Oxford: Clarendon, 1964), 112–98. **[2]**

Udovitch, Abraham L., *Partnership and Profit in Medieval Islam* (Princeton: Princeton University Press, 1970). **[3–4]**

Vogel, Frank, "Contract Law of Islam and the Arab Middle East," *International Encyclopedia of Comparative Law* (Dordrecht: Mohr Seibeck; Tübingen: Martinus Nijhoff Publishers, 2006), vol. 7, 3–76. **[3]**

Vogel, Frank and S. L. Hayes, *Islamic Law and Finance: Religion, Risk and Return* (The Hague: Kluwer Law International, 1998). **[3]**

Index